The New Architecture of Science

Learning from Graphene

The New Architecture of Science

Learning from Graphene

Kostya S. Novoselov
University of Manchester, UK
and
National University of Singapore

Albena Yaneva
University of Manchester, UK

World Scientific

NEW JERSEY • LONDON • SINGAPORE • BEIJING • SHANGHAI • HONG KONG • TAIPEI • CHENNAI • TOKYO

Published by
World Scientific Publishing Co. Pte. Ltd.
5 Toh Tuck Link, Singapore 596224
USA office: 27 Warren Street, Suite 401-402, Hackensack, NJ 07601
UK office: 57 Shelton Street, Covent Garden, London WC2H 9HE

British Library Cataloguing-in-Publication Data
A catalogue record for this book is available from the British Library.

THE NEW ARCHITECTURE OF SCIENCE
Learning from Graphene

ISBN 978-981-122-067-8
ISBN 978-981-122-068-5 (ebook for institutions)
ISBN 978-981-122-069-2 (ebook for individuals)

For any available supplementary material, please visit
https://www.worldscientific.com/worldscibooks/10.1142/11840#t=suppl

Printed in Singapore

For our parents
Tatiana and Sergey, Ogniana and Kostadin

National
Graphene
Institute
material needs a
revolutionary place
to grow.

Foreword

Graphene came into my life in 2011. I was Chancellor, and I got a message from Manchester University. It went along these lines: "We've got two Nobel winning scientists working here you must meet. They have got a plan to turn their amazing discovery into something that can benefit the whole economy, and they need your help to make it happen." I was intrigued and made my way to the research laboratory of Kostya Novoselov and Andre Geim. They explained to me the wonders of graphene, the material with incredible strength and versatility that was only one atom thick.

Their work, undertaken in a British university, had a huge number of possible applications in the real world. What they wanted, and what Manchester wanted, was for that research and development to happen in the country and in the city where the discovery had been made. But the sums of money that required needed the help of the Treasury. I was happy to provide it. For just as scientific discovery and innovation powered the first industrial revolution in Manchester two centuries ago, so it powers the technological transformation underway today.

This was the genesis of the National Graphene Institute that you see today. In the many visits I have made — from its origins as a construction site, to the moment of pride when I took President Xi Jinping of China there to show him what British science could achieve, to my more recent visits as chair of the Northern Powerhouse Partnership — I have seen the Institute go from a mere building, albeit an impressive one, to a living, breathing community of scientists, researchers, inventors and entrepreneurs. No wonder the world has queued up to take a look.

This wonderful book tells the story of the people behind the National Graphene Institute and, I hope, will inspire others to follow in their footsteps — so we go on discovering, inventing and making.

George Osborne, UK

HYDROGEN/ARGON
AMMONIA
METHANE
HYDROGEN
ACETYLENE
ARGON
OXYGEN
CLEAN DRY AIR
UTILITY NITROGEN
PROCESS VACUUM
CARTEN

Acknowledgements

We are grateful to all participants in this study: Sarah Haigh, Mark Bissett, Andrey Kretinin, Francisco Lopez-Royo, Rahul Raveendran Nair, Abhishek Mishra, James Fitzsimons, Chris Livingston, Lewis Le Fevre, Christopher Hyde, Ernie Hill, Stuart Lockwood, Olga Falko, Beverley Brown, Phil Higgins, Polly Greensmith, Richard Cutting, Daniela Sevelova, Kelly Stanford, and Vladimir Falko. John Whittaker, NGI Head of Operations, deserves a special mention: we thank him for generous professional input, many guided tours and interviews, as well as his precious helps in facilitating the participation of other NGI colleagues. Tony Ling, architect from Jestico+Whiles, provided valuable information and images on the project. We also thank Peter Blake for helpful consultations and advice.

Ben Blackwell, Brett Mommersteeg and Simon Mitchell, PhD researchers in Architecture from the Manchester Architecture Research Group (MARG), Manchester Urban Institute, helped at different stages of the development of this project. Last, but not least, we are greatly indebted to the team of World Scientific Publishing for their professional work on the book production: Kim Tan, Nargiza Amirova, Dr. Ng Yan Hong. Special thanks to Loo Chuan Ming for ingenious typesetting and to Sophia and Victoria Novoselov for proofreading.

Contents

Preamble

The design of laboratory buildings has often been steered by narrow concerns for efficiency. Praised as a place for securing the credibility of scientific claims, the contemporary laboratory is, however, far from being a neutral "stage" for the production of knowledge. To illustrate this, the book explores the architecture of one of the most advanced nanoscience labs ever built, the National Graphene Institute (NGI) at the University of Manchester (UoM), United Kingdom (Fig. 1). What is so special about the NGI? What makes it worthwhile of a book? Its exceptional features include: a clean room designed with a specific focus on graphene and other 2D materials, spread across two floors connected by a clean lift; a variety of open space laboratories and specialised labs with grey spaces that provide infrastructure for the exploration of graphene; and also, a number of social spaces and atria that ensure quality "breakouts" and promote communication. Although, what makes it most unique is that its design is the result of an exceptional partnership between the lead scientist of the NGI, Kostya Novoselov, and the architect Tony Ling, director of the London-based architectural firm of Jestico+Whiles. The design of the NGI is the upshot of a long process of discussions and negotiations, "a continuous fight" of scientists trying "to reduce the architectural features" and designers "trying to enhance them." Amazingly, this "battle"

1

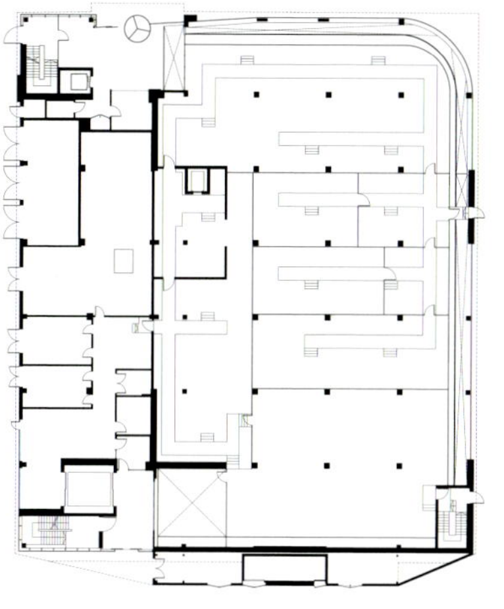

Fig. 1 (opposite): The National Graphene Institute (NGI) in Manchester, photo by Ben Blackwell.

has resulted in a happy building that fully functions today, a fine example of the new generation of high-tech science labs and their capacity to breed new collaborative research cultures.

Conceived as an alternative account of the making of the NGI building and its present-day dynamic lab life, the book draws on two reporters' voices. First, the voice of the lead scientist, Kostya Novoselov, who was closely involved in the planning and development of the building, recounts the main design moments and outlines the distinctive building features; second, the voice of the architectural anthropologist, Albena Yaneva, who studied the building and captured its working rhythm between 2017 and 2019, tells an ethnographic story about its lived reality. The graphene building is thus presented on two parallel stages: the stage of making [M] (design, development, and construction) and the stage of experience [E] (ways of dwelling in the different spaces). If the first narrative speaks on behalf of graphene and other 2D materials, presenting the visions of graphene's development, expanding a story about the scientific and technical rationale behind the building, the second narrative tells a tale of how the building is experienced now, speaking on behalf of all those who inhabit it and use its facilities on a daily basis. The two narrative planes, together and in synch, weave an argument about the importance of architecture for graphene research in particular and for the efficient organisation of scientific work in general. The unique story of the NGI sheds light on the design of the new generation of scientific buildings.

An exceptional building deserves a bespoke method of study. The ethnographic part of the story (marked as [E] for Experience) is based on the anthropology of dwelling and draws on a number of other voices through in-depth interviews with a range of scientists, architects, building managers, industry people, clean room and lab technicians, project managers, administrators, porters, and house service staff (30 interviews).[1] Additionally, it builds on ethnographic observations in

1 Participants include John Whittaker, NGI Head of Operations (4 interviews), Vladimir Falko, Director of NGI (1), Tony Ling, architect from Jestico+Whiles (1), Andrey Kretinin, Lecturer in Materials Physics (2), Mark Bissett, Senior Lecturer in Nanomaterials (1), Francisco Lopez-Royo, NGI Clean Room Manager (1), Rahul Raveendran Nair, Professor of Materials Physics (1), Richard Cutting, Senior

different parts of the building. Isolated and protected environments set barriers for an anthropologist to access and freely stroll in the spaces. To circumvent these restrictions and gain a better understanding of how the building works for various groups of "dwellers," she took ethnographic walks with the interviewees asking them to recreate their daily trajectories and the specific ways of engaging with the different features of the building (16 walks). This allowed developing insights into the different spatial practices and daily routines of dwelling that form the core of the laboratory life at the NGI. The anthropologist also conducted brief observations in different sites: visiting the clean rooms, wandering the viewing corridor, sitting in shielded labs, and witnessing the buzz of the busy Friday afternoons, when more than 100 researchers and industry people storm the top floor to attend the graphene seminars. From these short visits, the spatial dimensions of scientific work, the movements and the locales, became visible. The working rhythm of the NGI building was documented between 2017 and 2019; that is, two to four years after it was built as it gradually entered into a steady-state phase of functioning. During the ethnographic walks and observations, the anthropologist questioned people's attachments to the building, took numerous photographs to explore the different material arrangements, equipment settings, inscription techniques and the various design features that matter for them. Following the rhythm of scientific dwelling in its course, the ethnographic study advanced a different understanding of the nature of scientific buildings and shed light on the impact of architecture on nanoscience research.

Faculty Project Manager, Faculty of Science and Engineering (1), Sarah Haigh, Professor of Materials Characterisation, Director of the Electron Microscopy Centre (1), Abhishek Mishra, Postdoctoral Researcher at the Centre for Mesoscopic Science (1), James Fitzsimons, Technician (1), Chris Livingston, NGI Stores Manager and gas room technician (2), Lewis Le Fevre, Postdoctoral Researcher at the Department of Electrical and Electronic Engineering (2), Christopher Hyde, Senior Equipment Technician (2), Ernie Hill, Senior Lecturer & Assistant Director of The Manchester Centre for Mesoscience and Nanotechnology (1), Stuart Lockwood, Capital Projects Project Manager at the University of Manchester (1), Olga Falko, NGI Project Manager (1), Beverley Brown, NGI Administrator and acting receptionist (1), Phil Higgins, Senior Prototyping Engineer (1), Polly Greensmith, NGI Technical Manager (1), Gordon Royle, House Services Staff (1), Daniela Sevelova, House Services Staff (1), Kelly Stanford, artist in residence at the NGI (1).

Currently there are more than 250 people involved in graphene -related research in Manchester. The swift pace of graphene research follows a tree-like development; the NGI functions as the trunk of this intertwined branching, extending to the Graphene Engineering and Innovation Centre building (GEIC, completed in 2018), and other buildings like the Henry Royce building (currently under construction). A burgeoning graphene empire is spreading. A "graphene city" within the city of Manchester has emerged and continues to reshape its urban ecology[2] as we write these lines in 2019.

2 See the study of Ben Blackwell on the science-led urban transformation of Manchester, PhD dissertation, *Building a Graphene City: Infrastructuring a New Scientific Ecology*, The University of Manchester.

[M] Introduction: The Making of the Graphene Building

Graphene is the first two-dimensional crystal available to us, which was obtained experimentally only in 2003–2004.[3] Very soon after its first experimental isolation it became clear that this material will open a broad scope of research directions, which still grows even to these days (these words were written in early 2019). Among the most active fields are the applications in energy (batteries and supercapacitors), electronics, optoelectronics, composite materials, nanomedicine. Even a simple list looks very broad and, may be, eclectic, but there is a very strong progress in the development of all those directions. There are several reasons for that.

First of all, graphene is a very simple material — it consists only of carbon atoms arranged in the 2D honeycomb lattice. And yet, the same honeycomb structure guarantees very non-trivial electronic properties,[4] which can be easily calculated and experimentally verified. Also, because of the high strength and stability of the carbon-carbon bonds, experimentally obtainable crystals of graphene can be of very high quality, which allows a broad range of experiments to be realised in this material.

Second, because of its extraordinary properties (such as high mobility of charge carriers — important for electronic devices; high optical transparency; high mechanical strength, etc.) graphene is a

---

[3] Novoselov, K. S. *et al.* Electric field effect in atomically thin carbon films. *Science* 306, 666-669, doi:10.1126/science.1102896 (2004); Geim, A. K. Nobel Lecture: Random walk to graphene. *Rev. Mod. Phys.* 83, 851-862, doi:10.1103/RevModPhys.83.851 (2011); Novoselov, K. S. Nobel Lecture: Graphene: Materials in the flatland. *Rev. Mod. Phys.* 83, 837-849, doi:10.1103/RevModPhys.83.837 (2011)

[4] Castro Neto, A. H., Guinea, F., Peres, N. M. R., Novoselov, K. S. & Geim, A. K. The electronic properties of graphene. *Rev. Mod. Phys.* 81, 109–162, doi:10.1103/RevModPhys.81.109 (2009).

very promising material for a large number of applications: from optoelectronics to energy and from sensors to composite materials. This immediately attracted attention from industry and has already resulted in a number of real-life products which are either based on or utilise this material.[5]

Third, graphene opened the floodgate for many other 2D materials to be discovered and studied.[6] These days the family of such materials consists of dozens of different crystals and covers the full breadth of properties: insulators, semiconductors, semimetals, metals, superconductors, ferromagnets ... Furthermore, such materials can be assembled into the van der Waals heterostructures which opens a new direction in engineering of novel materials with on-demand properties.[7]

All these resulted in the exponential growth of graphene activity in Manchester — the place where graphene was first isolated. In a short period of time a large number of scientists with very different backgrounds became involved both in fundamental and applied research of 2D materials. It soon became obvious that the community would strongly benefit from having new research facilities.

Firstly, the process of working with any nanomaterials, especially those considered for electronic applications, require the use of the, so-called, clean rooms (spaces with well-controlled temperature, humidity, illumination, vibrations, etc.). But the clean rooms, where the original graphene research was conducted, were outdated, too small for the increased number of researchers and could not fit the new equipment required.

Secondly, because the research quickly diversified into the multiple, very different directions, some specialised labs were required.

---

[5] Novoselov, K. S. *et al.* A roadmap for graphene. *Nature* 490, 192-200, doi:10.1038/nature11458 (2012); Ferrari, A. C. *et al.* Science and technology roadmap for graphene, related two-dimensional crystals, and hybrid systems. *Nanoscale* 7, 4598-4810, doi:10.1039/C4NR01600A (2015).

[6] Novoselov, K. S. *et al.* Two-dimensional atomic crystals. *Proc. Natl. Acad. Sci. U.S.A.* 102, 10451-10453, doi:10.1073/pnas.0502848102 (2005).

[7] Geim, A. K. & Grigorieva, I. V. Van der Waals heterostructures. *Nature* 499, 419-425, doi:10.1038/nature12385 (2013); Novoselov, K. S., Mishchenko, A., Carvalho, A. & Castro Neto, A. H. 2D materials and van der Waals heterostructures. *Science* 353, aac9439-aac9439, doi:10.1126/science.aac9439 (2016).

For instance, research into energy applications would require dry rooms with strictly controlled humidity. Research in optoelectronics benefits from vibration-free dark rooms with laser safety systems included. Modern cryostats require a lot of infrastructure around them (cryo-free systems require supply of process cooling water, sometimes compressed air, and better to be placed in the noise-isolated spaces). Low current, highly sensitive measurements in electronics require shielded rooms, and so on. Furthermore, modern safety standards imply very specific requirements to the laboratory spaces and procedures.

Thirdly, the community would strongly benefit from a centre where researchers from different background could interact between themselves and with industrial partners, and where interdisciplinary research could be conducted.

Thus, through the efforts of Professor Sir Andre Geim, Professor Dame Nancy Rothwell, Sir Howard Bernstein, Lord Willets, George Osborne (then Chancellor) and Professor Sir Kostya Novoselov a decision was made to create the National Graphene Institute (NGI). The major tasks for such an institute are (not necessarily in the order of importance — which might depend on the particular preferences):

i) To increase the capacity of the current clean room both in terms of the equipment available, processes it can accept, as well as in the number of people which can operate in such labs at any moment of time.

ii) To create specialised laboratory, fit for the development of specific applications, such as energy, composite materials, optoelectronics, etc.

iii) To create a collaborative workspace where researchers operating in different branches of graphene science could exchange ideas, recipes, transfer technology.

iv) To create a collective space which would allow efficient collaboration with industrial partners, which would include both spaces for precompetitive and post-competitive research.

It should be noted that the physical building of the institute, completed in 2015, is only part of the whole graphene enterprise in Manchester. The most important component of the whole graphene activity are the researchers working in this field. In this sense, the National Graphene Institute has been operational for years, even though it didn't have its own building until 2015. Thus, the structure of the existing research groups as well as links between the groups had to be taken into account during the design and construction of the building.

However, the ambition of the NGI is to be able to push things even further than simply supporting the existing relations. Being a new technology means that a lot of new procedures, protocols and know-how around graphene arise every day. Successful and efficient transfer of the technologies between different research groups would make the whole enterprise much more fruitful and there is no better way to transfer technology than to share it at the workplace. Such cross-pollination will not only speed up the existing research but will also create new directions of investigation.

This created rather contradictory requirements for the building. It had to support multiple research groups with very different demands towards their laboratories, both in terms of physical requirements (vibration, contamination, facilities, temperature, moisture, etc.) but also in terms of accessibility to facilities (shared/non-shared spaces). Thus, how can we design a building that accommodates both isolated, specialised lab spaces and shared and flexible communal spaces? How can we design a building that will be adaptive and receptive towards novel ideas? These were the key questions, which emerged in the process of design, and we will address them in this book, presenting both the solutions and the challenges.

Furthermore, it is important to remember that the National Graphene Institute is only one of the pillars of the global innovation strategy around graphene in Manchester. It has been quickly realised that the strong team of researchers covering the broad range of expertise, combined with the strong traditions in engineering create a very attractive base for innovations in this area. It would be very beneficial for the city, the region and the country to capitalise on it through a coherent industrial strategy. The next pillar of this strategy is the Graphene Engineering Innovation Centre (GEIC), which is expected to evolve into the innovation and industrial park specialising in advanced materials.

The interaction between the building, research facilities, its users and its alignment to the broader strategy around graphene research and innovation is the major focus of this book.

An extra challenge: academics and industry people under one roof

One of the original goals for the NGI is to promote collaboration with industry and undertake industrial projects. The requirements from industrial partners, however, are often very much different than those from academics. In particular the difference is obvious when talking about collaboration and intellectual property. Only a small fraction of industrial projects are in the pre-competitive stage, when the ownership of the results is not as important as the know-how. In the vast majority of the work the major goal for industrial partner is to develop competitive advantage, which means strict confidentiality. At the same time, most often academics benefit strongly from openness, technology transfer, collaboration.

In order to satisfy requirements of both sides a variety of laboratory spaces has been provided in the NGI. Secluded laboratories (both with and without windows) allow control over access and thus can satisfy the strict requirements (particularly legal) on the access inside the lab. At the same time, open space laboratories have been provided, which give better utilisation of space, offer opportunity to install particularly bulky equipment and promote collaboration.

Still, the relation between academics and industrial partners is very complex and the structure of the building reflects only the very top of the whole maze of the interactions. Arrangements for a particular project depend crucially on the type and the attitude of the industrial partner, financial arrangements, goals of the projects, legal position of the University, interests of the leading academic, strategic interests of the NGI and many others. It would be too naïve to expect that such a relatively small building as the NGI could accommodate all possible requirements within its architecture, though the attempt was made to accommodate the most common ones.

[E] Experience of Design

The design of the NGI lived two lives: one for the scientists, another for the architects. Architect Tony Ling and his team from the London-based firm Jestico+Whiles experienced the challenges of designing the NGI differently from the scientists. Scientists "dwell" in buildings in specific ways. To learn about the nature of their practices, how they work, and to grasp their expectations, Tony listened to stories of many graphene researchers. For him the texture of the spaces and the surfaces grow from disparate influences. They should not only reflect the changing needs and preferences of different research teams, the vision of the lead scientist, Kostya, or the funding realities of graphene research, but also the complex properties of graphene and its projected development. As a scientific building, the NGI followed, what Tony calls, "an inside-out" approach whereby the form grew from the internal arrangement of the programme and its gradual transformation

Fig. 2: A scale model of the NGI building, photo Jestico + Whiles.

through the design development (Fig. 2). While describing the unique collaboration he had with Kostya in designing the building, Tony emphasizes how exceptional it is to have a client involved in the process from day one. They spent many hours working together and discussing every step in the design and the development of the building.

Although Tony had had experience in designing nanotechnology buildings (for the University of Southampton and the University of Sydney), he finds that "the main difference between the NGI and other nanotechnology-related buildings is the fact that they are generally part of the Physics department (…) whereas in the NGI, the sole purpose of it is to explore *the properties of graphene*, and also, the NGI has a policy of invitation of industry partners, who are given space within the building, to work with the academics at the university, to mutually benefit from the research."[8]

Graphene and its properties were at the core of the design concept. The architect had tried to understand as much as possible about the nature of graphene before his team started work on the building, but, as he shares honestly, "the actual, very detailed properties and mechanics of working with graphene are beyond our grasp."[9] Instead, the architects' main job, he explains, was to understand what kind of environments the scientists working on graphene needed, that is, what spaces are important for the practices in which graphene can grow and "dwell" alongside the scientists.

However, there are many challenges for designing a "home" for graphene and its scientists to "dwell" in together. One challenge that emerged from the very beginning, and endured throughout, was related to its size. There was a discrepancy between the expectation for a 5000 sqm building, according to the university's feasibility report, and a much larger building, calculated on the basis of the scientists' needs. The major reason for this is that such a research-intensive building will have a large fraction of space dedicated to services, and thus will have a large gap between the net and gross space. For six weeks the designers analysed the net to gross floor ratios, and the cost per square metre of

[8] Interview with Tony Ling, 23.06.2017.

[9] Interview with Tony Ling, 23.06.2017.

similar buildings with clean rooms that had been recently completed, producing different options and comparative scenarios. Finally, the tests proved that a larger building was necessary (7,825 sqm). As Tony recalls: "it was quite an intensive exercise to eventually challenge that the building was to be bigger."[10] While architects probed different scenarios, tested options and refined their working techniques, mobilised new tools and engaged in experimentation, the scientists fine-tuned their own expectations and the funders increased their budget. The proliferation of technical choices in design (e.g. the façade options, the seminar room arrangements), in turn, influenced design and aesthetic choices.

Architects spent a lot of time with the scientists to understand the specific requirements for the NGI. Due to the complexity of the building it took weeks of iterative interviews with the scientists, involving experimental layouts and 3D models to mediate between the architects and the scientists as the clients, and clarify what they wanted. Tony and his team engaged in a process of generating "experimental layouts of notional ideas," spatial tools for eliciting the opinions and desires of the graphene researchers (Fig. 3). The layouts, in effect, acted as prompts or tools for translation between these two domains, asking "is this what you mean?" Numerous discussions followed, from which both the architects and the scientists learned from one another. As a result of experiments and trials in the design lab, these images also served as a way of communicating the expectations of the scientists. They allowed the designers to learn from the scientists as clients and at the same time helped clarify issues related to the structure, mechanical, electrical as well as IT aspects.

Among the many issues that required an active exchange between design and scientific know-how, the "veil" (see chapter 13) was central. It was an expression of the process of organising the building according to its internal functions, an approach that Tony imagined as "inside-out." During this process, architects again made numerous models, both virtual and physical, of the whole building as well as of the different components of the building. They engaged in 3D modelling,

[10] Interview with Tony Ling, 23.06.2017.

Fig. 3: A prototype rendering of the NGI building, photo Jestico + Whiles.

and even produced a 1:50 model of the rear façade of the building to visualise how it fits together. The models illustrated different options, took into account cost and programme factors, and also the planning and university contexts. They, like the veil, showcased the "inside-out" approach: starting from a number of knowns, the building grows around the programme, taking a distinctive shape that follows its internal organization, a kind of crystallisation. While the design process of the NGI involved fine-tuning the tools and techniques of both architects and scientists, it also impacted the way the building mattered in the daily practices of graphene research.

1

[M] Location, Location, Location

Before we proceed to the explanations of the rationale behind the particular design solutions of the NGI, it is important to understand the administrative structure which exists in the University. Most academics in the University of Manchester are employed by a particular school: School of Physics and Astronomy, School of Computer Science, School of Material Science, etc. The way academics are divided into schools is mainly determined by the teaching activity. It happens often that in terms of their research activities academics from different schools are closer together than academics within one school. A couple of examples to demonstrate this: physicists who work in the area of non-linear dynamics would tend to collaborate more with people from the School of Mathematics; astronomers who design new detectors would have intimate relations with the school of Electrical Engineering. Institutes within the University act as "clubs," which assemble together researchers from different disciplines and are designed exactly to solve these discrepancies, gathering people by the projects, not on the basis of their teaching.[11] Researchers are attracted to the institutes because of access to shared facilities (which do not exist in the individual schools) and because of the ability to do collaborative, often cross-disciplinary, research and transfer technology between different projects.

Thus, it was crucially important to choose the physical location of the National Graphene Institute to be in close proximity to the schools whose researchers would be the major members of the Institute. Most of the academics would have some research activities located

[11] A number of institutes exist in the UoM and function in a similar way (ie the Manchester Urban Institute, Photon Science Institute, Manchester Institute of Biotechnology, etc.). They might or might not have their own building.

both in the schools and in the institute, and to allow easy access and communication the travel time between the two research locations should be within five to ten minutes. Considering that academics who are the most active in graphene research belong to the School of Physics and Astronomy, School of Chemistry, School of Material Science and School of Computer Science — the location of the NGI Institute should be central on the University campus (Fig. 4).

Fig. 4: Campus map. The map of the campus of the University of Manchester within 3 minutes walking radiuses around some of the buildings. Blue radius – the former School of Material Science; purple — the School of Computer Science (number 40 on the map); green — the School of Physics and Astronomy (number 54 on the map); green — the School of Chemistry (number 61 on the map). The present location of the NGI is marked by number 90. The blue arrow indicates the direction to the north.

Such potential central location presented a range of problems — it is not that easy to find a plot of land of sufficient size; it is difficult to build in the centre of the campus because, apart from the plot for the building, one requires an adjacent space for the services/storage during the construction; it is very likely that a lot of communications (water, gas, electrical, telecommunications, etc.) will be laid under the plot and thus have to be relocated; etc.

Also, the specifics of the building present additional problems. The most important component of the building is the **clean room**. Prior to the NGI the group of Geim, Grigorieva and Novoselov combined efforts with the groups of Prof. Ernie Hill and Prof. Tom Tomson in running the small clean rooms in the Computer Science building. Built originally for the needs of the data storage group in the Computer Science, it became the technology hub for the mesoscopic physics group of Geim, Grigorieva and Novoselov from 2001 and up to the moment when the NGI was constructed. Even now it is still used for students training and as out-spill clean room as well. Small (only about 250 m^2) and cosy, it hosted all essential equipment for small, dedicated operation. However, already in mid 2000 it was overcrowded with equipment, some of which was located in the chase areas. As the activity on graphene broadened and new types of devices needed to be produced, new technologies have been introduced which required dedicated equipment and space, and thus the question about expansion stood really sharply.

Clean rooms are the special type of laboratories designed for research on nanotechnology, mainly to prepare nanostructured devices. They require strict environmental controls in terms of temperature and humidity, stability of those parameters, cleanness of the air from any dust particles, illumination, vibrations etc. Such laboratories need a lot of supporting facilities (air handling units, extraction). In order to minimise the services, it makes sense to localise the clean rooms on one floor, rather than split them between different floors. Also, it is much easier to control the vibrations on the lowest floor of the building. Thus, the plot of land chosen for the Institute ideally should be able to fit the whole clean room on one floor.

Another solution, which would significantly help with the communications and logistics, is to have **several entrances to the Institute**. Having a large building means that people coming from the wrong side of the campus would have to go around to enter the Institute, which is not ideal, especially in the wet Manchester weather. So, several entrances which lead directly to the labs and the clean room would save time and improve communication.[12]

Thus, the largest square plot of land in the close proximity to the major departments, and one of the main arteriae in the city, Oxford Road, has been chosen for the location of the graphene institute.

---

[12] The GEIC, situated only a few hundred metres further away, turned out to be much more disconnected.

1 [E] Experiencing Movement

Location matters. It matters where the production of knowledge takes place. For the scientists involved in graphene research, being close to the main arteria of the city is crucial. Let us witness how they experience the location and how it matters for their daily work. As Rahul Nair, Professor of Materials Physics, explains, "this building is the best place for our experiments. We have a lab there, if you ask my students, for example, if I ask them to relocate from this building to any other building, they will not do it; they want to be *here*. Because they like their lab, they like the social space, they like the location — because it's really close to Oxford Road."[13] What is so important about *here?* What makes it work as a location? Indeed, the central position of the building facilitates quick transit as it connects the existing buildings on campus — Chemistry, Physics, Material Sciences — to the NGI as a hub for graphene research. Being connected and being in transit is significant. As a result, the multiple entrances and exits form a particularly important feature of the building for coming and going.

The two main entrances ensure connectivity and facilitate quick transit through the building. No time is lost. Instead, passing through it as if it were a street passage, but accessible only for those equipped with the NGI badge, turns it into an important "urban knot." For them, coming and going, entering and exiting is important. Sarah Haigh, Professor of Materials Characterisation, for instance, prefers the front entrance from Booth Street East. "I like sunshine," she explains. "Last Sunday I was here, and I was sat in the lobby at the entrance of the building [from Booth Street East] that has lovely glass doors (Fig. 5). On that Sunday I was sat by the reception for three hours doing some work, sat on the floor with my laptop, just because it was lovely, sunny;

[13] Interview with Rahul Raveendran Nair, 04.07.2017.

it was like being in a conservatory, wonderful, and the students were coming in and going."[14] Other scientists prefer accessing the building from the back entrance. It is "conveniently positioned because the bus stop is only a minute walk from here," comments Andrey Kretinin, Lecturer in Materials Physics. He continues: "I just come straight through the back entrance to the lab."[15] Most buses stop on Oxford Road; it is a central artery for Manchester. Bus 147, the campus bus, for instance, allows for the quick commute of academics and students around the campus. From the bus stop, it is only a minute walk to the back entrance. For Andrey, it is a straightforward passage from the rear entrance to his lab. The quickest route.

Yet, if you want to reach the front desk where Sarah was sitting with her laptop on the floor, you may not reach it as "the route from the back to the front of the building is confusing, you have to go up the stairs, you can't walk from the rear of the building to the main reception."[16] It is not the quickest route. Clearly the rear entrance is not meant for external visitors, but only for scientists and technicians who "dwell" in the NGI — who call it "home." The rear entrance takes them right to their labs or offices easily through the stairs or the large goods lift. However, it is also for VIP visitors. For instance, to greet the Chinese president or Prince William and Kate Middleton, the Duke and Duchess of Cambridge, NGI scholars welcomed them through the back entrance.[17]

Most of the external visitors, the guests, both Manchester staff and others, can only access the NGI through the front door (Fig. 5). A number of bureaucratic steps are needed for guests. They must register, sign in with their name, the date, the time of entry, the person who will be visited at the NGI, leaving an empty space for the time of exiting the building. Then, they receive a badge to take with them. It is only

14 Interview with Sarah Haigh, 10.07.2017.

15 Interview with Andrew Kretinin, 29.06.2017.

16 Interview with Richard Cutting, 10.07.2017.

17 There is also another back entrance/exit to the building from the east side used as a fire exit and also for the delivery of equipment and big machineries between Booth Street East and building number 33 on the map (see Fig. 4). It is also used occasionally for VIP visitors.

Fig. 5: The front entrance of the NGI building, photo by Albena Yaneva.

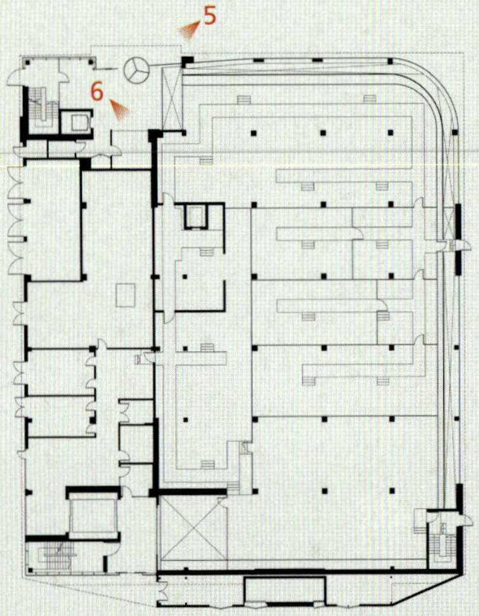

after passing through these steps of registration that they can enter the building. They go in, visit the building, and then exit it from the same front entrance, signing out. Singing in/signing out, going in/going out, up/down — these are the simple moves the external visitors perform. In contrast, equipped with a special card, the NGI "dwellers" can access from any entrance; their moves are more unpredictable: in, up (stairs or lifts), across and through (labs, corridors, atria), then out (from any of the exits). The card does something more than the visitor's badge: it opens lab doors and offices. Yet, each person's card opens different doors as most spaces are card protected. The travels of those who "dwell" here are not absolutely free. The administrators' cards, for instance, can open offices and meeting rooms, but cannot open the lab doors or the clean room. The researchers' cards open the lab doors of their respective group and the clean rooms; the technicians open the gas and storage rooms, and the doors to the roof. Access is variegated; there are different kinds of access, different itineraries. If anyone who "dwells" here wishes to get access to other spaces, they need to have a "good excuse" to get it and to pass through an induction process with the safety officer. Like the visitors, there are steps to pass through to gain access to where one does not yet have it. If we follow the daily flows of people and things, and the conditions for access, the different lives, the different spatial flows in the building themselves become accessible to us.

The building, as a whole, is always accessible for the scientists. The coming and going has no time limit. Equipped with their pass, researchers can come and work at any time, day or night, weekday or weekend. Let us witness for a moment the different flows of people and things going through the entrances and the exits.

Fig. 6: The receptionist Beverley Brown at the front desk, photo by Albena Yaneva.

At the central entrance, Beverley Brown sits at the reception desk (Fig. 6). She guards the NGI from unexpected visitors, greeting and registering every single person who enters the building in a big black or blue book. "It is a closed research facility," explains Beverley, "nobody is allowed to just walk in and wander around."[18] The blue book is for external visitors and

[18] Interview with Beverley Brown, 11.10.2019.

the black book is for university people who require permission to access the NGI building. It is there where we sign-in every time. Those who we visit inform the reception that they are expecting visitors. Beverley gets that phone call; she knows that somebody is coming and is prepared to welcome them. However, we cannot just enter. The NGI "dweller" comes down to collect us, to lead us into and through the building. The black book is important; it keeps the records of visitors for the entire year. Everyone signs in. After the ritual of signing in, we can finally go into the building accompanied by our host. The blue visitors' book is managed in a slightly different way. Each external visitor signs in by directly filling in the information onto a blue sticker (the carbon copy remains in the book). Beverley tears out the sticker and puts it on a lanyard for them. While the copy stays for the record, the blue original travels with the visitors on their badge. If, at any moment during their visit, the name and the type of the visitors is to be accounted for, that information can be easily traced back from the carbon copies left in the book. The blue badge/lanyard makes the external visitors visible at any time as they stroll in the building while the internal UoM visitors are less easy to detect. Still, we all need to sign out by adding the time of our departure in either book before exiting the building. Even gone, we remain visible inside the building.

The books (one for each year) are kept for a certain time in the records. Visitors are registered in a meticulous way in order to account for the number and type of people having access to the facility. This visibility is important. Reports on the use of the building and the kinds of people who access it are generated; this is to take an account of the life of it. Additionally, as Beverley explains, there is another kind of accountability: it is important to keep a trace in case "anything happens." Sometimes, it is necessary to locate the name of a visitor; they can use the books to trace them back. In a way, one never leaves the building without leaving a trace.

Watching Beverley greeting people at the reception desk, chatting with them, and sharing a laugh, tells a lot about the life of the building. Here comes Gabriella to see her on her way out; they comment on the cancelled Friday seminar. Here is Mark Bissett, Senior Lecturer in Nanomaterials and two other colleagues chatting and laughing, and Beverley is using this opportunity to remind them about a money collection for the Christmas "do." At the entrance and exit, as people come and go, she says, "when you see people you have to grab them," and while she sits at the reception desk, she catches up with everyone. As people move quickly throughout the building, passing by here, it is important to reach out, to slow people down. Occasionally, she stops and waves at someone who passes by the building. The glass architecture of the reception allows people walking by the building to see Beverley sitting behind her desk and greet her from afar. She explains, "these are all people from other buildings. As I have been to the University for a long time [she worked at the Physics building and the Electrical Engineering building before], I know quite a lot of people. So, they just pass and wave."[19] Even if passers-by do not know Beverley, as the transparency of glass has an inviting appeal, people tend to stop by, enter the lobby and ask questions when they feel lost on campus. Beverly is happy to help them find their way. As the designers' aim was to maximise and utilise all usable space in the building, little space was left for the reception desk. It is small, but its design is efficient; a cosy waiting area with conformable sofas for guests make it even more welcoming. People can come in and pause. The movement of the building slows down here.

At the back entrance (Fig. 7) we meet the "guardian" of the rear door, Chris Livingston, who is the Stores Manager and gas room technician. We do not have a card, so we wait. We wave at Chris hoping he will see us behind two layers of glass doors. Yet he is very focused on his work at his desk. Luckily, one of the technicians, Hannah, comes out and opens the door. We notice immediately the people who access the building from this side are of a different kind: mainly students and NGI staff, equipped with the access swipe card. Not people, like us, waiting and waving. Chris has many duties: he oversees the gas room, connecting the cylinders, and filling liquid nitrogen dewars, while also taking care of deliveries. He is not expecting visitors without card

[19] Interview with Beverley Brown, 11.10.2019.

Fig. 7: The back entrance of the NGI building, photo by Albena Yaneva.

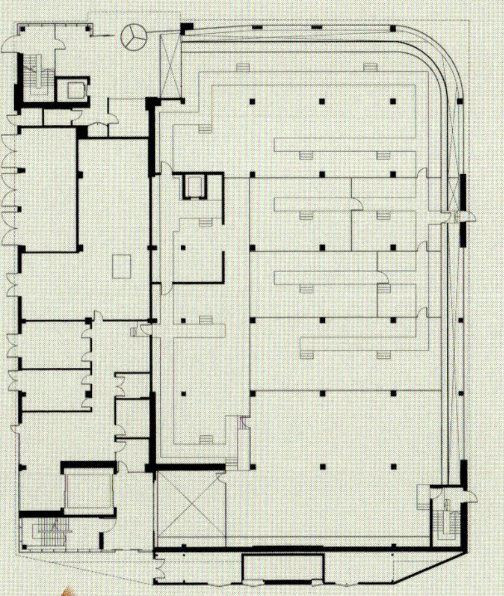

7

access here. While sitting at his desk and managing all these tasks, he remains visible, ever-present, through the glass door to anyone who accesses the building from the rear entrance. Like Beverley at the front entrance, Chris stands guard. He keeps an eye on those who enter the building. But his role is a little different. As he explains: "obviously the people coming from here usually know where they are going because they have the card access to go upstairs in the lift and through the door."[20] Those who enter here do not have to go through the same ritual to enter the building. Rather than signing into a book, the interaction is more informal, saying hello while passing through. However, his door suggests another difference. Like the glass façade, the glass door indicates accessibility, inviting visitors to rely on him as a first point of contact while entering the building. But, this "openness" changes when his door is closed. The closed glass door implies that he has different functions than the receptionist at the front desk (which is always open during working hours). There is also another door, a back door, that connects to Chris's office. This door is linked to the loading bay area where he, if he is not in his office, performs his other duties. Usually, he is there in the morning. Chris begins his day at 8.30 am, to welcome all the deliveries, the parcels with equipment, consumables and samples that the researchers need to continue their experiments.

Let's follow the students coming through the rear entrance: they come, wave "good morning" to Chris and go up the stairs. No time is wasted by waiting for the lift, especially if they only go onto the 1st floor. This entrance also provides access to

[20] Interview with Chris Livingston, 16.10.2019.

the clean room, and the researchers entering the building from here, instead of rushing up the stairs, take the elevator or use the stairs to go down, and "gown up" to go into the clean room. For the many scientists equipped with an NGI card, choosing between front and back entrance is not an innocent act: the side of the building they enter from guides them to different kind of processes related to graphene research, and to different sides of graphene itself.

In addition to the card holders, there are crowds of other people who want to access the NGI from the back door too. As Chris says, "sometimes I do see people standing outside the building because it is confusing. So, people will just stand there, and I will go outside and will say to them that they need to access the building from the front entrance. As you know it is a closed facility. They have to sign in; that's the protocol."[21] After Chris has directed them to the front door, they come and find Beverley and then go through the ritual of registering in either the black or the blue book. This happened more often in the early days of the NGI building. People who were fascinated by graphene would come to the building in the hopes that they could catch a glimpse. Rather than getting access to the building, however, they would have to visit online. Chris would direct them to the NGI website where they can find information about the material, or, if determined, they could see information about booking a tour of the building on specified open days. Even if these external visitors did sneak into the building, perhaps by sliding in behind others who have access, they would soon be trapped with nowhere else to go as they need cards to access the doors and lifts. Their visit ends here; one click of a button and they go out.

The buzz at the front or the rear entrances of a scientific building tells us a lot about its nature. It is where crowds of people and things enter and exit the building. Watch Chris for a moment as he prepares the deliveries in his office at the rear entrance (Fig. 8). This is where all the supplies arrive, and depending on their nature, Chris can tell what kind of work is happening in the labs. The supplies provide the means of seeing into the life of the building. He explains that he can

[21] Interview with Chris Livingston, 16.10.2019.

Fig. 8: Chris Livingston in the delivery room next to his office, photo by Simon Mitchell.

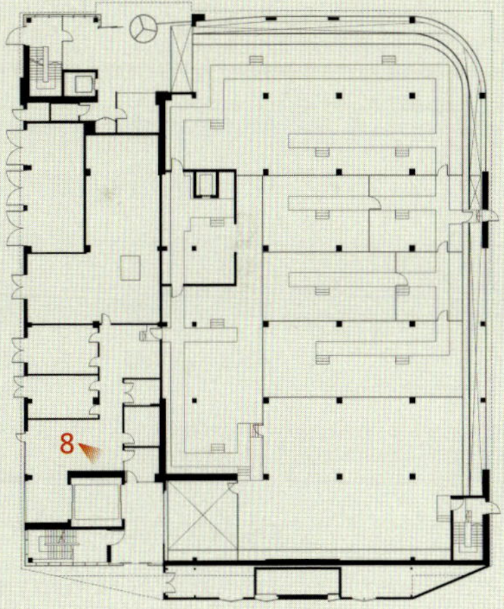

"get into what they [the scientists] are really doing in the labs when they purchase specific things, like gloves or argon."[22] Every parcel is received by Chris here, who unpackages them and sends them to the labs. But it is also where all the samples (the new kinds of materials or devices) produced in the NGI labs begin their own travels to other labs in the UK, USA, Europe, China or Australia. When a sample lands on Chris's desk, he must describe it carefully and pay heed, especially, if the item is hazardous. As he elaborates: "I do not know exactly what the work is and what the process is until they send a sample, because I send samples out all around the world depending on who they [the scientists] are collaborating with. That's how I get an idea of what exactly they are doing."[23] We look at the paperwork together. Today he has sent some graphene samples

[22] Interview with Chris Livingston, 16.10.2019.

[23] Interview with Chris Livingston, 16.10.2019.

on paper to the University of Cambridge. There is another one that departed to Australia. Chris fills in a form that describes the sample's weight, size, dimensions, and its destination. For the second sample, as it is going overseas, he also prepares a commercial invoice—a description for customs purposes. This paperwork is important. Just like those who need to register for access into the building, for the graphene-based sample to travel smoothly, to reach its destination, it has to be registered as well for travel. Without it, many researchers from around the globe could not continue their work. Describing the samples, preparing the deliveries' paperwork, Chris has an important role in the unstoppable rhythm of the global engine of graphene research. If, at the front desk Beverley is busy registering all humans attracted by the power of graphene, at the rear entrance, Chris is busy registering the nonhumans (supplies, equipment, samples) entering and existing the NGI to frantically travel the world.

Following crowds of people and things accessing the building from different sides, we can encounter the connectivity, the coming and going, that the location of the building affords. Far from being a static container of activities with a single façade/front entrance, the numerous entrances/exits make the building function as an active machine, accelerating the speed of transits, redistributing the flows of visitors, and regulating their trajectories in an efficient way. The building acts as an "urban knot" of the city network of research and industry, while simultaneously attracting crowds of external visitors. The many entrances and exits form an important feature of the new generation of scientific buildings and ensure a membrane-type of "porosity" that integrates it further into the dense urban fabric. The specific glass design of the entrances/exits succeeds in speeding up the work of the NGI "dwellers," while carefully filtering the access of the external visitors so as to protect the scientific work and ensure greater efficiency. By ethnographically following the movements around the front and the rear entrances, we also get a glimpse into the universal circulation of things and people that graphene research implies. From an urban knot, the NGI gradually turns into a global node.

2

[M] Square Shape

Another consequence of the location chosen (which is by itself a consequence of the proximity requirements) is the shape of the building. The small size of the plot of land available at the location chosen, and the prerequisite to minimise the number of floors (due to both cost and internal traffic implications) dictated that the building should occupy the whole area available. This explains the square shape of the building (Fig. 9).

9

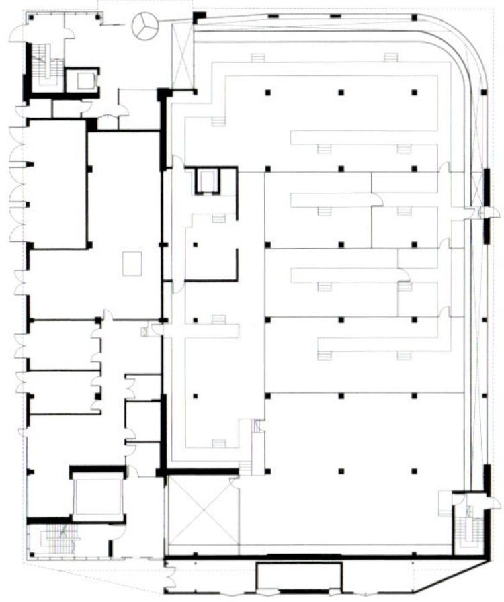

Fig. 9: The NGI, view from Booth Street, photo by Albena Yaneva.

The shape of the building has a consequence on the relation between labs and offices. The problem with a square building is the access to the daylight in the centre of it, which presented quite a puzzle to solve to the design team.

First, the laboratories which do not require daylight (or, better to say, which would benefit from being in the permanent darkness) have been identified. Those include optical labs (including space for Raman, infrared and FTIR spectrometers); Faraday cages. Optical labs are designed to measure very weak optical response from our materials and devices, and thus any stray light might be detrimental for the measurements where counting individual photons is the routine operation. The Faraday cages (or shielded rooms) are not that sensitive to the external light. But being basically large metal cases, they don't allow any light inside anyway, so it is logical that such labs are left in the darkness.

Thus, a set of such labs were logically placed in the middle of the building, still leaving large spaces which need to be provided with light. One solution here is the atrium. Such an architectural feature naturally makes the space more alive, creating illuminated areas. Another solution is to put offices along the perimeter of the building and to make the walls of the offices transparent. As the offices are only a few metres across, one could easily see outside from the interior of the building, effectively providing the interior labs with access to daylight (see chapter 8b).

3

[M] Vibration

Most operations in the field of nanotechnology and nanoelectronics are extremely sensitive to vibrations: production of devices which are only few atoms in size or imaging on the subatomic scale require extreme stability. Luckily, the bedrock on the site of the NGI is located at relatively low depth (6–8 metres), so the decision was made to dig down to the bedrock, establish an additional foundation on top of that and locate the most vibration-sensitive equipment right on top of that foundation. This way the clean room ended up in the basement.

Furthermore, to avoid vibrations from the busy road located to the North of the building — the most sensitive equipment (electron beam lithography, focused ion beam, scanning electron microscopy, atomic force microscopy, Raman spectroscopy, ellipsometry, etc.) was positioned in the south part of the building. In order to avoid the vibrations from the footfall the equipment is disconnected from the raised floor (which allows air circulation in the clean room) and placed on the so-called "elephant legs" — the metal pillars which are anchored directly to the slab.

Also, to achieve the VCB standard of vibrations throughout the building we have chosen relatively small grid and thicker slab across the whole NGI.

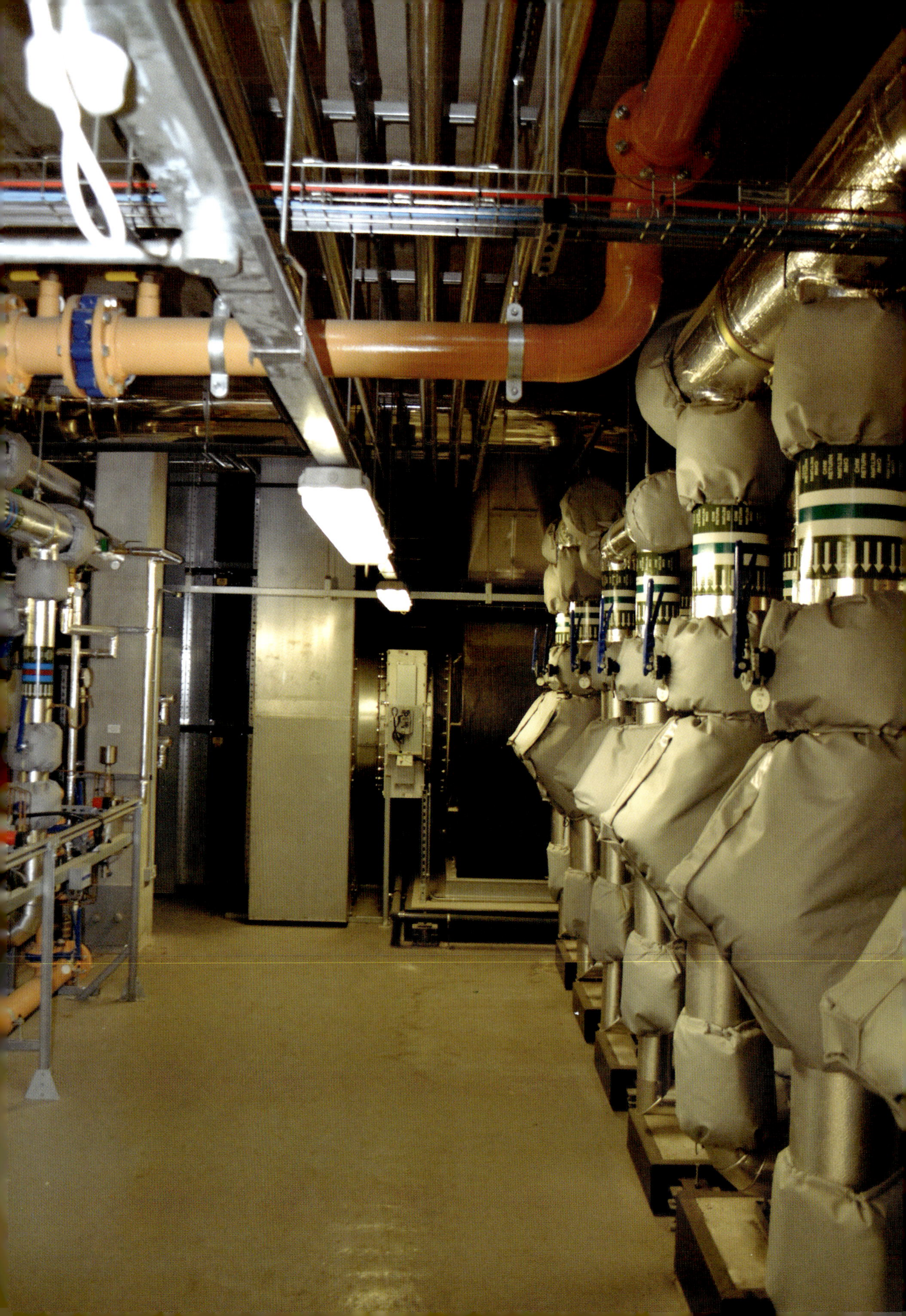

4

[M] Two for the Price of One

The clean rooms and the labs require a lot of services. Probably the most important are the air-handling units which bring air from outside, clean it from dust particles, cool it down to reduce the absolute humidity and then warms back again to the required temperature (21°C) to supply inside of the clean room. Apart from that there are solvent and acid vapour extract (which should be cleaned with scrubbers), process cooling water, ultra-pure water loop, compressed air, supply of multiple (21) gases, etc. (Fig. 10).

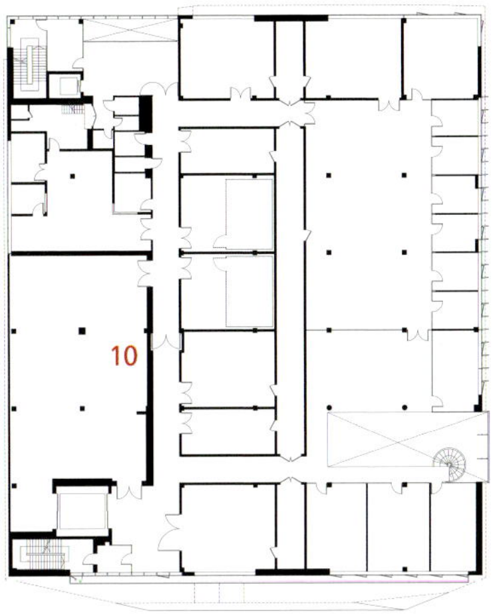

Altogether such service equipment is very heavy, includes a lot of pumps and produces a

Fig. 10: The Central Utilities Building, photo by Ben Blackwell.

Fig. 11: The Central Utilities Building, parallel pump sets for process cooling loop, photo by Simon Mitchell.

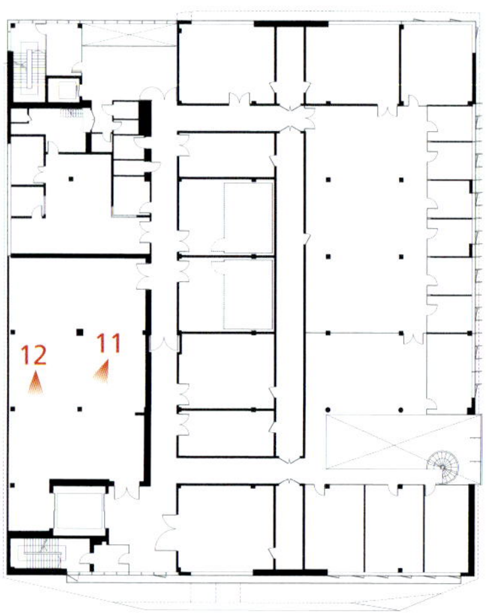

lot of vibrations, acoustic noise, heat, electrical interference (Figs. 11, 12). It was clear from the very beginning that if positioned close to the research equipment the crosstalk and interference will be very strong and the delicate experiments which are often carried out in the NGI can be ruined.

To this end a decision was made to make **two buildings** under the same roof, completely disconnected structurally. The smaller one along the west side of the construction will be occupied by the services (it was named the Central Utilities Building or CUB) and would be separated from the rest of the building by a 50mm gap. This would isolate the research part of the building from the heavy machinery in the CUB. Even though the CUB and the main building are connected through the foundation, the bedrock is massive enough, so the vibrations are not transmitted through the ground.

Such separation into the CUB and the main building also serves another purpose. It helps to split the responsibilities clearly. Whereas it is the responsibilities of technicians and research staff to look after the laboratory equipment, the facilities are usually serviced by the central estate department in the University. Thus, having the research and the service facilities to be separated into different buildings creates a clear demarcation line in terms of responsibilities and access privileges, which significantly simplifies the operation and the management of the building.

Fig. 12: The Central Utilities Building, parallel pump sets for primary building cooling, photo by Simon Mitchell.

4

[E] Experiencing the Hidden Building

To understand how the second building (the CUB) functions let's witness two scenes:

Scene one: On the roof

May 2019. At the end of the day we visit the roof of the building with Christopher Hyde, a Senior Equipment Technician and Olga Falko, NGI Project Manager. Here again, the access is limited and secured through the card pass to avoid "too many people going on the roof."[24] Only about a dozen people have access to the roof, the 4th floor, and the 2nd floor plant rooms (as well as the -2 plant rooms below the ground

Fig. 13: The "plant" on the roof: acid process extract and abatement system, photo by Albena Yaneva.

[24] Interview with Christopher Hyde, 31.05.2019.

Fig. 14: Foreground: acid extract; background: primary cooling coils, photo by Albena Yaneva.

floor). As we walk across it, we discover it is not just a simple roof. Everything above the level of the concrete finishes and the steel work is a plant area (Fig. 13); there is cladding around it in order to cover "the ugly structures," jokes Christopher, "it makes them look a lot nicer." He shows us the power supply as well as the solvent and acid extracts that clean all of the solvents and acids before they are emitted into the air (Fig. 14). Christopher points to equipment on the roof: "these are the three chillers that chill all the water, [and] two expansion ones in case we need more to retrofit them. These are the solar panels for power generation."[25] What an impressive industrial spectacle! Yet, with the steam coming off the extracts, billowing into clouds in the air, it creates the impression of pollution. With this impression, we find ourselves in danger of resorting to the industrial metaphor — one that Manchester, as a city, is increasingly trying to shed itself of. Yet, Christopher corrects us: "people think that's pollution but once it's gone through this system

[25] Interview with Christopher Hyde, 31.05.2019.

it's all perfectly clean."[26] It is a clean cloud. Perhaps another metaphor is necessary.

This entire plant on the roof is connected with the central utilities building (CUB)—the invisible building within the NGI. We picture, for a moment, how that giant hidden network of pipes goes all the way down to the storage with the solvent extract and the acids; it runs smoothly on every floor with offshoots feeding all the labs and further down to the clean rooms. Now, we can connect the dots; there is an immense web of gases traversing the whole building, ending up here on the roof. A hidden infrastructure that is missing from accounts in design literature, however, its impact on architecture and the functioning of buildings is indisputable once you go inside the NGI, and follow the practices of its inhabitants, like Christopher, who make it visible.

Scene two: Monitoring the NGI

November 2019. John is at his computer, and as he clicks, explores the NGI building through the Building Monitoring System (BMS) to inspect the building performance (Fig. 15). As the NGI Head of Operations, John is in charge of facility management and engineering development. He looks after a number of buildings: the NGI and the IT building with its old clean rooms, and he also has access to the GEIC building. The BMS is used by Estates[27] to monitor every building across the campus, which becomes noticeable as alarms go off. Sitting at his desk, John monitors the functioning and behaviour of different buildings, with the recording of all the data available over periods of 24 to 48 hours. Within the NGI, he examines the humidity levels across the building, and conducts performance checks of the clean room, inspecting the temperature, the room pressure, the pressure of the ducts, and to see whether any alarms have been set off. From here

[26] Interview with Christopher Hyde, 31.05.2019.

[27] The Directorate of Estates and Facilities forms part of the Professional Services at the University of Manchester and it is the Directorate's duty to manage the University estate. It is in charge of constructing new and refurbishing existing buildings as well as the development of imaginative and innovative landscapes on campus.

Fig. 15: The building manager John Whittaker (in his office on the 3rd floor) using the BMS on his computer, photo by Ben Blackwell.

he can also check the temperature of all of the laboratories on the 2nd floor on the basis of data logged, and the temperatures of the primary cooling loops of the different equipment, as well as many other parameters. This system allows John to "stroll" through the building without having to leave his office on the 3rd floor; he has a "snapshot" of all the computers, of the different rooms' behaviours, without having to go there — even the roof where we have just visited with Christopher and Olga.

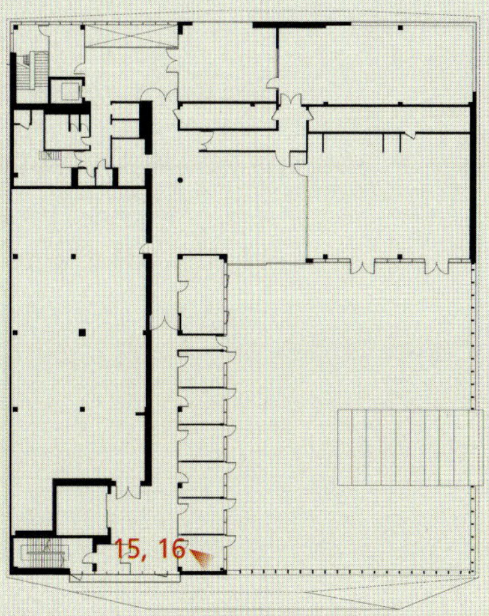

Fig. 16: John Whittaker using the BMS in his office, a zoom into the Acid Exhaust System, photo by Ben Blackwell.

Instead of going up there in the rain, John stays and oversees the extract levels from his cosy office overlooking the garden on the roof terrace. He can zoom into the acid extract system (Fig. 16), the gas and pressure metres. Opening different windows on the huge computer screens, John can delve down into deeper individual zones as well. Each floor is its own zone. The BMS also allows John to travel across the campus, again, from the comfort of his office. In case an issue is raised by the scientists or technicians from other facilities, he can check on the system right away.

Here, the whole "graphene ecology" on campus resurfaces onto John's computer as he clicks buttons, checks systems and zooms in to inspect parameters. An unstoppable rhythm of performing buildings, gas systems and mechanical circuits. Like the hidden infrastructure of the NGI, here is another hidden system that connects the ecology together. A functioning ecology of flows.

5

[M] Solutions Dictated by the Process

There are other important factors which have been taken into consideration early on during the design stage. Such fundamental constrains impact strongly on the design and pretty much determine the final look of the building. Below we will consider some of these constrains.

a. Floor loading

It is always tempting to design the labs to be as universal as possible: provide full scope of services in every corner of the building; arrange high ceilings in each room; design maximum floor loading on every floor, etc. In reality one can gain significantly in cost and construction time if the services are engineered smartly, alike labs are combined close to each other and relevant rooms are placed in the vicinity of the services they use.

Distributing the floor load across the building can reduce the cost dramatically. It seemed logical that the very top floor should have significantly lower floor load than the others, especially in conjunction with the decision to have a roof garden. Then the activities, which do not require heavy equipment can be placed there. The first candidates are administration offices (offices of the academics should be located close to students and labs). Any cafeteria, pantry, meeting rooms must go there as well, which would also allow people to utilise the roof garden fully (Manchester weather permitting). Among the other facilities which can go there is the chemistry room. Typically, equipment is not very heavy in this sort of activity, so such decision seems logical.

b. Chemistry room

There are other considerations as well which brought the chemistry and furnace rooms to the top floor. For instance, proximity to services are crucially important, as it allows one to save significantly on cost. There are two major services one can consider: gas supply and extraction. There are two gas storages available in the NGI. One on the ground floor, close to the delivery area, and another is on the roof of the building. The latter is for future proof mainly, it hasn't been planned to be used from day one, but the communications have been laid during the construction, so it could be brought into operation very quickly. To ensure independency, it has been decided not to use the clean room ultra-pure water (UPW) loop, and rather use its own, located in the grey space adjacent to the chemistry room. So, the gas supply justifies two choices for the chemistry room location: either the top or the ground floor.

At the same time, another important service is the extraction. A dozen fume cabinets will require both solvent and acid extraction and furnaces in the furnace room need intensive heat extraction. Thus, the size of the ducting can be significant, so minimising the length of the ducting is an important cost- and space-saving exercise. This immediately dictates the top-floor disposition of the chemistry and furnace rooms — as much as possible closely to the extraction and scrubbers on the roof.

Another consideration comes from the necessity of planning for the worst. The building is filled up to the brim by the safety features, and yet, accidents do happen. Chemistry laboratories are probably most prone to accidents: fire, explosions, toxic contaminations, etc. In particular, one would like to avoid having explosions in the lower parts of the building: the pressure wave will damage all the floors above and below. At the same time, should an explosion happen at the top floor — the roof will be damaged, pressure released, thus minimising the destruction to the floors below. It is the hope of health and safety services and all the scientists that this consideration will never be checked in practice.

One argument against placing the chemistry laboratory at the top floor is that it might be a bit smelly at a time and thus the proximity to the kitchenette and coffee room is not desirable. Also, people getting out of the chemistry room need to be encouraged to wash their hands as thoroughly as possible, especially before taking any meal.

Still, the advantages of having the chemistry room on the top floor outweigh the inconveniences of having it close to the cafeteria. To this end special precautions have been undertaken to mitigate the possible issues. The entrance to the chemistry room, which is right in the middle of the common area on the top floor has been separated from it by a glass corridor. This allowed to keep the possible odours (good or bad) contained in the lab. Also, it discourages people to rush directly to the coffee machine upon exiting from the chemistry laboratory, directing them towards the washrooms instead.

c. Storage and goods lift determine the orientation of the building

In a square building like NGI, the CUB part can go practically to any side: north, south, east or west. There are minor considerations, like situating the viewing corridor connected to the clean room alongside the main roads. And the main entrance should preferably be from the Booth Street East (see the plan on Fig. 4). But the main practical consideration about which side the CUB building will go was given by the location of the loading bay.

In the building like NGI the loading bay and storage rooms are of crucial importance. With 100+ people in the building the goods traffic can be significant. Furthermore, being at the forefront of research, NGI is expected to have a regular influx of equipment. Occasionally this equipment has to be preassembled outside the labs, in order not to interfere much with the active research processes. Additional problem is the large traffic of gases for the clean rooms and laboratories: it is the responsibility of the store's manager to order and connect those, as well as return the empty bottles. Finally, it is most logical to co-locate the storage rooms with the goods lift.

Such a lift in a research-intensive building needs to be able to deliver all the current equipment as well as the one that will be brought up in future. The largest machine by size for the initial installation was the Vistec electron beam lithographer EBPG 5200, with a height of 2.3 metres and lateral dimensions of 1.53m × 2.17m. Whereas it is practically impossible to foresee what kind of apparatuses will need to be brought up in the future, one can think practically and guess that some of the service equipment might malfunction and thus need to be replaced. Especially it concerns the equipment in the CUB. Although the CUB is fitted with removable panels facing the outside, which can be taken out to facilitate access to the equipment, sometimes it might be more convenient to use the goods lift. So, the weight capacity of the lift was chosen to match the weight of the air handling units. That is how the NGI got a 3.5 tons combined goods/ passenger lift.

The best location for the delivery bay is the West side of the building. Delivery lorries would block traffic if the bay is located on any other side: in the North it is the busy Booth Street East road; in the East — the access to the Aquatic centre car park; and in the South — it is the exit from the car park of the Prospect house. The entrance from the service road in the West side of the NGI seems most logical: traffic there is rather infrequent, so any long parking of the large lorries, which might block the road temporarily during loading/ unloading will not be critical.

It is also clear that a 3.5 tons lift needs to go to the CUB. This way it will minimise the impact of the vibrations produced, will be closer to the equipment in the CUB (in case the faulty one need to be removed and the new one installed) and also it would not eat up the precious space from the laboratories and the clean rooms. That is how the fate of the CUB has been decided — it should go to the West side of the building.

a. Location of the atrium

Atrium is an important feature of the NGI, serving several key functions: it provides light into the interior of the building; creates focal point in the building, used for meetings, relaxation, etc. Surely it eats up the useful space, but there are arrangements made which would allow eventual conversion of atria into laboratory or office space. Yet, the location of the large atrium in the building is by no means random. The most sensitive and delicate equipment in the clean room (electron beam lithography) is located closer to the South part of the building, as far away as possible from the busy Booth Street East — the main source of vibrations. At the same time, such equipment is also sensitive to magnetic field and electromagnetic interference, so it should be located further away from the laboratories where the use of strong superconducting magnets (20 Tesla, or possibly even higher in the future) is anticipated.

Thus, it is logical that atrium would be situated directly above the electron beam lithography machines, avoiding the interference between different experiments.

6

[M] Design of the Storage Rooms

The design of the storage rooms and the delivery bay deserves a special attention. The reason is that in the NGI the store has multiple functions. Apart of regular delivery of goods, it also manages supply of chemicals, gases, liquid nitrogen, sending back the chemical waste. In the NGI all of this is managed by one person, so the store should be quite ergonomically organised.

With the clean rooms using 21 different gases — their supply and exchange is quite an operation. It is important to have continuous supply of all gases, so we used two-bottles on auto-exchange system with purging, with several bottles on standby. The storage for both full and empty bottles and the gas supply rooms are next to each other, which simplifies the bottle exchange process. Furthermore, rooms have doors from outside of the building (in addition to entrances from inside of the store). This should potentially allow the delivery company to bring full and collect empty bottles without using the main delivery gates and possibly even without bothering the store's manager. Another key feature of the storage room is the large gates. The gates are designed to accept goods which are much larger than the size of the lift — this is in order to account for packaging, which might be very bulky on delicate high-tech equipment (in order to protect it from vibrations and possible damage). The NGI has two delivery gates, right next to each other. One is directly opposite to the entrance to the goods lift in order to facilitate easy movement of the goods/equipment. Another, right next to the first one, leads to the main storage area. The storage area is equipped with a hoist for easy management of the heavy goods.

As mentioned above, the NGI has two entrances to facilitate more efficient flow of people. The South entrance (or the rear entrance) is used mainly by people moving to/from the Physics and Chemistry buildings and has a quick access to the entrance to the clean rooms. This entrance is unmanned, meaning that access is by security cards. However, it is always useful to monitor the entrance to mitigate possible access, security and technical issues. To this end the office of the store manager has a door and a window which lead directly to the entrance hall (see chapter 1, Fig. 8). This allows the manager effectively to take over porter functions of the South entrance as witnessed earlier in chapter 1.

One of the most important and complex services in the NGI is the supply of the gas and liquid nitrogen. Delivery of liquid nitrogen into the building is done by 70 litres transport vessels, which are filled at the special bay right outside the South entrance. It is the function of the store manager to facilitate the dewar filling and delivery to the particular lab of the NGI. Thus, the close proximity between the dewar filling point and the office of the store manager is essential. Delivery of nitrogen to the large storage vessels outside the NGI is done by an external company. The arrangements are such that the delivery person has access to the storage vessels and can fill in liquid nitrogen without bothering the store manager or even outside office hours.

6

[E] Experiencing the Flows

Fig. 17: Cabinets with gas cylinders in the storeroom, photo by Albena Yaneva.

Let us follow the work of Chris in the storage rooms for a moment. Visiting the gas room, we contemplate a landscape of cabinets that store gas cylinders (Fig. 17). Another complex infrastructure, but this time, with pipes (Fig. 18). Chris describes this infrastructure: "there's pipes leading through the ceilings and through the floor that go to various laboratories and clean rooms for the lab users to have access to gases. So, there are not many cylinders within the lab areas. All the gases will be used from down here."[28] Have a look at the different cylinders. Chris is in charge of ordering, storage, transportation, and installation. After ordering the chemicals, he tracks the delivery and when they arrive plans their installation in the cabinets. As the toxic gases might be dangerous, Chris usually liaises with the technical staff, the lab technicians or the cleaning staff, and they help with the installation; "it's a two-man job," he explains. Christopher whom we met earlier on the roof and Chris take care of the gases together and help each other. When required, they also do the installation of cylinders upstairs, in the labs, and are in charge of the connection with gauges that are set up in the labs.

One of the purposes of liquid nitrogen facility is to provide gas nitrogen to purge and clear the lines of any toxic or flammable gases.

[28] Interview with Chris Livingston, 01.12.2017.

Fig. 18: Chris Livingstone and the gas cylinders in the gas storeroom, photo by Ben Blackwell.

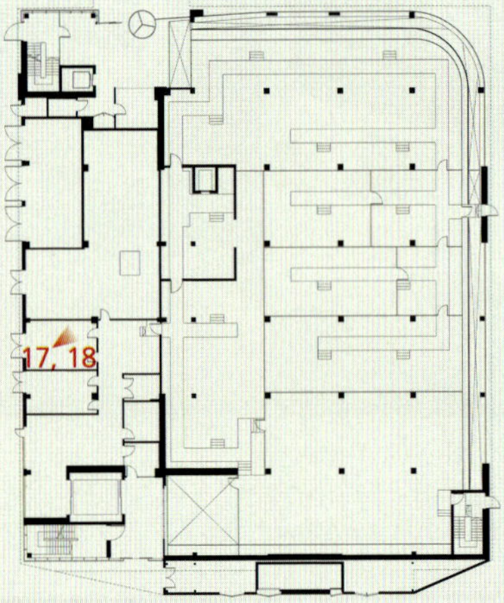

Dealing with liquid nitrogen is a delicate process, especially during transportation, as it goes into the lift and from there to the various labs. We are dealing with an extremely dangerous nonhuman agent here: if liquid nitrogen leaks it could suffocate researchers and technicians. It is extra dangerous to have leaks in a tightly enclosed environment as it can cause rapid asphyxiation. Chris is aware of this. Always cautious, he never travels in the same lift with the nitrogen vessel. A good and sensitive alarm system helps him detect leakages; it is an important ally in preventing possible harm. The alarms are connected to John's laptop. Using the BMS to monitor the building, as we have just witnessed, John can see the alarm signals at any time. The same goes for the quantity of liquid nitrogen: a record on his computer shows that a "fill" has been done overnight or in the early morning. Here, in the gas storeroom, we are at the other end of this sophisticated high-tech system for monitoring building performance. Chris has his own routine: he clears the toxic lines out and purges them with nitrogen, removes all of the excessive gases and reconnects them back to the labs. This is all done electronically from the gas room (Fig. 19). Connecting the parts, he pushes a button and all the sensors start reading. In the event of a fault, it cuts off automatically and prevents the system from causing danger.

Swimming in the quiet of the daily routine, hidden in cylinders and cabinets, the gases become present and remind us of their existence only when the alarm goes off, signalling a leakage or any other problem. Once the alarm goes off, Chris has to check and investigate what the problem might

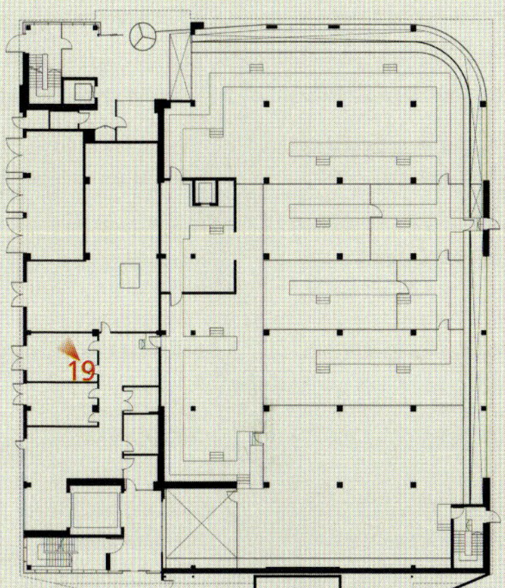

Fig. 19: Chris Livingstone working in the gas storeroom, photo by Simon Mitchell.

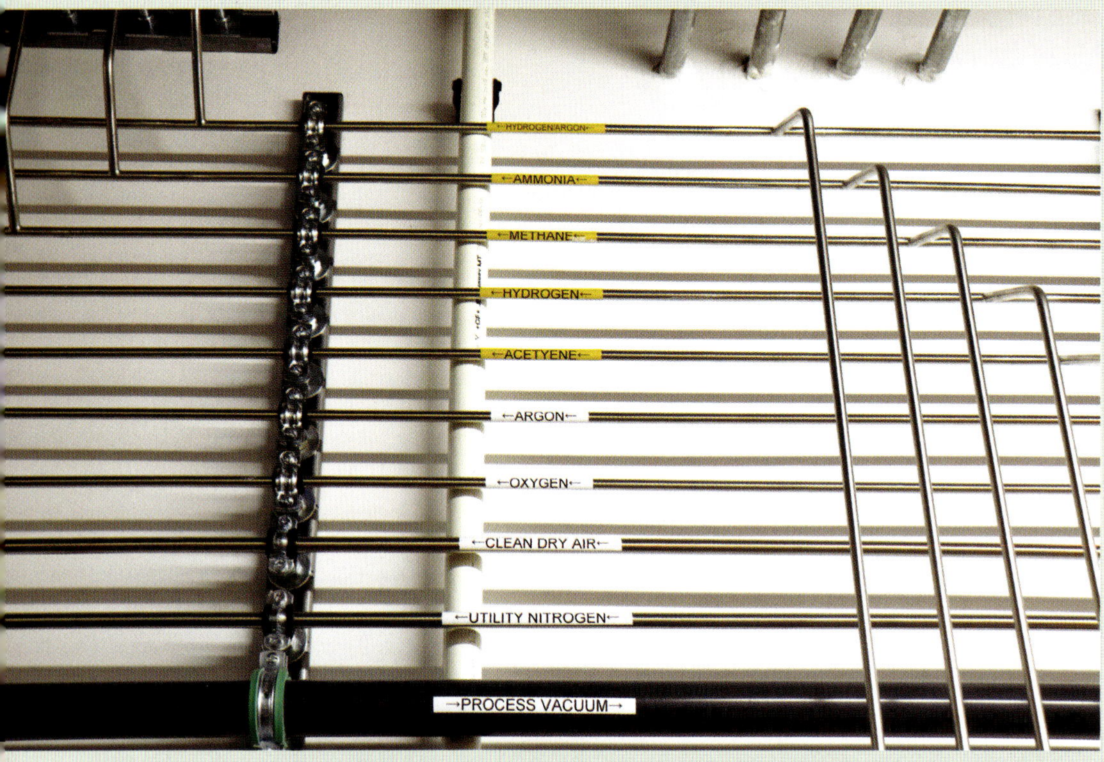

Fig. 20: Pipes with the different gases used at the NGI, photo by Simon Mitchell.

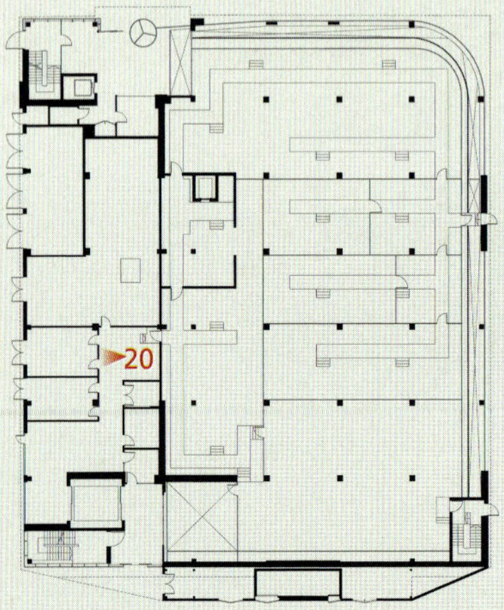

be. This may be due to a fault with the cabinets; they are highly sensitive. It may also be due to an excessive flow, which happens if one of the lab users are working in the lab and turn on the taps. There may be too high of a gas flow in the pipework, and the pressure is not adequate enough to push it through — and the alarm is sounded. There may be other causes that restrict the flow of gas to the labs. Whenever and for whatever reason the alarm goes off, Chris is there to trace back, identify and solve the problems.

The most common gas regularly ordered by Chris is pure argon (Fig. 20). Argon as an inert gas frequently used in experiments with materials which can be easily oxidised; it is used extensively in the clean room for the glove boxes and other rigs.

Every two weeks, four or five cylinders of argon are delivered to the NGI. Helium is the second most common, followed by mixed gases (e.g. hydrogen mixed with argon), hydrogen on its own, and then different grades of nitrogen follow. Other special gases, like chlorine, methane and toxic fluorides are ordered, but not as frequently. One cylinder of these gases could be "on the line" for 12, or even 18 months. While the gases are used differently, the least used gases only have to be ordered every two years or so. The frequency of gas delivery depends entirely on the nature of work of the lab users and their needs. All of these gases are vital for the working life of the labs.

The technicians are there to control their movements and installation and ensure that there are no interruptions in the workflow. Commenting on their role, Chris says, "sometimes we are the unsung heroes because if we don't do our work, they [the researchers] won't be able to do any experiments."[29] No scientist can access the gas and the storerooms for safety reasons. Accessibility, as we have seen above, is restricted. It is Chris's "kingdom" and access to this "kingdom" is controlled with the swipe card to restrict access to people who may walk in and "fiddle" with the equipment. If technicians finish work at 5pm, the lab users still can be in the building until much later, and that is when a lot of the problems can occur. Often Chris and Christopher are greeted in the morning with a problem and they are required to fix it immediately. The flow of lab work is to be restored. This is why Chris has access to the entirety of the building as he needs to be able to help with problems that may arise in the labs. He can enter into any part of the otherwise invisible infrastructure. As the utilities are constantly renewed, gases are filled, and systems are updated, the course of graphene research runs with an unstoppable pace. This pace is maintained and cared for by technicians and the alarm systems. The flow of gases, interconnected alarm signals and safety features are continually monitored through the sophisticated computer system witnessed in John's office.

Another way to sustain the unstoppable course of graphene is by ensuring that it is constantly supplied with any consumables

[29] Interview with Chris Livingston, 01.12.2017.

necessary. Next to the gas room, where we met Chris, there is a store where researchers can "purchase" some basic supply "paying" through accounts, linked to their research grants. There is also a storage room for deliveries. This is all part of Chris's "kingdom." We understand now why everyone knows him. Here is a student coming to purchase some solvents. In that store one can find all sorts of products that are used in the labs: from clean room and lab consumables ranging from gloves and beakers to test tubes and masks and overshoes. Chris says proudly: "I have a varied range of items to cover the needs of students. So, this works as a principle, instead of them ordering stuff and it will take two to three days. I basically have all of the stuff here and they can purchase it immediately. I have various solvents so that they can continue with their experiments."[30] When Chris receives the deliveries at the two large loading bay doors, anything could be found in the parcels — from cylinders and large pieces of equipment, to solvents and gloves. Yet, nothing is really stored in the gas room and the solvents store for a long time but are rather swiftly put in circulation to ensure the "beat" of graphene work is never put on pause.

[30] Interview with Chris Livingston, 16.10.2019.

7

[M] The Key Lab: Clean Room

The major component of the Institute is the clean room with a total area of about 1,500sqm. All the nanotechnology processing is done in such laboratories where temperature, humidity, vibrations, air contamination are strictly controlled. This is absolutely necessary when dealing with devices much smaller than the thickness of a human hair. The change of temperature even by a degree would change the chemical and mechanical processes involved in the fabrication of nano-devices and will lead to mistakes and make results non-reproducible. The same can be said about humidity, dust and vibrations.

Control of vibrations is one of the major functions for the modern laboratories and is especially important for the clean rooms. Modern electron beam lithographers allow resolution below a nanometre, and it would be a pity if it is spoiled by vibrations. There are several major sources of such disturbances. First, the external, environmental vibrations, caused by nearby traffic, for instance. Another one is the internal equipment itself. As the NGI was planned to be loaded with heavy-duty machines, so the vibrations from them could be significant. Vibrations of the structure of the building might be important as well, especially for tall constructions with large span of the grid. Finally, the footfall of the people, however insignificant, can be crucial if specific precautions are not taken. There are very specific, sometimes elaborate, ways how to fight each of those sources. The most efficient way of avoiding vibrations is to use a thick slab. However, it is very uneconomical if we want to achieve the vibration standard better than VCD (Fig. 21). An alternative is to place the clean room with all the vibration-sensitive equipment on the lowest floor, thus using the ground to damp the vibrations. One could potentially build the foundation directly on the bedrock. If the building is connected semi-rigidly to such bedrock, the bedrock itself becomes part of the foundation, effectively increasing (dramatically) the mass and the thickness (important for increasing the bending rigidity) of the foundation.

To this end the site chosen for the NGI has been investigated. It turned out that approximately 4 metres below the ground level the soil consists of a very dense sand, which eventually turns into Sherwood Sandstone at approximately 8 m deep. The bearing pressure of such soil is around 700kPa, which is sufficient for good damping and supporting of the heavy building.

In order to test the local vibrations and the damping properties of the local soil several accelerometers have been placed in 4m deep shafts on the potential site. The results of the test suggested that such soil can satisfy VCD requirements, and by some parameters even VCE and NIST-A requirements (Fig. 21). So the decision was taken to excavate the ground to about 8 metres deep and build the clean room in the basement. In order to combine the waterproofing and antivibration properties a thick (500mm) slab with a studded drainage

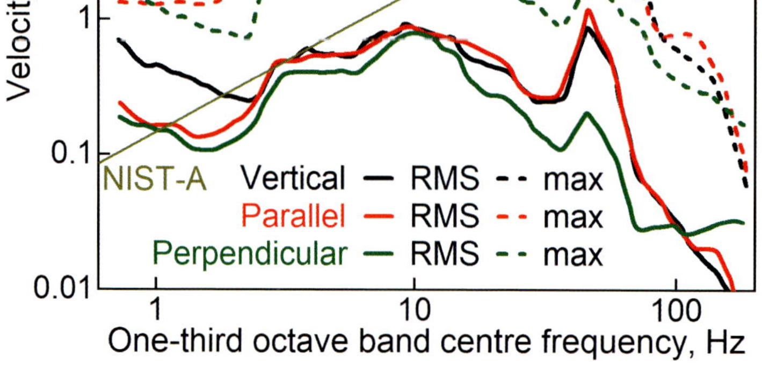

Fig. 21: Results of the vibration study of the site from a 4m deep pit at the site.

membrane which is covered by 250mm thick structural floor has been arranged.

Another issue to be considered is the proximity to the busy road. The NGI is adjacent to a street with a lot of traffic from the north (Fig. 4). Thus, an early (during the initial planning) decision was made to place the most vibration-sensitive equipment (electron and atomic force microscopes, electron beam lithography, focused ion beam machine) closer to the south part of the building.

Solution to place the clean room in the basement presents several minor, though annoying problems. First of all — access to the daylight. Whereas it is not crucial from the point of view of energy saving — clean room consumes so much power anyway that saving a few hundred watts on illumination doesn't make any difference — but it is crucial from the point of view of human perspective. Wearing the not very comfortable and awkward to dress-in overall doesn't make you want to get in and out of the clean room too often, so people spend extended periods of time inside. Especially during the short winter days people can spend from dawn to dusk inside the labs not seeing the daylight practically at all.

To mitigate this issue, it has been decided to place a viewing corridor along the north and east parts of the clean room and arrange large windows at the ground level so the daylight could penetrate inside of the clean room. Such solution brought multiple benefits. Apart of the access to the daylight, people from outside could see what is going on inside of the clean rooms, thus promoting our work. Considering that the NGI is situated right between the largest car park on the campus and the Aquatic Centre, a large number of visitors pass by the NGI every day. The capacity of the car park is a bit shy of 10,000 cars. At least half of the people who park there are from outside of the University. It means that 10,000 external visitors pass by the viewing windows every day. Seeing the active nanotechnology work with complex and shiny nanotechnological equipment is probably the best way to promote science. The walls along the viewing windows are capable to accept TV screens, posters, information billboards which further explain and advertise the NGI and University activities. Also the viewing corridor is rather heavily used. The NGI is one of the flagship projects for the UK science and is probably even more popular outside the UK (especially in China — thanks to the visit of President Xi in 2016). So the viewing corridor is a simple way to introduce the work inside the clean room without the need to dress up in the clean room overalls. The viewing corridor also serves as a separate, emergency barrier from the moisture which might come through the walls. Also, it is used as an additional fire escape.

People passing by only have a glimpse at what is going on in the clean rooms, which allows scientific activities to remain visible yet, not completely decipherable by the general public. This could tempt people to learn more about the NGI and graphene, thus increasing the power of the building.

The site chosen allowed enough space in the basement to accommodate the clean room sufficiently large to be able to fit all the equipment desired. At the same time, the nature of the research work is such that it is never possible to predict the future requirements. To this end a decision was made that extra clean room space for future proof should be arranged. Such space was placed on the 1st floor and linked to the major clean room (in the basement) by a clean lift. The reason for the lift is the equal opportunity requirements which would prohibit a simple staircase. Currently, just five years after the launch of the building, about 50% of this expansion clean room is already occupied.

Having people from different branches of science working under the same roof is a rare opportunity and it would be a crime not to use it. After all, it is the multidisciplinary research which often brings most exciting breakthroughs. But how can one make people talk to each other? There are several solutions envisaged in the NGI. The first space that actively promotes communication is the clean room: students from different groups all use the clean rooms. It is a true melting pot of ideas. Nanotechnology work requires constant improvement of the recipes and development of the new ones. People working next to you always can see what you are doing and can help with an advice from their own experience or, contrary, can use your newly developed recipe in their own work.

7

[E] Experiencing Clean Lab Work

The building is "very technology intensive," according to Fran Lopez-Royo, the clean room manager, as a "high proportion of building volume is dedicated to the provision of technical facilities."[31] The clean room plays an important part in it; it forms "the heart of the building." Like a self-contained building inside of a larger building, the clean room provides a sealed environment with high requirements for vibration and other intruders that can disrupt the practices of the scientists. For the architect, the clean room and its technical performance is absolutely paramount for the building's success. All of the scientists appreciate this state-of-the-art clean lab — it stands out for them. Rahul explains: "you cannot find such a big clean room in any other University. It's very unique to this building."[32] "What is very special about the NGI," confirms John, "is the scale of the clean rooms, the building is 8,000 sqm of which 1,500 sqm is clean air space."[33] Other universities may have a 2–300 sqm clean space; it is typically a floor, or several rooms, in a department. Previously, the University of Manchester also had similar kinds of clean rooms, where the isolation of graphene happened in 2004. But now, the NGI clean room is seven times the size of the old clean room, which makes it almost an industrial size facility. It is where most of the experimental work is carried out. As the building plot does not allow a larger clean room, two clean rooms were designed, one is about 1,100 sqm (in the basement) and the other one is about 400 sqm (1st floor) with a plant floor in the middle where the clean air is made.

When the building opened doors in 2015, the large clean room in the basement was used by the University scientists, and the smaller clean room on the 1st floor was used and shared by the industry

[31] Interview with Francisco Lopez-Royo, 04.07.2017.

[32] Interview with Rahul Raveendran Nair, 04.07.2017.

[33] Interview with John Whittaker, 22.06.2017.

Fig. 22: Upper clean room, 1st floor, photo by Ben Blackwell.

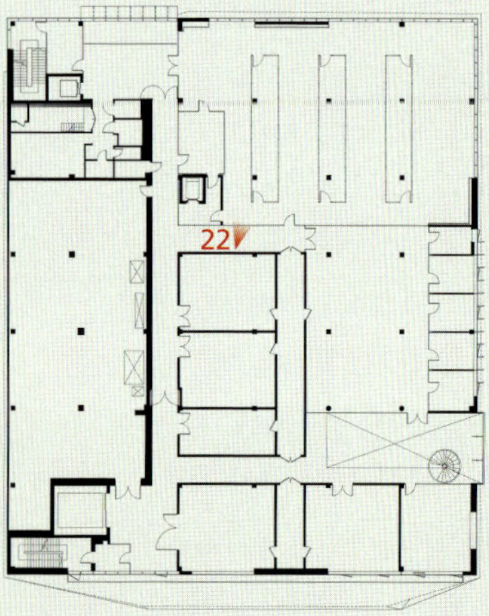

partners invited to work in the building (this area for industry-based staff was used as such until 2017–18). Soon they realised that they needed much bigger facilities for industry-related work and an entirely new building. This is the GEIC building which opened doors in 2018. A visit to the clean room now shows that while in the basement the lab rhythm is relatively quiet, on the 1st floor, the upper clean room is busy (Fig. 22). What used to be an area for industry-based staff is now a preparation zone where we witness a lot of students and postdocs spending large amount of time. When they complete the preparation, they take their substrate, go down with the clean lift, put it into the machine and leave. It might take an hour for that process to complete. The basement is silent again. In a few hours the researchers go back to the preparation zone to start another sample. As this hectic rhythm of sample preparation is entirely hosted on the 1st floor, it remains invisible for the viewers walking in the glass corridor in the basement, or the Mancunians strolling along Booth Street.

A modern, bespoke building is important because, as Fran puts it, "you get better clean rooms if you purposely design the building to house the clean rooms from day one, rather than convert or refurbish an old, more classic or conservative type of building with a different atmosphere."[34] Or, as Mark explains, "the way that I have always thought about the NGI is that actually it's a clean room that a building was built around. So, the clean room is very much the heart of the building and pretty much the building's primary purpose is housing it."[35] Moreover, while there are clean rooms for other kinds of materials and types of scientific activities, the NGI clean room was "designed with a specific focus on graphene, or other 2D materials. And this is what makes it unique compared to other buildings."[36] The clean room is designed for specific fabrication processes.

Clean rooms are categorised into different classes: class 100, class 1000, or class 10,000. That is how scientists differentiate between the different clean rooms. The number indicates how many particles larger than 0.5 micrometres are contained in a cubic foot of air. Class 100 indicates a very high-quality clean room. Class 1000 and class 10,000 indicate that there are more particles in the air, and thus less clean. The NGI is equipped with class 100 and 1000 clean rooms. Although the small quantities of graphene used here are not dangerous to work with, every possible measure is taken to ensure that any processes which might release particles are conducted in fume hoods, which have

[34] Interview with Francisco Lopez-Royo, 04.07.2017.

[35] Interview with Mark Bissett, 30.06.2017.

[36] Interview with Andrey Kretinin, 29.06.2017.

particle filters so that no particles can escape. This is important for two reasons: to have the particles contained for health and safety reasons, and to avoid contamination of the clean areas. Clean rooms are clean because the air within them is filtered continuously; the particle count is really low; the exhaust, the inlet and outlet are clean; and the air itself circulates without "strangulating." It is a zero-dust environment that also has very high specifications in terms of anti-vibration control, radio frequency control, humidity control and temperature control. Clean rooms, in other words, are clean because they are monitored, measured, tested and controlled. But this also means that they are fragile and are continuously maintained.

Planning the clean room

Very early in the design and planning process, architects and planners had to decide where to locate the clean room. During the site investigation, they discovered that the bedrock of that area was only about 4–6 metres below street level. Thus, one of the first decisions that was made by Tony was "the clean room to be placed below street level."[37] This is tied to the need to reduce the amount of vibration that could find its way into the space. Since the material — graphene — is studied at a very small scale any kind of vibration could disturb the experiments. In the NGI building, vibrations are successfully minimised through the design (as seen in chapter 7[M]). Let's compare it to the London Nano Centre. It had a similar problem because of trains rumbling underneath the building creating vibration. In this case, the architects eventually resolved the problem by putting the building on springs that dampen out that vibration. Luckily, at the NGI, the circumstances of the site avoided excessive vibrations. A happy coincidence. Reflecting on the planning of the clean room, Ernie Hill, Senior Lecturer and Assistant Director of The Manchester Centre for Mesoscience and Nanotechnology, recalls that they "didn't have that problem here [at the NGI], the basement is sitting down on a sandy bedrock and there is no vibration essentially. In fact, the class of vibration is one above

[37] Interview with Tony Ling, 23.06.2017.

Fig. 23: The old clean room in the IT building, photo by Albena Yaneva.

for what we designed for."[38] Thus, the location of the NGI clean room in the basement — the fact that it is 4 metres below ground level — considerably contributes to the anti-vibration quality of the space. This key initial decision on the location was jointly made between the design teams, structural engineer and NGI lead scientists, and played a driving force behind the rest of NGI's design.

Ernie was closely involved in the planning and design of the NGI clean room as he had extensive experience with the old clean room facilities; it was part of the work on 2D materials carried out by the Centre for Mesoscience and Nanotechnology, which Ernie set up together with Andre Geim in 2002. Due to his experience, he was the best person to understand the requirements for the new facility. In the old building, there were also two separate clean rooms; this caused issues because stepping out of one clean room to then step into another, moving in between, the scientists could eventually contaminate the cleanliness of the rooms (Fig. 23). As a result, the researchers had to change in and out of their clean clothes in order to be able to pass between the two rooms. This slowed them down. To avoid the

[38] Interview with Ernie Hill, 14.06.2019.

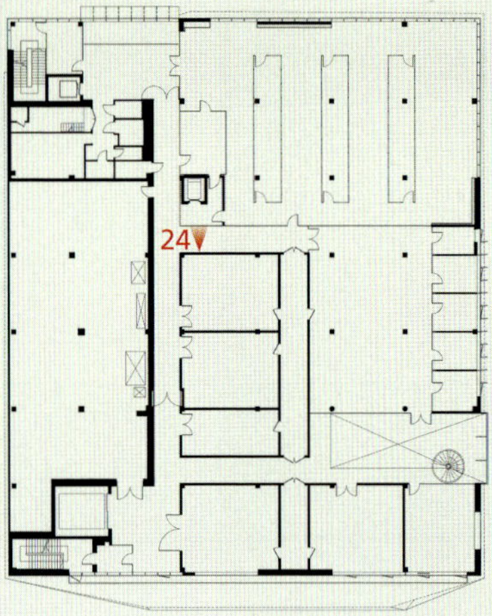

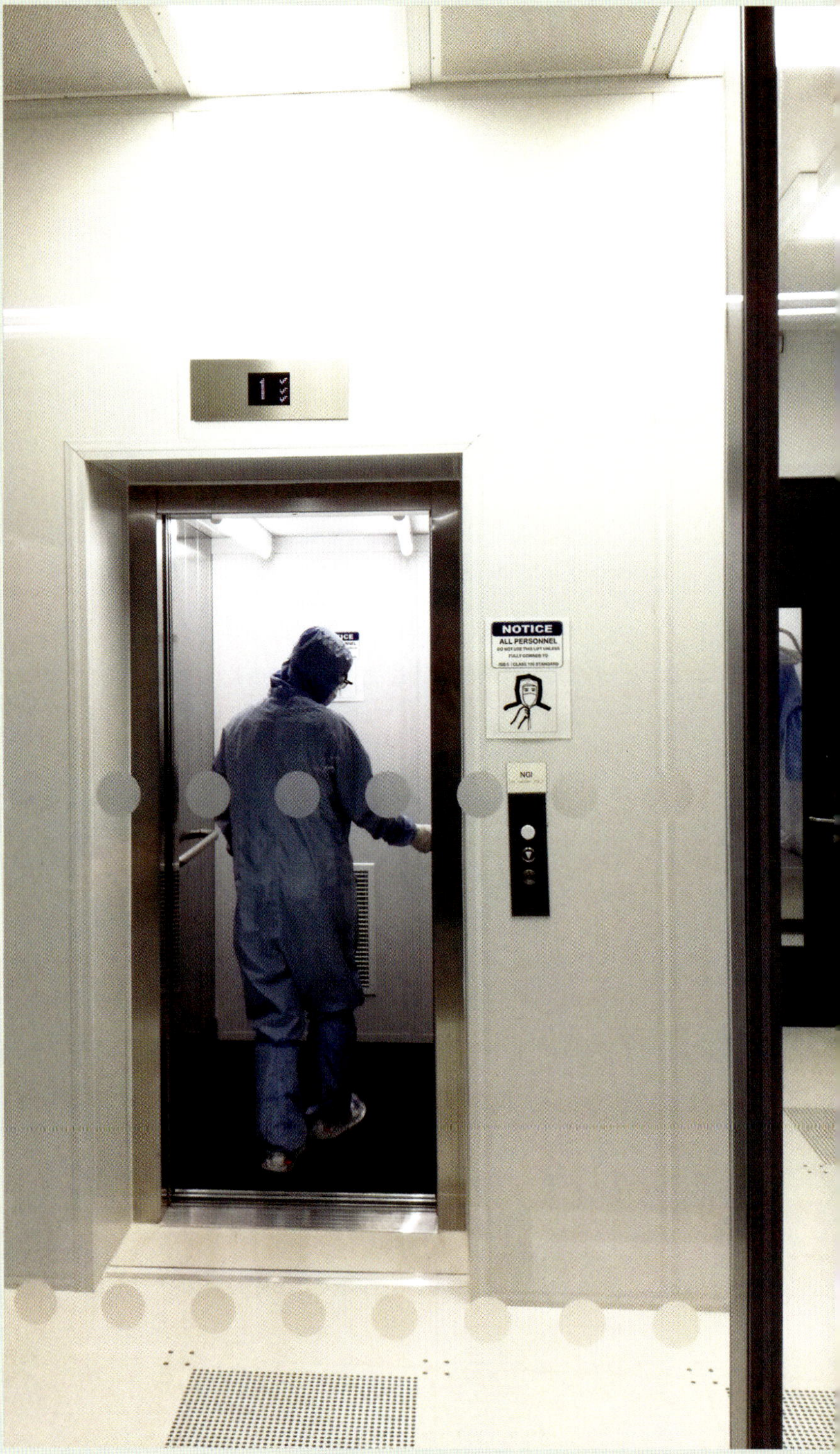

Fig. 24: The clean lift on the 1st floor, photo by Albena Yaneva.

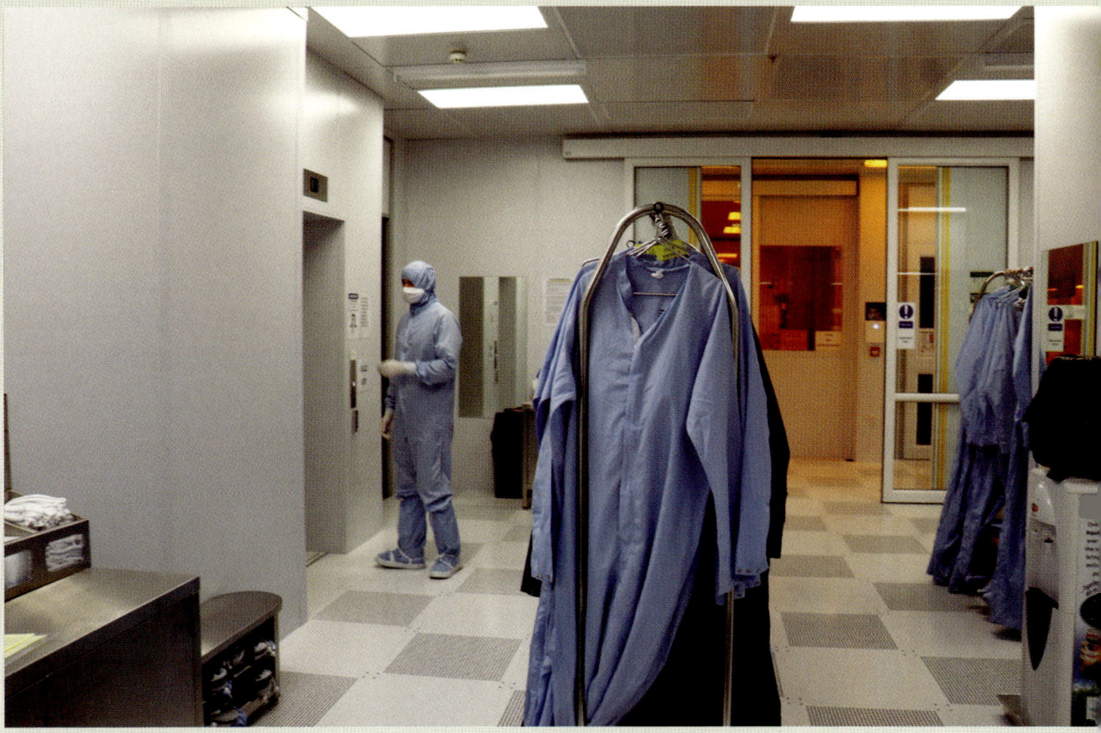

Fig. 25: The clean lift in the basement, photo by Simon Mitchell.

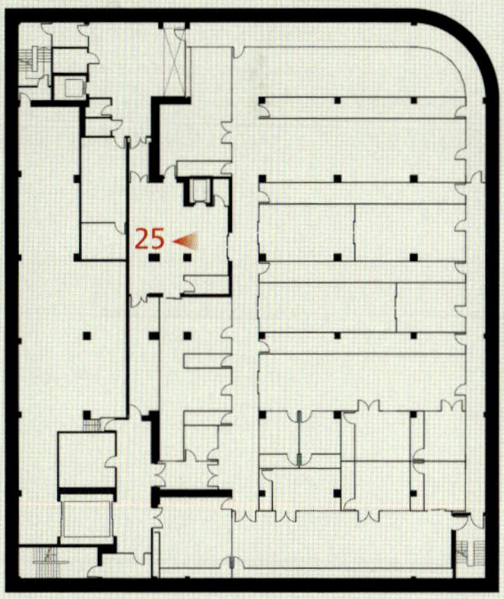

inconvenience, they started using "short-cuts in one clean room to avoid using proper equipment in the other clean room."[39] In the attempt to prevent this from happening at the NGI, it was important to connect the two clean rooms smoothly so that scientists could move without changing between the two floors. How do you do this between floors? You design a clean lift (Fig. 24).

For some scientists, the best part of the NGI clean room is the clean lift that connects the two facilities swiftly (Fig. 25). As Mark says, "people are just excited to catch the clean lift up and down."[40] This speeds up the process. An additional concern for the Estates, recalls Stuart Lockwood, Capital

[39] Interview with Ernie Hill, 14.06.2019.

[40] Interview with Mark Bissett, 30.06.2017.

Projects Manager at the University of Manchester, was to ensure that people in a wheelchair or who have mobility disabilities have access to the spaces. This was an initial concern from various points of view: in order to get planning permission from Building Control, as well as an internal criticism from Disability Services at the university. "We needed to make sure that all people can use it [the clean room]," he explains, "that's why we put the clean lift in."[41] The lift itself looks exactly like any other standard lift, except that it is sealed. It has 5 filter units that filter the air while people are inside in order to reach the cleanliness criteria. And yet it is very unique: it is the only clean lift in the UK (there is another one in Ireland). It is especially useful as it saves time. People no longer have to physically leave the space, change, go up a lift, change again, in order to continue to work on an experiment. The clean lift smoothly continues the uninterrupted course of graphene research. Experiments can keep running.

In the process of planning and designing the new clean rooms at the NGI, scientists recurrently built on lessons that they had learnt from working in the old clean room. These spaces were full of "fairly ancient equipment" and were overcrowded. "We would have 10–12 people working in a small bay. And they were getting underneath one another's feet."[42] Everything was so compressed and tight. When it got very busy with people opening doors or standing behind doors, they had to warn researchers not to "dash through doors" and to constantly remind them to "take care." Watching over the research centre on a day-to-day basis, Ernie witnessed the growth of graphene-related work and how it began to take over the whole centre. The more projects, the larger the number of researchers, the more crowded the clean room became; soon, "graphene" became too large for this space. The need to expand the facility and upscale the technology became obvious to them, along with the awareness that the space was becoming unsafe for the researchers. It grew, effectively, stretching into a new dedicated building.[43]

---

41 Interview with Stuart Lockwood, 3.06.2019.

42 Interview with Ernie Hill, 14.06.2019.

43 Currently, the old facility is still being used and researchers can move between the two buildings to use different equipment. In the old clean room, the focus

Ernie, together with Peter Blake[44] and Kostya Novoselov, wrote the clean room specifications, working closely with the company CH2M Hill that did the main clean room design and with the contractor who built it. He "knew what they [the NGI people] wanted in terms of the requirements for graphene. You have to be quite rigorous at separating out the various processes and make sure there is no cross-contamination."[45] Drawing on his previous experience, Ernie helped a lot with the initial specification and the design work. A central criterion that he proposed was to ensure there was "good circulation space": "you don't want everything to be too tight for health and safety reasons." More space for circulation is crucial, not only to give room for air in the space to circulate, but also for the researchers and for graphene to grow.

The viewing corridor

As the clean room had been "sunken into the basement," it was important to ensure that it also does not go entirely underground, visually isolated. A viewing corridor that curves all the way around the clean room was designed. It is two-storeys high and is entirely glazed at the street level (Fig. 26). It establishes a connection with the outside world. Ernie played an important role in the design of the viewing corridor too. Traditionally, clean rooms are enclosed, and closed off from the outside world — turned into black boxes themselves. But, the corridor at the NGI is not entirely to connect with the outside, to the busy street or those who pass by the building. As Ernie was involved in the design of the old clean rooms in 1990s, he had had experience with clean rooms that were connected via a small corridor. These facilities were also used for teaching purposes, and so the small corridor allowed them to show students what was happening inside without having them get dressed up to access the rooms (Fig. 23). This became a factor considered in the design of the NGI corridor

is on general nanoscale work and it is used for teaching purposes too, whereas the clean rooms at the NGI are focussed on 2D materials.

44 Peter Blake is a researcher at the NGI. He was instrumental in designing the building and the clean rooms in particular.

45 Interview with Ernie Hill, 14.06.2019.

Fig. 26: The basement clean room, a glimpse at the viewing corridor on the left, photo by Albena Yaneva.

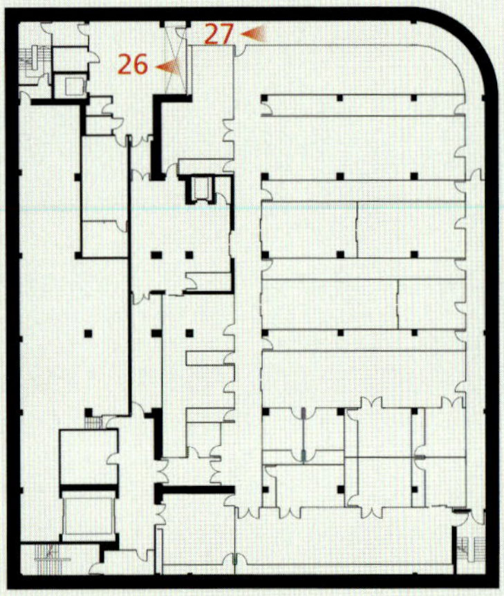

(Fig. 27). But it has other roles. Some researchers call it "the presidential corridor" as it is where President Xi Jinping was photographed with the lead scientists Kostya Novoselov and Andre Geim, and the Chancellor of the Exchequer, at the time, Mr. George Osborne. It has many functions indeed: at once presidential, for viewing, but also as a fire escape corridor as it opens to the street at the East side of the building.

The viewing corridor also plays an important role in facilitating disciplinary fusions. Researchers from different disciplines can come at any time

Fig. 27: The viewing corridor: basement clean room on the right, Booth Street, on the left, photo by Ben Blackwell.

and witness the activities in the clean rooms. John explains that this is part of the open nature policy of the building. It is how discussions often start around simple questions of curiosity triggered by the visit: "what does that tool do?", "why is this room yellow?", "why are we filtering UV light from photolithography?" During a walk John often hears the scientists wondering and exclaiming: "Oh, I never thought photolithography involved that technique!", "Oh, actually it's just an electron beam microscope with some modified components from it!"[46] That is how chemists, physicists, material scientists and others, walk and wonder. These moments of surprise and little discoveries become central points for discussion in the corridor; and from there they spread to the rest of the building. Before it even catches the gaze of random passers-by in the street or curious external visitors, the viewing gallery, much as the other spaces in the NGI, brings together various scientists from different disciplines, and makes them change working attitudes and epistemic habits, and eventually, impacts their ways of addressing research problems.

The architect reflects back on the process: "the last thing we wanted was to design a sort of black-box and some building buried in the ground."[47] Now, the corridor and the open windows going up to street level bring natural light into the clean room. When scientists work in the clean room, they see daylight; they feel connected to the city rather than being "buried," isolated in a dark black hole. Thus, bringing the light in, the corridor provides conditions that are important for the working environment for scientists, technicians and industry people. Researchers share that now they could stay in the clean room virtually all day, apart from coming out for lunch, and they never feel depressed. They constantly compare with other clean rooms that they have worked in before where access to natural light had been an issue. As Ernie explains, "people don't like working when there is no natural light for an entire day. It isn't very nice."[48] And the clean room manager Fran elaborates, "it's a brilliant aspect of our clean rooms here, the fact that

[46] Interview with John Whittaker, 22.06.2017.

[47] Interview with Tony Ling, 23.06.2017.

[48] Interview with Ernie Hill, 14.06.2019.

you allow researchers and people working in the clean rooms to feel a bit less oppressed in that they have a window to the outside world."[49] The glass connection makes the clean room open, welcoming and the lab life of the many blue-gowned scientists in it, more enjoyable.

While inviting the light and the weather in, the glass also brings the gaze of the public strolling around the building. Thanks to the corridor, when passers-by walk by, they can look down, through two layers of glass into the clean room and can see what is happening inside and can literally witness "science in action."[50] What they see is not just high-tech equipment and blue-gowned human figures working in a lab, but, importantly, they witness that "public money" is being used in a sensible way. They can see it in action. As Stuart points out, a lot of campus buildings turn their back on their neighbours, and do not encourage engagement with the public. This concern was important during the planning stage. Taking into consideration these discussions, the NGI is one of the first buildings in Manchester that "opens up to the public." For Stuart, the aim was "to encourage that relationship with the general public — our neighbours — and for somebody walking past to see and wonder: 'Oh what are they doing? Can I do this? Can I be part of that?'"[51] The NGI design encourages this train of thought, and has inspired a number of other buildings on campus that followed this trend.

Once in the building, visitors can use the viewing corridor to have a closer peek at "science in action." Guided by NGI staff, groups of guests closely inspect the premises, the different coloured bay areas, the giant shiny machines and sophisticated microscopes as well as the movements of the blue-gowned scientists and technicians between spaces. What can they see through the windows? Can they hear anything at all? Can they grasp a rhythm of graphene research? Yet, for an untrained eye, it is often hard to identify what a particular piece of equipment does or distinguish between researchers; visitors can hardly recognise the

[49] Interview with Francisco Lopez-Royo, 04.07.2017.

[50] Latour, B. *Science in Action: How to Follow Scientists and Engineers through Society*. Cambridge, Mass.: Harvard University Press (1987).

[51] Interview with Stuart Lockwood, 3.06.2019.

full scale of the work in the clean room. Sarah often takes people for tours around the clean corridor. During the tour, she stops at places and explains: "this is e-beam lithography, it does this, that, etc."; "this is someone from the Raman lab…"[52] They look in, try to find the beam, the microscope or the scientists behind the blue dress; yet, all researchers look the same in their gowns; the technologies look alike to the external viewer. In spite of the exposure both machines and people share a symmetrical anonymity.

While letting people look in, the viewing corridor also provides an excellent opportunity to protect the clean room from the outside world. Since the building opened doors, the crowds of visitors at the University of Manchester have increased. However, crowds of visitors pose a risk to the research; in particular, they risk introducing particles and other intruders into the clean room. Therefore, the viewing corridor is also a means "to minimise the amount of people that go into the clean room."[53] When a small group tours the corridor, the researchers know that they can be seen at any time, but they cannot be heard; likewise, they cannot hear what is being said on the other side of the glass about them and graphene during the guided tours. Visually connected, yet, sonically isolated and sheltered. It is a clever way, elaborates Stuart, to allow people to be there but "without disturbing any of the research." He continues to describe its benefits: "they [visitors] do not have to get changed, dressed up to go into those spaces; they can see them from outside."[54] The visual contact with people outside the lab does not interrupt the research rhythm, and it actually contributes to the stronger fortification of the clean room research world. The open, porous, membrane-like type of architecture facilitates wider connectivity while ensuring that random people cannot physically enter the building. Access, as we have seen, is slow, mediated, bureaucratically loaded, and includes strict procedures for signing in at the reception desk and for dressing up. In fact, very few people go inside the premises of the clean room and turn into gowned figures. The more visually connected and visually open the clean room is, the more protected its cleanness

52 Interview with Sarah Haigh, 10.07. 2017.

53 Interview with Francisco Lopez-Royo, 04.07.2017.

54 Interview with Stuart Lockwood, 3.06.2019.

Fig. 28: The viewing gallery, view from Booth Street, photo by Albena Yaneva.

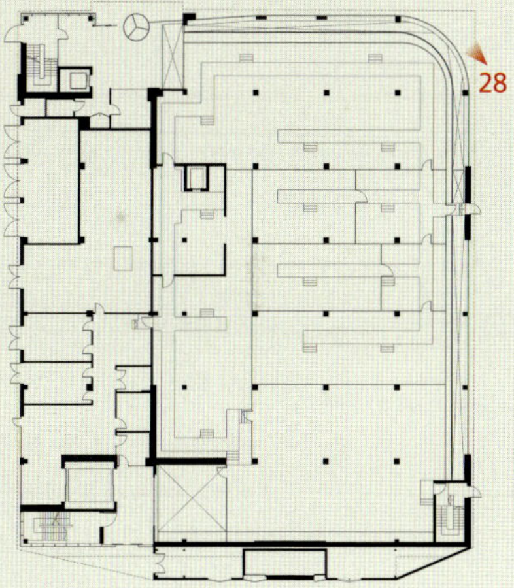

remains. A well-functioning scientific facility is not a crowded one, but one that finely regulates the balance between openness and enclosure.

The glass surfaces also enable visual connections between lab and city life and allow their interaction. Passers-by often stop to also contemplate art on display in the upper windows of the gallery (Fig. 28). Commenting on this aspect, artist in residence Kelly Stanford clarifies: “It’s not often that you come across architecture for a research institute that allows the public to see the work that goes on in the labs, let alone double as an exhibition space for art. I feel that the introduction of art into the viewing gallery is excellent as before it was just a cold concrete cavern, whereas now it’s being used as a space where art can draw attention to the science being done.”[55] Some pieces displayed show photography of the scientists working with the

[55] Interview with Kelly Stanford, 13.12.2019.

graphene material, while others focus on the people behind the work and reference past interdisciplinary collaborations such as the hyper realistic bee illustrations. Research, we witness, does not simply flow out of the fantasia of isolated brilliant minds; it happens here in front of the bewildered eyes of urban viewers, and it emerges from society's anticipation of the applications of graphene. The city of Manchester does not usurp the world of graphene; it rather expands the work of science. It is this mutual reflection and amalgamation of scientific and urban experiences that is wonderous as we walk around the glass surfaces, generating a dazzling spectacle.

Maintaining the cleanness

Although glass provides opportunities for openness and visual communication with the outside world and allows researchers to overcome the inconveniences of a contained environment, it is in the very nature of the clean room to be enclosed and isolated for the following reasons. First, there is a constant air flow going through several stages of filtering (200–300 changes per hour), where 10% of the air leaves the clean room and fresh air comes from outside of the room to refresh it. Second, the amount of particles needs to be monitored and controlled below a set value. Third, the temperature and the humidity is controlled. Forth, the air pressure inside the clean room has to be slightly higher than outside; the reason for this, explains Fran, is that "there's always going to be slight openings. It's obviously impossible to create a clean room that's 100% airtight, so you want to make sure that the air pressure inside is a little bit higher, so that any air is going out rather than coming in."[56] The idea of maintaining all these different pressures is to manage the amount of particles in the room in order to avoid falling out of the category of the 100 class into the 1000 class, rather than the other way around. The 1000 class area has a slightly higher pressure than that of the main gowning areas. The different seals ensure that a constant flow of particles leaves the clean room, and that nothing goes in.

[56] Interview with Francisco Lopez-Royo, 04.07.2017.

Although Fran's main responsibility is the clean room, he also monitors changes in the entire building as "anything that may have happened in the rest of the building may affect the clean rooms"; as the "heart" of the building, the clean room is integrated and responds to the rest of the NGI. He makes sure there are no issues with the 21 different gases as well the nitrogen supply, the compressed air, the ultrapure water — all located in the plant room. Fran also deals with all of the operational issues in the clean room. Small operational meetings with the technical staff at the start of the day help ensure that everyone knows what they are doing before starting up the services. "It's like being in a factory," he jokes. We can follow Fran going around the viewing corridors several times a day; he occasionally uses the telephones installed in the viewing corridor so that he can speak to people inside the clean room if needed. Most of the days he is able to go into the clean room to spend a couple of hours inside. Yet, when he is not able to do this, the viewing corridor allows him to monitor the activities inside the clean room. We witness another way for glass design to speed up communication, and from there the pace of graphene research.

Fran's technical team spends at least 50% of the time in the clean room and the rest of the time at the desk. When they are in the clean room, they use also the clean room computer to make sure they communicate on progress and on current developments in the clean rooms. Thus, the communication between the clean room and the outside is continuous. Their aim is to "keep the instruments operational, and the processes working in a repeatable manner so that researchers don't have to waste time in problem-shooting."[57] The priority is that scientists focus on their research, their ideas, and experiments without having to worry about possible complications caused by the machines or that the lab is not properly maintained. Fortunate to have a sufficiently large team in the clean rooms to help them, NGI researchers can continue their work without interruptions. The technicians support this workflow by maintaining the equipment, protecting it from improper usage. The clean room technician James Fitzsimons explains that his

[57] Interview with Francisco Lopez-Royo, 04.07.2017.

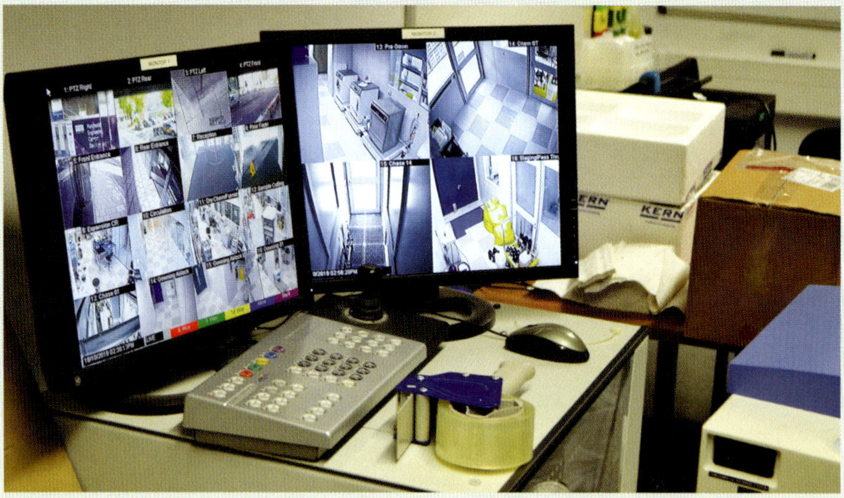

Fig. 29: The technicians' room in the clean room, BMS monitors used by the technician James Fitzsimons and the clean room manager Francisco Lopez-Royo, photo by Ben Blackwell.

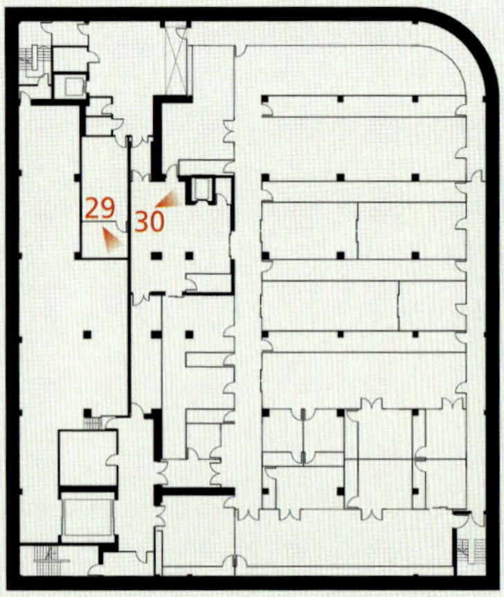

role is to help scientists so that they "don't affect the equipment negatively."[58] As the equipment is very delicate and expensive, a single piece of equipment tends to be used by, in some cases, 20 or more people in contrast to a standard lab where only two or three people may use it. Therefore, it is imperative that the equipment is maintained professionally by technicians and experimental officers, who do not discriminate between humans and machines, treat them with equal care, and keep this process operational. The entire support infrastructure of the labs is organised in a way to allow researchers to spend long hours at a continuous speed without any downtime.

Let us follow the work of James. He spends a considerable time inside the clean room (ca. 70 – 80% of his working time). When he comes in the morning, he first checks the BMS. Just like John who uses the BMS to monitor the NGI

[58] Interview with James Fitzsimons, 28.11.2017.

building, James uses the system to oversee the clean room parameters (Fig. 29). Then he runs to the lab. He walks around "checking different things," this time in the space itself, like the temperatures, the humidity, and the consumables where they are materially situated in the room. After he has made sure that all is "running" properly, James returns to his computer, sits down, and checks emails that he has received with regard to pieces of equipment or training that researchers might have requested on specific equipment. Afterwards, he performs the revolving and regular maintenance tasks: once a month he maintains the chillers, the spin coaters; once a week he checks the ultrasonic baths and cleans them. He also makes sure that everything is clean and put together in the facility. In addition to the sophisticated equipment, simple things like the doors and hinges have to be checked as he walks around the clean room. Everything has to be in place. He explains: "everything should be in order to avoid rubbing that will generate further particles."[59] These little maintenance tasks are done in a revolving schedule and last a few hours. After this long maintenance ritual is completed, James goes back to his computer to catch up on admin work, purchase orders and other tasks related to the maintenance.

Compared to the standard labs, the clean room requires a very strict control of "what can go in and what comes out of the lab" as well as in terms of "keeping the infrastructure running." The regular maintenance James performs is crucial to ensure that the main part of the facility is kept clean and to the highest standard, and that nothing degrades over time. "In the clean room," he states, "we really have to think about the impact of any work we do, so we have to plan all of our work in such a way that it has minimal impact on the clean room."[60] Simple technical tasks are much more time-consuming and rigorous here. For instance, when they have to install a new piece of equipment, they have to slow down, and think about all of the possible risks of creating and spreading particles into the clean room, which would be disruptive. For instance, how to avoid drilling through a wall to install a pipe. The wall would send little particles out into the clean room. Therefore,

---

[59] Interview with James Fitzsimons, 28.11.2017.

[60] Interview with James Fitzsimons, 28.11.2017.

James and his colleagues from the technical team find other methods for the installation that will have minimal impact on the clean room environment. Although this sets new challenges for the technicians, it also makes them think "outside of the box," to find creative solutions.

To fully maintain the cleanness of the clean room, it has to be cleaned like any other space in the NGI. The cleaning equipment is already there. To access the rooms, the house attendants "gown up" like anyone else before they enter the general area. They first put red shoe covers on to avoid carrying any dirt with them when entering (Fig. 30). There is a barrier and to cross that barrier they have to put blue shoe covers over the red shoe covers. Watch Daniela sitting on the stainless steel bench near the barrier, she has her red shoe covers on; then she grabs one blue shoe cover and puts it over her right red shoe cover; then standing on one leg before the barrier and one leg after it, she steps over the barrier and puts the blue shoe cover over the left feet. Only then can she enter into the gowning area where she puts her face safety mask, a hair net, a hood, a blue gown, and special boots over her blue shoe covers. House attendants and technicians have dark blue gowns. The only body part that one can see is their eyes, the rest is covered to stop contamination. There is a very delicate process for passing through the threshold into the clean room. The house attendants often laugh: "you've got to do this palaver so that you can just go and clean the floors." Once in the clean room, they empty the bins and take them out. They spray IPA (isopropyl alcohol) on the floor, a product known to be highly effective as a solvent to remove a variety of contaminations; they use a special soft mop and the IPA evaporates very quickly. Contrary to expectations (as if a clean room should always be clean already!), cleaning a clean floor is not an easy job, but rather a tedious procedure, and the slightest contamination must be wiped off. The house attendants also wear special blue bracelets with sensors that open the door; these avoid skin contact that could leave behind traces and contamination as they touch surfaces. Some of the

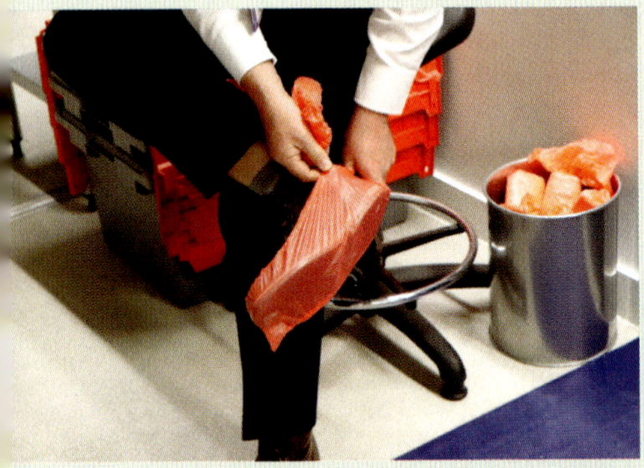

Fig. 30: Red shoe covers, photo by Simon Mitchell.

rooms have potentially lethal hydrofluoric acid: no one can simply go into these rooms. A "danger" sign on the room warns everyone working in that part of the clean room and the door is only activated by a blue bracelet; whoever goes there has to follow a certain protocol and all house attendants are aware of this. Thus, just like the simple technical maintenance procedures and the installation of equipment described by James that have their own challenges, the mundane operations of dusting and washing floors set their own trials due to the controlled environment of the clean rooms. Equipment and 2D materials are protected from dust and particles that humans can eventually bring in; bodies are isolated in gowns to minimize harmful effects on the clean environment. Both humans and machines have to follow special rituals and respond to "danger" signals just as doors and surfaces react to sensors and alarms.

Lab work in the clean room

Researchers spend different amounts of time in the clean room, depending on the type of work, type of fabrication and its complexity. Sarah is the Director of the Electron Microscopy Centre here in Manchester, where they have around 20 microscopes. Yet, if she wants to use the electron microscope in the NGI, she must travel to the NGI clean room. She explains, "I can't just walk in and check it. I have to be in the clean room to use it."[61] As it takes a lot of time, as we have seen, to enter the clean room, she usually sends her PhD students to use the electron microscope. However, the fact that 20 researchers can use one piece of sophisticated equipment, and not all of them are experienced, can cause problems. As she says, "you cannot be an expert in everything, and there are experts who specialise just in electron microscopy, and you often rely on others to help you with the equipment."[62] The technical staff at the NGI fills in this role: they are "experts in all of the machines

---

[61] Interview with Sarah Haigh, 10.07.2017.

[62] Interview with Sarah Haigh, 10.07.2017.

that enter the clean room."[63] They learn how to take care of the new equipment. For instance, the FIB [focused ion beam] has not been used in the clean room before and it is very new for the technicians. They are required to learn its intricacies, how it can be used, what it does. The clean room is full of a varied assembly of instruments, specialised equipment, scientists with expertise, and technical staff looking after sophisticated machines.

Let us take a look at the scientists working in the clean room for a moment (Fig. 31). Dressing gowns make the researchers unrecognisable; like the nanomaterials, people, too, need special protection, as we have seen, to access the controlled environment of the clean room (the air composition, temperature, humidity and air pressure control affects them as well!). There is a symmetry between the nanomaterials and the researchers. However, the key role of the blue suits is to cover human bodies to protect the clean room from the deleterious effects of bodies. Unable to access the clean room in their normal attire, humans perform a whole dressing ritual prior to the entry: carefully a face mask is placed over their mouth, a hairnet on their head, and then putting their dedicated gown on, covering themselves fully from toe to head. While they protect the environment, both the dress and the mask considerably restrict their bodily activities; the dress limits their movements in space, whereas the face mask does not allow them to breathe as normally as they can breathe outside.

Robed in this way, Abhishek Mishra, Postdoctoral Researcher at the Centre for Mesoscopic Science spends most of his time in the clean rooms while working on his experiments, and then in the Raman spectroscopy lab on the 2nd floor. He explains his role: "I'm mostly responsible to fabricate the devices. So, I really spend a lot of time in the clean rooms. Maybe six to seven hours per day."[64] Once Abhishek finishes the device fabrication, he has to "characterise" it. The devices are taken from the clean room and moved to other labs in the NGI, where the characterisation tools are placed. If, for instance, the device is meant for optical research, its characterisation can happen

[63] Interview with Sarah Haigh, 10.07. 2017.

[64] Interview with Abhishek Mishra, 21.11.2017.

Fig. 31: Scientists working in the clean room, photo by the University of Manchester.

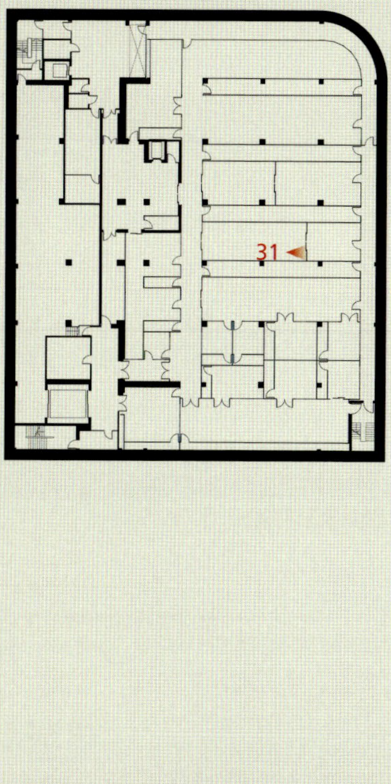

in the optical characterisation lab. The lab time is structured by the conditions of work. The ritual of dressing and undressing the light blue gown separates clean room researchers from the other facilities. It turns Abhishek into an anonymous blue gowned scientist when he enters the clean room to fabricate a device akin to the device he works on that is equally anonymous, uncharacterized. When he takes the dress off and puts his own clothes on, Abhishek turns into a recognizable individual moving to the specialized Raman lab; while the device is being characterized there, and as it gains specificity, the researcher also enhances his singularity. Taken in this amazingly symmetrical dance, people and devices circulate hectically between labs. Although these rituals slow down the transition between spaces, they ensure that the work is done according to the regulations of each place and both human and nonhuman participants in this process gain the capacity to act that is needed.

If, in the specialised labs, researchers can work long hours, in the clean room, they must respect the normal hours (usually from 10 am to 5 pm) as the technical staff, who take care of the equipment, needs to be around. If, in the other labs, scientists can work alone, in the clean room no one can work alone after 5 pm or during the holidays, due to health and safety reasons. It is expected that there is at least one other researcher using the facilities of the clean rooms. This is the only restriction, but it is very stringent. In addition to health and safety reasons, it has other effects. More lab users in the room means more possibilities to share techniques and have more exchanges. Once in the clean room, the processes take their own time; time runs uninterruptedly as precision is crucial. Reflecting on the rhythm of work in the clean room, Fran adds, "some of the processes are quite long by their nature. So, a user might start a process on one of their samples, maybe for instance a wet etching process that might take several hours. Users might generally leave their samples in the wet etchant and then leave the clean room."[65] Today Abhishek is etching silicon in the clean room, which takes two to three hours once he has dipped it into the solvent. During these hours he can focus on something else or discuss results with colleagues, or he can go out, get a coffee, and do some reading, then, after some time, return to the clean room. Yet, according to the clean room rules, all scientists should leave a note with their name, telephone number, a description of what they have left there, what day they left it and time, and when they are coming back to collect it. "If there is no such a requirement," comments Abhishek, "you can stay out of the clean room as long as you wish and come back in the evening."[66] Yet, he knows that if he has started a process (sometimes the waiting time is shorter, maybe 30 minutes), he needs to be there

[65] Interview with Francisco Lopez-Royo, 04.07.2017.

[66] Interview with Abhishek Mishra, 21.11.2017.

after the completion of the process — otherwise, he will worry about the sample and the risk of degrading it. In any case, when he goes out of the room, he labels his things, clears up his working place; he is aware that he should not leave his things unattended. Fran makes sure everyone does this.

Here, again, a symmetry is established. Remember the tedious process of signing up at the front desk, making everyone's visit accountable (date, name, time spent in the building). Just like humans who enter and exit the building on a daily basis, samples and flakes are registered and traceable as they enter and leave the clean rooms. It is in the process of being registered that they exist. They begin a different life. Yet another slow ritual of signing out and registering the sample is added to the gown ritual. It is the flake (and the related lab processes) that structures the time spent in the clean room and the need to account for its movements and trace its trajectory. All of the slow rituals of entering and exiting the lab, ensure that the clean room is used as efficiently as possible and by everyone who needs it.

Compared to the old clean room, the NGI clean room has a lot of space for manoeuvring and for discussions amongst researchers. Abhishek recalls that the old clean room was very narrow, and that they "were limited by the space, not many people were allowed, or able to work in the clean room at a given time."[67] More space allows more researchers to be alongside one another at the same time and thus offers a greater chance for the exchange of ideas and recipes for experiments. But it also means that more tools can be accommodated and as a result, "the waiting time is reduced because of the increasing amounts of tools."[68] Overall, this leads to a quicker pace of graphene research. In addition, as the clean room is used by a number of research groups who benefit from the facilities, it is entirely managed by the faculty's technical support team in a professional and timely manner. In contrast, the standard specialised labs are mostly used by a single research group, who is responsible for maintaining the equipment while the technicians maintain the systems in the building (e.g. the house

[67] Interview with Abhishek Mishra, 21.11.2017.

[68] Interview with Abhishek Mishra, 21.11.2017.

vacuum system, the process cooling system, the ultra-pure water) and supply the labs. Accommodating different research teams, the clean room acts as a catalyst for new collaborations, allowing scientists from various fields to rub shoulders with one another and facilitating the transfer of knowledge between them. In addition, it facilitates exchange with smaller companies who need access to a clean room as they cannot afford to build their own (bigger companies will probably have their own clean rooms). The same goes for the equipment. As Mark explains: "we are trying to make sure we have equipment that the SMEs [small and medium enterprises] wouldn't otherwise be able to get access to."[69] Facilitating collaboration, the clean room speeds up technology transfer through the co-existence of lab and industry partners.

Thus, the large, lit and accommodating clean rooms enable more researchers, industry people and equipment to be housed, and to connect in a flexible way, allowing experiments to run smoothly, quickly and efficiently. An entire network of technicians and alarm systems, mobilised, coordinated, running, ensures that the lab infrastructure is relentlessly maintained to aid an unstoppable rhythm of research: the constant flow of supply of gases, constant cleaning of the air, constant control of temperature and humidity, constant survey of the equipment, continual monitoring of the performance. This all affords "freedom of the research," as James puts it, and he continues: "if I'm doing a good job in the clean room, the technicians are doing a good job in maintaining the labs, then in theory, it goes unnoticed in that the researchers are able to get on with their work. [...] But generally, people only notice when something is not working. They don't notice when things work smoothly, and we are running it well enough."[70] As we listen to James, we realise that this versatile experimental inventiveness and research exchange is achieved through the many restrictions, rules, protocols and control systems that the invisible crowd of technicians put in place. The better they run it, the more invisible they become. Here is another contradictory, yet, productive feature that sustains the specificity of the clean room. Just as the glass design allows scientists to see the

[69] Interview with Mark Bissett, 30.06.2017.

[70] Interview with James Fitzsimons, 28.11.2017.

external world and to be seen from the outside, and it makes possible for the lab to remain protected and simultaneously open to collaborations, its infrastructural design maintains the subtle balance between a freedom of investigation and the multiple constraints of the controlled clean environment.

A tour of the clean room

Pockets of activity in the clean room can be witnessed in the morning between 9 and 12 am, and between 2 and 6 pm in the afternoon. The lab could be also very busy between 8 pm and midnight. Let us have a quick tour and see what happens in different bay areas and zones of the clean room at one of the peak moments of the day: 2.30 pm.

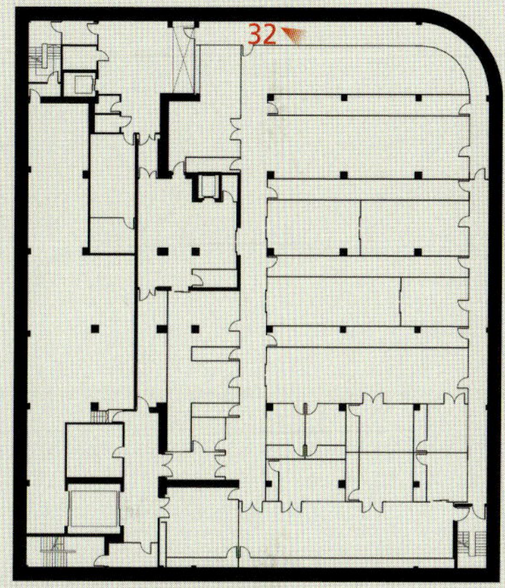

First, we stop and witness the PECVD growth in the clean room, a plasma-based system to grow different materials. The graphene growth in here might take four hours, but it is done on a wafer scale rather than a small scale. The

Fig. 32: The technician Maddy checking the growth rate of graphene in the clean room, photo by Simon Mitchell.

Fig. 33: The furnace in the clean room, photo by Simon Mitchell.

researchers set the process running and leave upstairs to do more preparation. Maddy, the technician in this area, is looking through the view port now, checking the growth rate (Fig. 32). She sees that the plasma is still there so she has to come back. She goes in the other room and comes back after a while. This is a fairly typical procedure. John explains, "we have some furnaces on the 3rd floor, but we couldn't put them here as these are very dirty. Here [in the clean room] these are the same furnaces, but they are about five times the price of the other ones (Fig. 33). They are all made of different materials because the materials will give off dust and we cannot have that in the clean room."[71] The clean room furnaces are made of glass and ceramic whereas the furnaces upstairs are made of thermalite brick, which cannot be used in the clean room. Every other piece of equipment here is made from stainless steel or other "no shedding" materials. Even the simple design features, like the chairs, have to be made in a special way; the seats are all leather as leather does not shed particles. Even regular paper is forbidden. Maddy writes her notes on special clean room paper that looks like shiny tracing paper. As we watch Maddy working in the clean room a number of other people stroll around her dressed in differently coloured gowns: dark blue for the technicians in the facilities and light blue for the users (both scientists and industry people). The

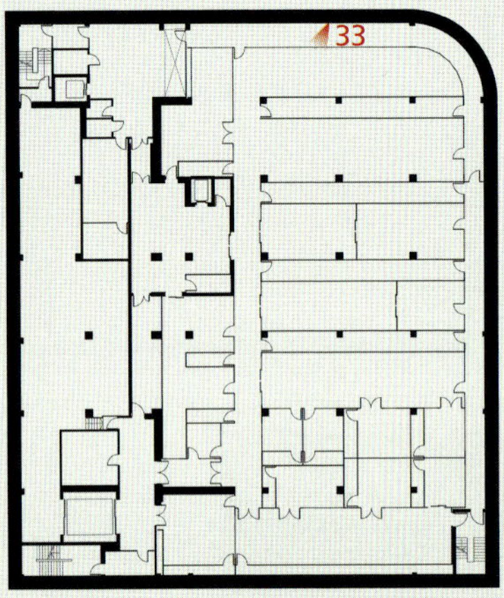

[71] Interview with John Whittaker, 16.10.2019.

colour indicates the distribution of roles; it also enables quick reactions in case of emergency situations as users know immediately who to go to and who to contact for help.

Here is the yellow bay area (Fig. 34). The "yellow room," as it is known, is where optical lithography takes place (photolithography) and it is where complex patterns, which determine the structure of the samples, are drawn in resists[72] with high intensity UV light. The yellow colour is not a random design choice; rather, the yellow appearance is a result of UV light being blocked from the room as it can damage this delicate process. In the yellow area we find Andrew, the experimental officer for this area. Even when the researchers are not here and not using the instruments, Andrew sticks around to make sure that everything is working. He will come and investigate issues and problems reported to him by users of this bay area.

In immediate adjacency to the yellow bay area sits the orange bay area (Fig. 35). There are a few chemists working in this area. Wet chemistry involves a lot of substrate cleaning, a lot of preparation, and some etching. Here is Eva in her light blue gown, demonstrating a new chemistry process. The green gowned person has an additional sheet overtop her light blue gown because she is using phosphoric acid and is about to do an "aggressive" process. Next to it is an HF (hydrofluoric acid) area, which is currently empty. It is highly controlled due to the aggressive nature of HF that has the capacity to go through anything, even glass. This is a space that the house attendants cannot access. At we continue the tour, we see the service bay for electron beam lithography, colour-coded in green (Fig. 36). It is similar to optical lithography, but a beam of electrons is used to expose resist instead of UV light which results in much better spatial resolution.

As witnessed in this quick tour, the distinctive colour design (different outlines around the doors, plaques, lighting) helps lab users organise their

[72] Optical lithography is very similar to the old-fashion photography. A layer of photosensitive plastic (resist) is deposited on a sample. A pattern is then projected on the resist with UV light. Depending on the nature of the resist, either the exposed or non-exposed areas can then be removed in special chemicals, resulting in patterns in resist, which can be used for further processing (using as a mask in etching, or thin film deposition, etc.)

Fig. 34: The yellow bay room for optical lithography, basement clean room, photo by Ben Blackwell.

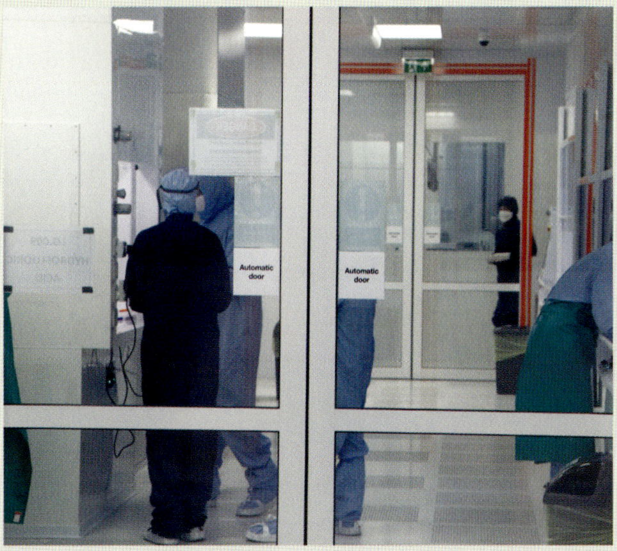

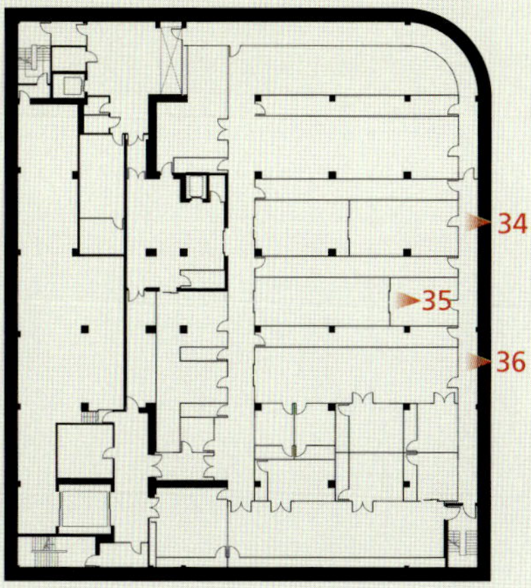

Fig. 35: The orange bay area for wet chemistry, basement clean room, photo by Simon Mitchell.

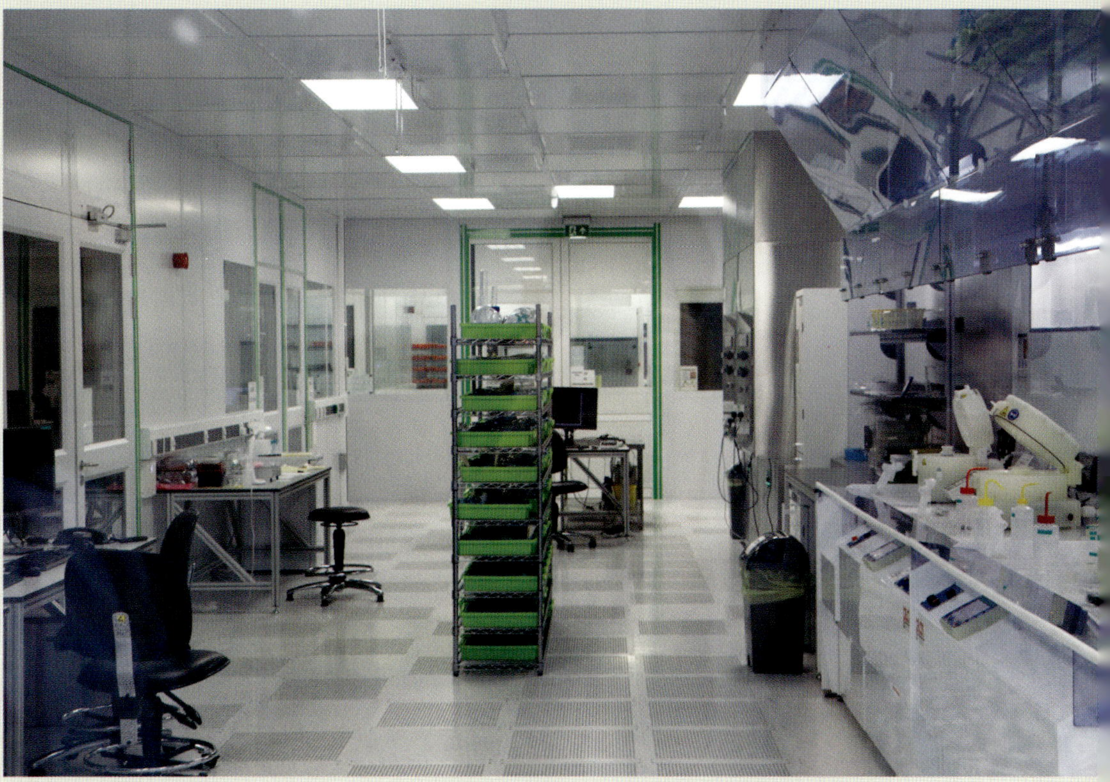

Fig. 36: The green bay area, wet preparation area for electron beam lithography, basement clean room, photo by Simon Mitchell.

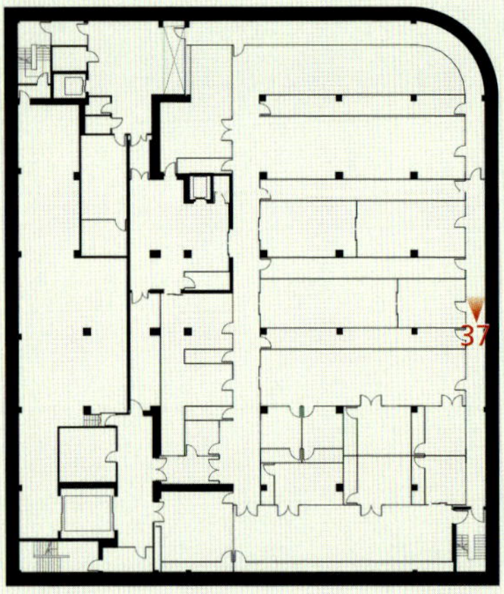

activities in these highly controlled environments (Fig. 37). In addition to the spaces, the glassware labels and equipment, trays and benches are also colour-coded in green, orange, and yellow. The colours signal that these areas are unique: all of the activities related to particles are separated out completely from the work on the flake transfer and from lithography. It also warns lab users that they should not be mixing things and that the chemicals residing in the green coloured area, for instance, could have an effect on the chemicals residing in the yellow area. The design of the bay areas reinforces this message. "It's what we call process control,"[73] clarifies John, as a way to prevent cross-contamination that could be critical. Thus, the strict colour coordination is there to allow a smooth coordination of all activities. In other words, we could say that the aesthetics has a significant functionality.

The probe station testing area of the clean room is used to precisely measure the electrical properties of devices fabricated with graphene and other 2D materials. We notice computers, there sits a dual-beam FIB, one of the high-end electron microscopes with a FIB used for nanofabrication. Here is a scientist cutting sections out of a sample for preparation to go into a transmission electron microscope to inspect the atomic layers inside it. This allows him to identify chemical compositions. We can see one screen flicking away, and here is a matrix map on the right-hand side screen, with four green dots. This indicates that the process is now running. This fairly typical procedure is performed on a regular basis. Many chairs are arranged around

[73] Interview with John Whittaker, 16.10.2019.

Fig. 37: The corridor, colour-coded doors for the different areas, photo by Albena Yaneva.

the computers suggesting there is a group of researchers using the space. Ending the tour of the clean room along the corridor we can conclude that although everything looks like a normal lab from the outside, equipment, furniture, paper, materials as well as humans all have to be specially prepared for the conditions of the clean room to prevent them from ruining the carefully-balanced environment. All bodies and machines, as well as the mundane operations of cleaning, technical maintenance, experimentation, communication and writing remain constrained by the cleanness and are supposed to simultaneously generate more cleanness so that all participants in the lab work can operate efficiently.

8

[M] Variety of Labs

The NGI has two types of labs in addition to the clean room: specialised enclosed labs and open shared labs. The open space labs are not specialised, in a sense that those have an easy access only to the standard set of services distributed through the adjacent grey space. At the same time, some of the labs are highly specialised: they enjoy special services in addition to the standard set.

Most labs potentially allow installation of one acid and one solvent fume hoods (though this capacity can be redistributed between near-by rooms). Also, standard labs are provided with compressed air, process nitrogen and process vacuum. Most of the grey spaces are supplied with process cooling water and helium return line (in case a helium liquefier will be installed in the future). Also, there are connections to two types of clean earths in the grey space (one which uses the same grounding as the rest of the electricity supply and one which uses completely separate grounding).

Chemical laboratory and furnace room have a significantly larger capacity in terms of extraction (acid, solvent or heat) and supply of gases.

Then there are optical rooms, which only differ by the preinstalled laser interlock system which puts a shutter on the laser in case the door is opened. It also allows separate programmable access to the room for authorised personnel.

The low noise laboratories have preinstalled Faraday cages, which have a potential to be galvanically isolated from the rest of the electrical circuit in the building and connected to the clean earth. Data transfer is arranged through the optical interface.

Recently, due to both research and industrial demand, additional chemistry room has been set up where research on chemical modification of 2D materials and their applications in energy storage are being performed. This demonstrate the flexible nature of the design principles utilised in the NGI. In order to set up such a lab a significant capacity of both acid and solvent extracts have been diverted. The system of the supply services through the grey spaces allow one to do it reasonably easily.

8a

Standard Labs

[E] Experiencing Self-Contained Environments

At the NGI different scholars (chemists, physicists, material scientists) and industry people all work together on graphene and 2D materials projects either in the large clean rooms where we have seen them above or in different laboratories (standard and open labs). As Rahul puts it "the building itself is more concentrated on laboratory space."[74] Compared to the large clean rooms (with multiple users, ca. 65–70 at the moment), which are wholly managed by the technical support team, the standard laboratories are "centred around one area of excellence."[75] While in the clean rooms, the regulations and requirements for maintenance are very strict in terms of keeping the infrastructure running, in the labs the requirements for maintenance, health and safety are still important but, less strict. The adaptability of the labs is the key feature: each of them is built to be very flexible in terms of what it can be used for. This is important as the research groups at the NGI grow and shrink very rapidly because of the dynamic nature of the scientific work. The lab architecture therefore follows the groups who, in turn, follow the pace of research. Flexibility also implies that although the labs are designed in a way that they are optimised for graphene, they can accommodate any other work in nanoscience.

Multidisciplinarity is performed here in full swing. The NGI is different from other buildings, John explains, because "in physics you would have physicists working in an environment settled predominantly for physics, in chemistry you would have an environment predominantly settled for chemistry, and the building is settled for chemistry control. And it is a different risk and risk management as well; there's a particular ethos in risk management in chemistry than there is in physics, there are

[74] Interview with Rahul Raveendran Nair, 04.07.2017.

[75] Interview with John Whittaker, 22.06.2017.

different hazards, you have different thought paths. When they come into a building like this they have to consider both sets of risks, they consider both sets of technologies."[76] As we listen to John, we witness that multidisciplinarity translates at the level of building design through the co-existence of different types of labs, technologies, inspection equipment, thought processes, outcomes, and algorithms. And they need to be placed together under one roof. This is in a way what makes the NGI unique. Making physicists and chemists work together is a difficult process as it requires the careful design of the co-habitation of diverse lab settings and technologies, with their distinct hazards and risk management strategies. The fusion of various kinds of research is unusual. Far from following the simple principle of "one discipline in one laboratory," as a multidisciplinary building, the NGI accommodates eighteen standard labs, each with different activities, making possible eighteen different "mixtures of disciplines."

To facilitate these mixtures in order to efficiently explore the unknown applications of graphene a large number of labs is needed in addition to the clean room: two chemistry labs, metrology, prototyping, microscopy, two low noise electrical measurements, energy, composites, furnaces, membranes and nanofluidics, digital fabrication, two optical, Raman spectroscopy, sample preparation, and two industrial labs.[77] In a way, this makes the building self-contained, as Vladimir Falko, research director of the NGI, argues and its strength is that it has many complementary facilities for the fabrication of devices (electronics and opto-electronics, nanocomposites, and printable electronic systems) invented within its space, characterised and then developed as prototypes for possible industrial use. This combination of practical, well-thought out flows of well-designed labs and infrastructure enables an accelerated speed of activities.

Some of these labs are specialised (e.g. the energy lab); others are general, for example, the lab for digital fabrication, where graphene

[76] Interview with John Whittaker, 22.06.2017.

[77] All these laboratories have different combinations of services. However, if required, many of them can be converted one to another by adding additional services, supplied from the grey spaces.

and 2D materials are printed onto fabric to create so-called "smart fabrics." In this lab there is a mixture between material sciences and chemistry. Some labs are small; others are large with 10–20 operative researchers coming from four or five disciplines working together in one room and interacting with each other at a local level. Some labs do not have access to natural light (labs in the centre of the building), like the optical labs; the experiments performed in their enclosed space require dark conditions where the light is removed completely. In the shielded rooms, researchers are sheltered from electromagnetic interference. The enclosed windowless labs are also perfectly suited for commercially sensitive research. All the other labs have windows connecting them with the outside.

Strolling around the campus, dividing his time between the Material Sciences building, where he teaches undergraduate students and where he has another office, and the NGI, Andrey can truly appreciate NGI's architecture as one whose "design is directed through what we [the scientists] need for our [their] graphene research."[78] As one of the first scholars who moved into the building in 2015, he has a fair share of experience dwelling in it as he spends most of his time here, in close proximity to his lab and his ongoing experiments, and the clean room. He elaborates:

> "Here we have laboratories where we can measure, and we have chemistry rooms with the fume hoods, with the wet benches where you can handle chemistry. We had some difficulty in the Schuster Building [the Physics building] but here we have a dedicated chemistry lab where we can carry on the experiments which wc were unable to do in Physics or it was very difficult. When the Physics Building was designed and built, they thought it was going to be about physics experiments.[79] But now we're in a such a multidisciplinary stage of research where

[78] Interview with Andrey Kretinin, 29.06.2017.

[79] When the original Shuster building was built back in 1898 it was qualified as being "the largest and most completely equipped in this country." See "The New Physical Laboratory at the Owens College, Manchester," *Nature*, October 27, 1898, no. 1513, vol. 58, p.621.

> we need to look into chemistry, look into market fabrication, look into physical characterisation, and they should be brought all together. It was difficult in Physics and it's probably the same difficulty when you work in Chemistry: you have a lot of chemistry space but no laboratories for physics. Here it's all brought together in a very close vicinity, so you don't need to go from one building to another, and everything is, sometimes, on the same floor."[80]

Listening to Andrey, we witness again how the multidisciplinarity, necessary for exploring the applications of graphene, requires the co-existence of different types of labs that were traditionally partitioned into separate fields and located in different buildings. In contrast, at the NGI everything is within seconds walk. Having everything "on tap" is very convenient, especially in chemistry, explains the technical manager, Polly Greensmith, as "you haven't got to move gas cylinders in. You haven't got to have vacuum pumps with background noise — it's on tap! It's part of the facilities. There are more fume cupboards than you can shake a stick at. There's lots. You don't need to share, because you've got a whole one."[81] The spacious labs and the infrastructure "on tap" facilitates the speedy course of graphene work in the labs enabling many different kinds of fusions.

In-built infrastructure

Let us follow another permanent "dweller" of the NGI building: Rahul. Prior to moving to the NGI, he was in the School of Physics, but now he is working fully on graphene, in the area of membrane technology. While the clean room was operational since the opening of the building in 2015, some of the individual labs, like Rahul's, opened in 2016 and only became fully operational in the first half of 2017. His team is working to develop graphene-based membranes for different kinds of separations (water filtration, gas separation, or functional coating). To

---

[80] Interview with Andrey Kretinin, 29.06.2017.

[81] Interview with Polly Greensmith, 16.10.2019.

develop these applications, Rahul needs to collaborate with industrial partners. Here is how his day unfolds: "In the morning I go to my office in the Physics building, and after that, in the afternoon/evening, maybe after 4pm, I come here and then I interact with students and see what is going on in the lab and discuss with them. Most of my students are sitting in this building."[82] Rahul has an office, shared with another colleague, where he meets PhD students. You can often see him staying late to finish his work. The NGI is the best place for his experiments. The brand-new facilities of the lab with in-built gas and vacuum facilities needed for Rahul's work on membranes speed up its tempo. He explains, "we don't need to bring extra gas lines into the lab which causes a lot of safety concerns and the University now is not allowed to store any gases inside a lab. So, these kinds of problems are solved already in this building, so that's why I'd prefer to stay here."[83] And that is why he stays late. It also makes his work stress free: "you don't need to worry about electrical and gas connections, you don't need to worry about anything for the next few years because everything is in-built."[84] With time, and the many evening shifts, Rahul and his students have developed an attachment to the building: "if you ask my students for example, to relocate from this building to any other building, they will not do it; they want to be here. Because they like their lab and the social spaces."[85]

And while Rahul and his students can be spotted working in the evenings, Sarah is often here on the weekend. The labs are open on Saturdays and Sundays, and if scientists have permission to work, they can access them. Most of the experiments cannot be done on the weekend as they require that researchers work in pairs for safety purposes. Sarah's experiments, however, allow her to work alone. As she explains, "some experiments we do are very safe, there's almost no risk at all, and so it's like being in an office and you have a machine in front of you and you press some buttons. So, it's no more dangerous

[82] Interview with Rahul Raveendran Nair, 04.07.2017.
[83] Interview with Rahul Raveendran Nair, 04.07.2017.
[84] Interview with Rahul Raveendran Nair, 04.07.2017.
[85] Interview with Rahul Raveendran Nair, 04.07.2017.

than me being sat on my desk."[86] So that is why we can find Sarah often here on the weekends.

Interestingly, the labs are not owned by any researcher or group, instead they are "used." Whenever a device is available it can be used so that more than one group or researcher can benefit from it. This flexible use implies "people filling up empty slots of equipment, office spaces and laboratory facilities whenever possible and without restrictions; the only restriction is when a space is occupied."[87] Thus, the NGI has a dynamic approach to space both at the level of ensuring the flexibility of spaces (labs change easily from one type to another type) and the flexibility of the use of space (users change swiftly working sites). This double flexibility allows scientists to easily change their teams: they group and regroup; they turn labs into offices and back, and perform any spatial modifications they need so they can feel more comfortably and work more efficiently. In addition, the research groups can tailor their own labs to ensure a quick turnaround: when one group moves out, another one can move in very rapidly. Space follows the pace of research. Walls and partitions are ready to engage in a dance of endless re-configurations.

The speed makes the NGI an ideal place for experiments. The ease of using the labs in terms of gas lines, water and power supply and extraction systems contributes to that speed. It is often mentioned by the lab users as being a valuable feature, especially in contrast to other facilities. The giant superconducting magnet, recently purchased for the NGI, for instance, requires a very specific arrangement to be performed around to create a higher magnetic field and test "how materials behave" under those conditions. The lines with cooling water, gases and electricity are all in proximity, coming from the grey room. A simple movement ensures its branching into the lab infrastructure. We can literately witness how space re-configures itself around the magnet. If this "on tap" infrastructure was not there, cylinders would have to travel between buildings. At the NGI, everything is set, as soon as researchers are in their lab; they can turn on their gases and

[86] Interview with Sarah Haigh, 10.07. 2017.

[87] Interview with Vladimir Falko, 21.06.2017.

use them straight away. That is why, explains Andrey, "it's much more convenient to work in these laboratories, from a practical point of view, because of the way infrastructure is designed and how it's actually put around the laboratories. So, we have very easy access to everything we need for our experiments, and this is very rare in scientific buildings. I haven't seen much of it before."[88] The comparison with buildings with more traditional architecture imposes itself again.[89]

To do characterisation, Abhishek, who we saw moments ago in the clean room, uses the labs on the 2nd or 1st floor where he analyses the data. Once he has finished making a device in the clean room, he comes out to characterise it. If the device is meant for optical purposes, we can see Abhishek carrying it to the optical characterisation lab to characterise it and get the data; according to the results, he needs to modify other devices. He also often uses the Raman spectroscopy lab on the 2nd floor (Fig. 38). This is an enclosed lab specifically designed for light sensitive experiments. This lab is used for characterising or measuring 2D materials, like graphene. Here we can find the multi-beam Raman that has four different laser lines. There is also a single beam Raman. These high-powered lasers all form a fairly comprehensive Raman facility, all placed on a floating air table for low vibrations. The lasers go into a common optics array, and then they are diverted down through the Raman spectrometer into a microscope. The results go onto the computer and the characterisation is completed. The lab is quiet, tidy and modern. Kelly compares it with the Schuster building, where she has done lab work with Kostya using Raman spectroscopy to analyse paint pigments and binders. The Raman lab here is "by far more modern and cleaner. The spaces in Schuster will often be large rooms where multiple different things will be worked on at once. Whereas the NGI offers more privacy and security for individual projects."[90]

Working in the cosy and secure environment of the Raman lab, scientists spend long hours; it is not unusual for the measurements

---

[88] Interview with Andrey Kretinin, 29.06.2017.

[89] For an analysis of the architecture of the Shuster building, the Physics building on campus, see "The New Physical Laboratory at the Owens College, Manchester," *Nature*, October 27, 1989, no. 1513, vol. 58.

[90] Interview with Kelly Stanford, 13.12.2019.

Fig. 38: The Raman spectroscopy lab, photo by Ben Blackwell.

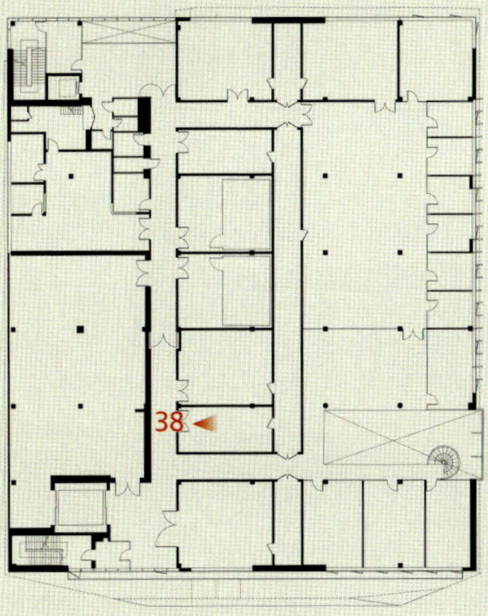

to run for eight or ten hours, especially in the evening. On the coordination board we can see who is mapping their sample at the moment and when they are expected to finish. This could happen anytime — 1.30pm in the day or even 2am in the morning. Each researcher books a session in the Raman lab for a certain time slot — one hour or four hours. On the board we read: "Nicky is using it until 1.30." The next lab user knows when to come and start his/her mapping. That is the reason we do not see crowds in these labs. The time is carefully planned, and the lab message board contributes to the fine and smooth orchestration of the working rhythm. The board acts as a simple and efficient organizational device; the small scale of the lab and the scope of the work does not require special design tricks to facilitate workflow (such as the solutions witnessed in the large clean rooms: colour coordination, prevention of cross-contamination, bracelet-access zones, etc.). In addition, the enclosed nature and the windowless character of the Raman lab does not offer the same social setting for lab work as in labs with large windows (in fact entire walls of windows) like the chemistry lab (Fig. 48) and the furnace lab (Fig. 47) on the 3rd floor, or the energy lab (Fig. 39) on the 2nd floor where the experiments are not light sensitive and the generous daylight and active contact with the city (campus buildings as well as Manchester icons) generate a unique working energy.

Retrofitting and maintaining the labs

Life for experimentalists is made easier as the NGI has its own mechanical workshop and an army of technicians who can help researchers at any

Fig. 39: The energy lab: window connection to the city, photo by Albena Yaneva.

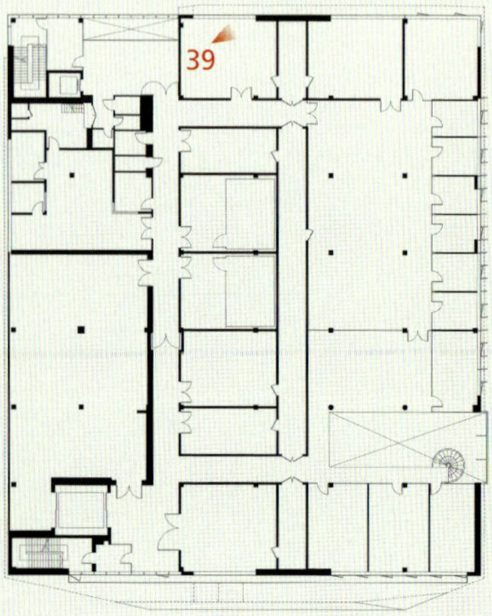

time. "Here, everything is automated," Abhishek points out, "we do not need to do anything. We just need to operate the machine to carry out a specific recipe. Everything else is taken care of by the technical staff."[91] If scientists want to modify something on the lab set-up, they do not need to hire subcontractors, which can take time. Instead, any changes can be all done "in house," on the spot.

The retrofitting of the labs happens often as modifications from the original lab's purpose impose themselves as crucial for the progress of the work. Meet the technicians who help them in the retrofitting venture on a daily basis: Chris, whom we

[91] Interview with Abhishek Mishra, 21.11.2017.

met in the gas room, is in charge of technical storage; Lisa is a senior lab technician (in charge of chemistry, the furnaces, the more scientific side of it) and when she went working at GEIC she was replaced by Hannah; Phil is in charge of prototyping in the workshop; Christopher is the "operations job man," as the other Chris calls him: "if we get new tables that need to be built up for the labs or in the grey space, Christopher is the one to help. Say, for instance, there was a pipe that burst. He'd be your man."[92] Polly is the technical manager for labs and facilities, and, as such, she manages the technicians (Christopher, Phil and Hannah) who cover the different labs (everything from the clean rooms up). She has worked at the university for 22 years and she has spent 18 months at the NGI. Compared to the Material Sciences building (where Polly worked before as a chemistry technician), which was re-purposed to be made into a lab, the NGI is a purpose-built space "where everything is done from the architecture up, and it really works."[93] Nevertheless, technicians still have problems to solve. Polly is in charge of the servicing and does the annual maintenance to "make sure all the checks are done so that nothing goes wrong." Small things still go wrong. At 8am in the morning, you can often see Polly and her team in the kitchen, holding an informal chat about "what the day's going to bring." Informal meeting works better for such a small team, they prefer to touch base on a daily basis. Polly explains that during these meetings they are "talking about problems, or what had happened yesterday, or what's coming up for today."[94] Problems of a different nature have to be solved promptly, for example that "someone is complaining that it is too hot," and they have to investigate, check the chillers on the roof, check the sensor in the lab, the control panel, etc. In another situation, there is a gas leak, the alarm goes off, and Polly and her team have to put things in place. Sitting at her computer, just like John, looking at the BMS, Polly can remove the problem from a distance, sometimes even from home (during the weekend and the holidays); she checks the system and the computer controls, she oversees the building to make

92 Interview with Chris Livingston, 01.12.2017.

93 Interview with Polly Greensmith, 16.10.2019.

94 Interview with Polly Greensmith, 16.10.2019.

sure all lab facilities are up and running so that all graphene scientists can continue their experiments without disruption.

Let us follow one of the technicians after he has left the morning meeting in the kitchen. A problem in one of the labs has been signalled: "the temperature blowing out at 29 degrees in this room" and the technician Christopher helps the scientists. Commenting on his role in the labs, he says "I'll first do a little bit of diagnosis, check if the solenoid valve is open and if not then I'm onto Estates. So, I deal quite closely with Estates."[95] Christopher also makes sure the lab equipment is installed. He spends the day with the researchers, checking that the equipment is up, available, and doing the tests with them to make sure it is fully functioning.

The lab doors are massive and close automatically. This system keeps all the chemicals and vapour smells inside the labs, to be extracted. Four to five air changes occur every hour and this regular air change is done so that a certain level of humidity is always maintained, and the temperature is always within a proper range (plus or minus half a degree). This is important, because, as Christopher explains, "when you're doing research you want to know that if you have your sample you can keep to your parameters for the amount of chemical you're using and you'd want to know that the room you're in can't affect your samples."[96] This can be controlled through the BMS. Christopher logs onto it and takes a snapshot of the whole building, clicks on each floor. He can see what the temperature is in every single room and lab and can adjust it accordingly. He elaborates, "we can easily have a look on just a computer screen anywhere in the building. This is how the building is working without us going around and saying, 'so where's the problem?' and trying to chase it through the building. We just look at a computer screen; it's all there for us ready to go. And then once we find if there is a problem we can go and adjust that straight away."[97] The system maintains a very pure gas supply, which is crucial for graphene research. The purity of the gas is an indication that the

[95] Interview with Christopher Hyde, 15.12.2017.

[96] Interview with Christopher Hyde, 15.12.2017.

[97] Interview with Christopher Hyde, 15.12.2017.

results will be good. Christopher also helps researchers connect the gases from the grey spaces to the labs, and elbow the pipe work down in, and then into the regulator. Once the equipment is installed the researchers can regulate their own pressure for every gas. Here is Christopher, going to the labs, liaising with the researchers and having different discussions around safety ("is it safe if we install in here?"), around ways of doing things ("this is how we're planning on doing it"). Scientists want to know what the limits are. They want to know all about services that come into the room: "how is the room fed," "what they can do to the room," changes like lowering the tables, changing the compressed air supplies, moving the regulators. Then Christopher starts getting the pipework set up, moving the labs around, planning the risk assessment if the lab needs to be changed, doing full installation of seven gas lines, for water, the vacuum system, and so on. If someone, for instance, uses carbon dioxide and they want to change that line to a different gas, Christopher can purge that line with nitrogen — clean it out and prepare it quickly for use again. If they need a certain level of gas flow, he gets that gas flow for them. If equipment needs to be installed, he gets everything ordered and has everything ready to go. If some researchers need to get on a piece of equipment quicker because one of their experiments has gone wrong, and an external company is coming with an installation only in a week, then Christopher has to do the installation even quicker by himself. All scientists rely on the work of Christopher and the other lab technicians. All the built-in structures commended by Rahul, everything Andrey needed for his superconducting magnet is put in place by Christopher. As we have seen many times already, the technicians at the NGI are important conductors for the speed of graphene research.

If technicians facilitate daily maintenance and retrofitting of the labs, in a quick, efficient and almost imperceptible way, without questioning it, the scientists are consulted and constantly questioned on the key design decisions related to the architecture of their labs. Just like Andrey, Mark, has an office in the Material Sciences building as well as an office here in the NGI. Mark leads one of the research groups here and they use a communal lab on the 2nd floor.

Fig. 40: The composites lab, photo by Albena Yaneva.

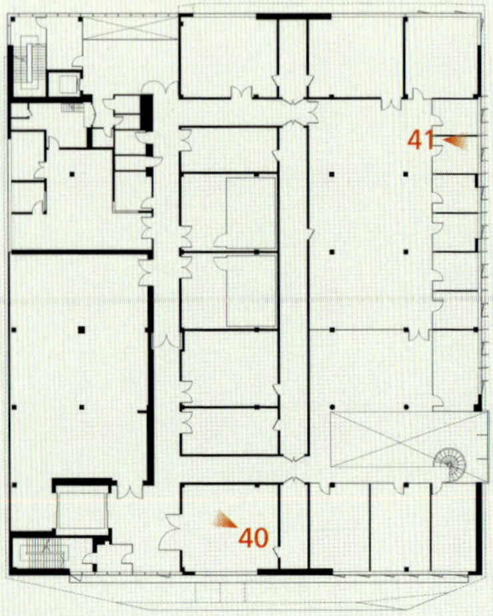

He praises the compact aspect of the building. "Generally, I quite like having my group near the labs, all of the equipment we need is in one building, so that outweighs any inconvenience to me, having to walk between buildings."[98] In fact, he only walks between buildings to meet his undergraduate students and teach (in the Material Sciences building), and then back to the NGI to meet his group of researchers; teaching and research remain separated in the different parts of the campus. Mark is an expert in energy storage (research on batteries, super-capacitors and system integration for electric vehicles) and he also does

[98] Interview with Mark Bissett, 30.06.2017.

composite materials (for aerospace and automotive applications). In both cases, it requires putting graphene or some other 2D materials into the energy storage devices or lightweight composites. As his research is divided into those two streams, he works in the energy lab and the composites lab on the 2nd floor (Fig. 40). His team also uses the chemistry and furnace labs on the 3rd floor. The labs are also divided into communal spaces for all of the groups to use. Only some groups and a few companies have dedicated labs. As they develop their research in energy storage and composite materials, Mark's group uses six or seven different individual labs across the NGI building.

Fig. 41: Scientist Mark Bissett showing the plans of his new lab at GEIC, photo by Albena Yaneva.

Follow Mark as he fetches the blueprints for his new lab in the GEIC (Fig. 41). The floorplan across the whole building is completed, and Mark will have a new lab there. I catch him at the moment when they are purchasing equipment to be moved as soon as the building opens (in 2018). We discuss the design of the lab and he is trying to work out what equipment is going to go where in terms of the flow of space and utilities, and where they need three phase power or an extraction system. He explains, "So, we've had several meetings with the architects and their team. I don't know anything about architecture, I just care about the lab [laughs]. There is always an interesting compromise I guess: the architects want to have very large open space and they want it to look very nice, but as scientist, I look at it and think I purely want to hear much more about its functionality and its health and safety. Like, if I'm doing some process here with explosive or dangerous gases, I don't want a large open lab that can spread or cause a damage."[99] Listening to Mark as he inspects the blueprints of his new lab at the GEIC, and compares it with the NGI, we witness

[99] Interview with Mark Bissett, 30.06.2017.

to what extent space is for him, not about a big and open aesthetically pleasing container, but rather about flows, about extraction and power systems, and circuits of utilities. It is this flow that makes the lab work efficient. The more open the plan is, the bigger the risk for spreading explosions or causing bigger damages in the event of an accident. How all these flows and potential hazards are regulated will imply a different type of aesthetics. The need to have contained, but well interconnected, spaces makes the lab successful.

As we saw at the beginning, the NGI is "a compromise between what is needed in terms of science" and "what architects want." As Mark explains, "there's always a limitation for lab space and office space across, at any university, so we care about getting the most equipment and most people we can in, per floor or space. But scientists also tend to be very territorial, we don't like sharing [laughs]. We're always worried. It's a very competitive industry, especially in the case of graphene where Manchester is obviously very popular for graphene and it has attracted 250 graphene researchers. But it also means we're all in competition with each other, and we're in competition for grants, and so we don't necessarily want to share too much of our space with other groups or people."[100] In designing a science lab, conflicts are inevitable. On the one hand, there is the need to have an efficient use of space and the NGI is a congested building with as many facilities as possible accommodated under one roof. A congested structure means sharing facilities – offices, labs. Yet, on the other hand, the competitive nature of graphene research conflicts with the idea of "sharing." This tension between the open and protected nature of the scientific work again defines the spaces here. At the moment of designing and planning the NGI, Mark recalls that the academic groups suggested to "put more partitions in, to put dividers in, to have separate offices," and the architects were "no, no it should be big and open and much more collaborative," and the scientists were like "no, no, we want to be separated" [laughs]."[101] These two drives between openness (that is how architects translate the need for graphene research to be collaborative) and seclusion (that is how

[100] Interview with Mark Bissett, 30.06.2017.

[101] Interview with Mark Bissett, 30.06.2017.

scientists reaffirm their need to preserve their territory, their results, their innovations) are successfully balanced in the design of the NGI building: "it's somewhere in the middle," states Mark. The containment of research work, results, and risks remains an important feature of the new generation of lab buildings while the overall design should communicate openness (like the viewing gallery in the clean room).

A visit in the energy lab

Let us visit the energy lab on the 2nd floor to understand how a lab is "fed." Lewis Le Fevre is a postdoctoral researcher with a background in physics, who is looking at solar cells and designing energy storage devices.[102] He focuses on the chemistry side and designs large devices like batteries, super-capacitors, among others. This work could be placed between blue sky research, basic fundamental research, on the one side of the continuum, and the industry level pilot line scale, on the other. As he explains, he makes "sure that we see the same improvement in the big devices that we see in the small devices."[103] Here is his lab (Figs. 42–43); the equipment is new and has the highest specs available in this area of research. Everything looks immaculate; only the black spots on the white cupboards disclose the intensive rhythm of work; graphene makes its presence known through this grey powder. There are seven registered users in the energy lab who use it as their primary lab, and they do the entirety of their research here. Other researchers visit the lab occasionally to use some of the equipment; thus, in total we can see about 12 people in the energy lab in 2017. In 2019 there are now around 20 lab users.

The lab is designed to have stacks of equipment on top of each other, which makes for a more efficient use of space. A lot of new equipment was purchased in the last couple of years as the funding increased between 2017 and 2019, and companies have become much more interested, especially British ones, in the work of the NGI energy

[102] The first interview was conducted when Lewis was still a PhD student (2017). He has completed his dissertation and is now working at the NGI as a postdoc.

[103] Interview with Lewis Le Fevre, 14.12.2017.

Fig. 42: The energy lab, photo by Albena Yaneva.

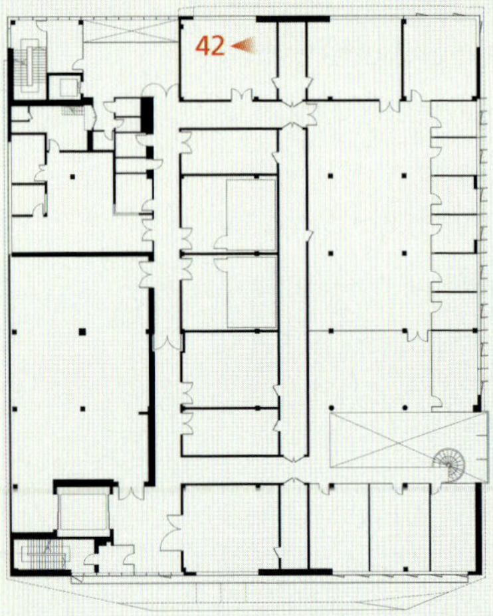

team. The lab swims in light and Lewis enjoys looking through the large windows; in fact, an entire wall of windows brings daylight in and connects the city views with the researchers working here (Fig. 39). "In the morning you have a lot of light," explains Lewis and he continues, "you have much more light compared to chemistry labs in traditional buildings on campus where you have one or two small size windows, but never a wall of windows."[104] The light improves the researchers' well-being without interfering with their experiments. As Lewis points out, "none of the experiments we do are light sensitive, and we only focus on closed systems."[105] Parts of the wall are painted in a joyful orange colour reflecting the day light (Fig. 42).

[104] Interview with Lewis Le Fevre, 13.11.2019.

[105] Interview with Lewis Le Fevre, 13.11.2019.

Initially, the architect suggested using orange for the façade, but the black colour was chosen at the end to maintain the shiny and mysterious profile of the building. Nevertheless, the orange colour remained in the labs, and some yellow walls can be spotted in the atria.

In contrast, the chemistry lab where Lewis worked previously, in the Chemistry building on campus, was very different; for him, it was very dark. There he shared space with 25 other researchers. As he expounds, "I don't know how to describe it. It felt more cramped with big things. It felt like you were constantly walking over things or people to do anything. The space there was nearly all being used up by other people and myself. Equipment, as well."[106] Comparisons with this working space makes Lewis appreciate the new energy lab here at the NGI. He spends at least seven hours a day here, and only two hours in the Chemistry building. Here he is: he comes straight to the lab in the morning, and he sets some experiments. He can leave a performing experiment or start a new experiment for some analysis and then leave it running for an hour, two hours, or even a day. Then he goes out of the lab onto the roof terrace to have lunch as the experiment runs its course. Yet, he explains, "If it's raining, or I've only got twenty minutes to wait, I'll start doing analysis on the communal computers we have in the lab. We have five communal computers in there."[107] All of the equipment is run from a computer, but Lewis or any other researcher from that lab can simultaneously use the computer for data analysis as long as no one else needs it to start another experiment (Fig. 43). Speed is something that can be witnessed in this daily lab rhythm again as we follow Lewis. In the Chemistry building everything is slow. Lewis describes the slow pace as follows: "if it's Monday, you thought of an idea, you wanted to do an experiment, sometimes you'd have to wait until Thursday before you can use the equipment."[108] No waiting is needed at the NGI; experiments follow ideas promptly. The high spec equipment facilitates quick thinking and ensures speed of experimentation and results.

[106] Interview with Lewis Le Fevre, 14.12.2017.

[107] Interview with Lewis Le Fevre, 14.12.2017.

[108] Interview with Lewis Le Fevre, 14.12.2017.

Another way to speed up the course of research is at the level of the analysis. There is a system for that, which can run multiple samples. In the Chemistry building, Lewis can only run one sample at a time and wait for weeks while it completes, whereas here he can run several samples at the same time. As they have become much busier, they now have two machines for multi-scale testing which allows him to test 30 samples at a time. Thus, numerous samples are analysed simultaneously and the chances to get good results quickly multiply as well. As we come across the various "dwellers" of the building, speed is ever-present. Speed runs through the veins of the entire building, from the entrance through to the gas systems and the multiple samples analysed simultaneously. The proximity of computers and experimental set-ups intensifies the discussions. When Lewis and his group have an experiment running, they all gather around the screen and discuss it together, trying to establish whether they see something strange, or if, as he puts it, the experiment "is not doing what we thought it would do."[109] Most of his colleagues in the lab work on the same project, and discussions unfold around the computer at any moment. They often plan experiments together, or they analyse their methods or procedures.

Working on similar projects and in the same lab space allows them to see each other very often. They have a lot of fun together: they bet on their experiments, develop different lists, like a project "to-do list," a list of things to be done before Christmas, etc. The lab is full of written scripts all around the equipment surfaces and the walls. On the glass surface of the fume hood we can see formulae and "instructions of how to do the testing" (Fig. 43). As Lewis says, "it is actually easier to show people how to do things by visualising it rather than explaining and talking."[110] These inscriptions replace the verbal communication between the scientists. There is a direct connection between the colourful formulae on the huge writeable black wall right in front of the lab (Fig. 44), which explain "what is going on in the lab," and the written instructions of how to do specific testing on the glass window of the fume hood inside the lab. The inscriptions outside the lab are meant

[109] Interview with Lewis Le Fevre, 14.12.2017.

[110] Interview with Lewis Le Fevre, 13.11.2019.

Fig. 43: Background: a fume hood with writings on the glass window; foreground: Lewis Le Fevre analysing data on the computer, photo by Albena Yaneva.

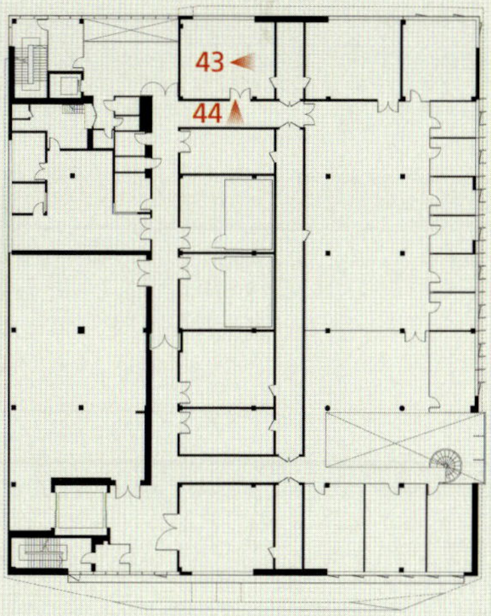

Fig. 44: Lewis Le Fevre in front of the black writeable wall opposite the energy lab, photo by Albena Yaneva.

Fig. 45: The lab layout of the energy lab drawn on the wall, photo by Albena Yaneva.

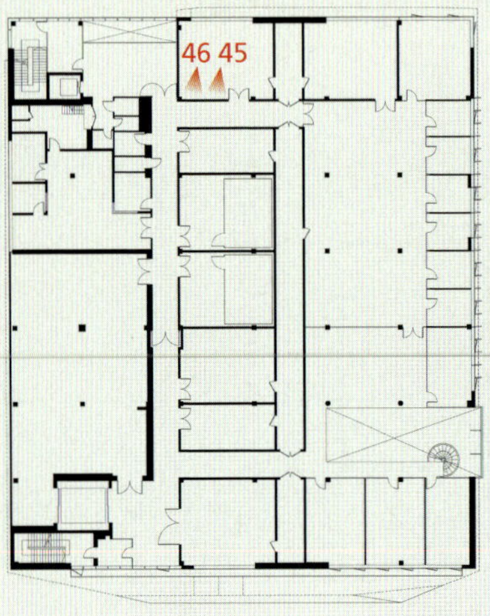

to the other groups and interested visitors of the NGI, they replace communication with the world outside the energy lab. In addition to these, as researchers cannot write directly on the white walls, which are not writeable, Lewis and his colleagues have bought white rolls and stuck the hand-made white boards on the wall using sticky tape to create another surface to write and scribble formulae and visual instructions. New writable surfaces are added to the lab, as the existing ones are all in use, for different purposes, and never enough. Further down, we see a plan of what "each section of the lab does" drawn skilfully and presented in a user-friendly way on the orange wall behind the sink (Fig. 45). Looking at the lab diagram, you can see the

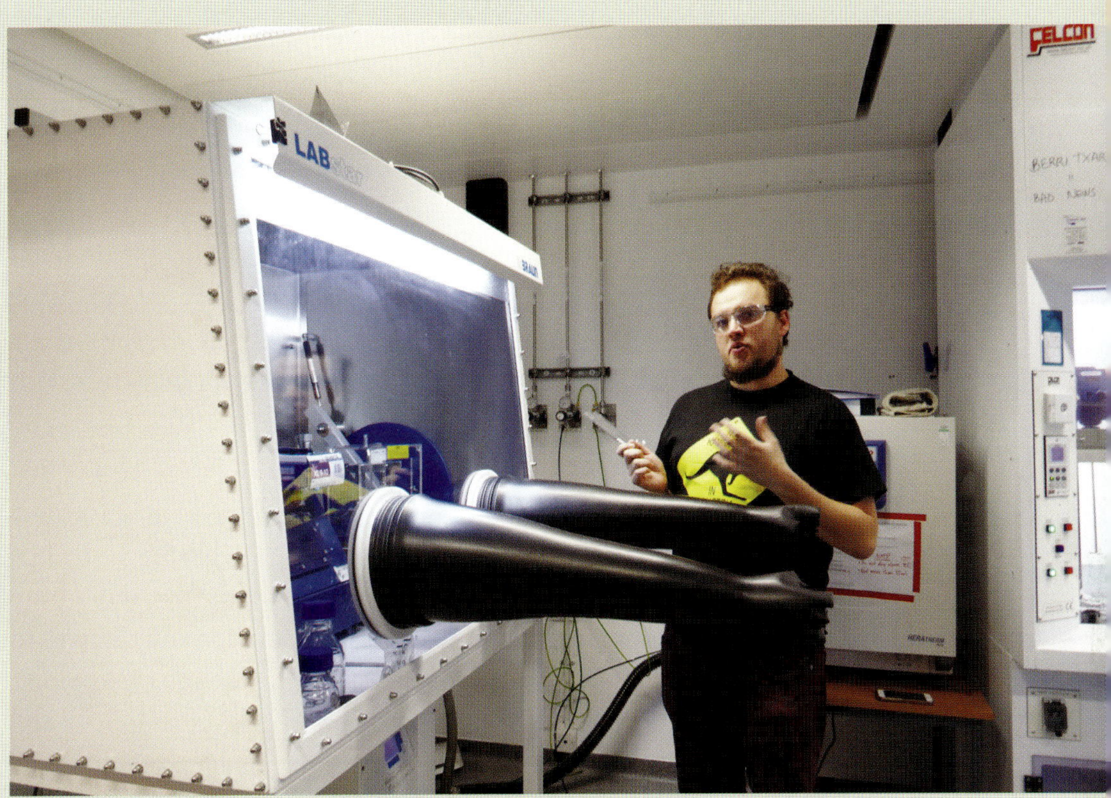

Fig. 46: Background: writings on the top of the fume hood; foreground: Lewis Le Fevre showing the new glove box workstation in the energy lab, photo by Albena Yaneva.

different areas (like preparation areas, testing, analyses, etc.) and this plan helps scientists to figure out the lab organisation; as Lewis elaborates, "it is a lot easier as we are trying to improve the flow."[111] Then, on the top of another fume hood, high up on the white surface of it, we can witness some handwritten Basque words and their translation into English (Fig. 46). These are the traces of a Basque postdoctoral researcher teaching her energy lab colleagues different Basque words, just for fun; we read "Berri Tzarrak + bad news" (the name of the Basque rock power trio). Lewis, in return, teaches them some slang English words. These inscriptions bear traces of informal communication among the lab users. As Lewis sums up his lab life: "what I do in the lab is run experiments, analyse data, discuss results, and have a joke with the

[111] Interview with Lewis Le Fevre, 14.12.2017.

other people."[112] That precise summary can also be read through the scripts and formulae drafted on glass, paper and wall surfaces — even the façade, as we will see — throughout the lab. The atmosphere of the work is convivial; the daylight and all facilities contribute to the joy of science as witnessed in the lab routines.

Like other scientists, Lewis appreciates the fact that he does not need to carry a bottle of CO_2 across the building (like he did in the Chemistry building where gas supply is not centralised). Everything is provided here, in every location, by the dedicated infrastructure that makes the gases for different experiments always available. Lewis and his colleagues have input from the technicians in terms of supplies: the house vacuum system, the process cooling system, the ultra-pure water. Yet, the technicians' "obligation and responsibilities end when they have supplied the different systems."[113] Lewis' research group is responsible for maintaining the energy lab and for any changes to the lab equipment and the shared computers (unlike the clean rooms where the equipment is used by lots of different research groups and is maintained by the technicians). The lab arrangement, written scripts and instructions, just witnessed here, bear traces of the very specific way scientists have appropriated the space and have mobilised it in the collective distribution of lab duties and responsibilities. This material architecture effectively replaces all kinds of speech: from informal chats to pedagogical instructions, from technical inductions to official scientific discourse. As no time is wasted to re-tell the obvious, the known, design helps the lab work to speed up its course in search of the unknown.

Labs on the top floor

There are two labs on the 3rd floor in proximity with the social spaces: the furnace and the chemistry labs. Take a quick look at the furnace lab and witness scientists growing graphene (Fig. 47). This graphene

[112] Interview with Lewis Le Fevre, 14.12.2017.

[113] Interview with James Fitzsimons, 28.11.2017.

growth room has several high temperature CVD[114] furnaces running at about 1200 degrees of heat. Because of the high temperature and the use of flammable gases in this lab, it is assessed as high risk. We see some researchers doing the substrate preparation, setting the growth to go over night and then leaving the lab. The researchers might spend 15 minutes for the preparation while the crystal growth can take anything from minutes to days. That is why there are a lot of people going in and out of the lab. The surfaces are prepared at the kneeling furnaces where, by heating copper up, the surface is made flat. Chemicals are forbidden here due to the high temperatures and the risk of spillage. The furnace lab is connected to the chemistry lab on the 3rd floor and users can go from one lab to another through a connecting door. Both rooms have limited access. Let us have a quick look there too (Fig. 48). As Andrey explains "the chemistry labs are all isolated; they have to have special air control, special fume hoods."[115] The chemistry lab is placed on the 3rd floor, as Polly explains, because "you always try and put the most hazardous things near the top of the building because the extract is shorter."[116] This is an important health and safety requirement because of the nature of the experiments and processes conducted there. John recalls that the original plan was not to have any active laboratories on the 3rd floor. Yet, they ended up with these two labs. There are a lot of risks with smells and chemistry spillages which requires good lab management. This lab is managed, looked over, at 8 o'clock in the morning; all of the meetings are held at that time before other users of the building arrive. This staggered approach to running the lab does not apply to the labs on the other floors. Yet, even before management comes, the design itself prevents the smells from spreading and the spillages from happening. The floor of the chemistry room is sunk at points with in-built drains so as to divert chemical spills. The two labs are placed at the outer perimeter of the building. There is a grey space and a corridor, between the labs on the one side, and the social area

---

114 CVD stands for Chemical Vapour Deposition. In these systems reactants are delivered in vapour form to the hot substrate, where they react, resulting in a particular chemical or material.

115 Interview with Andrei Kretinin, 29.06.2017.

116 Interview with Polly Greensmith, 16.10.2019

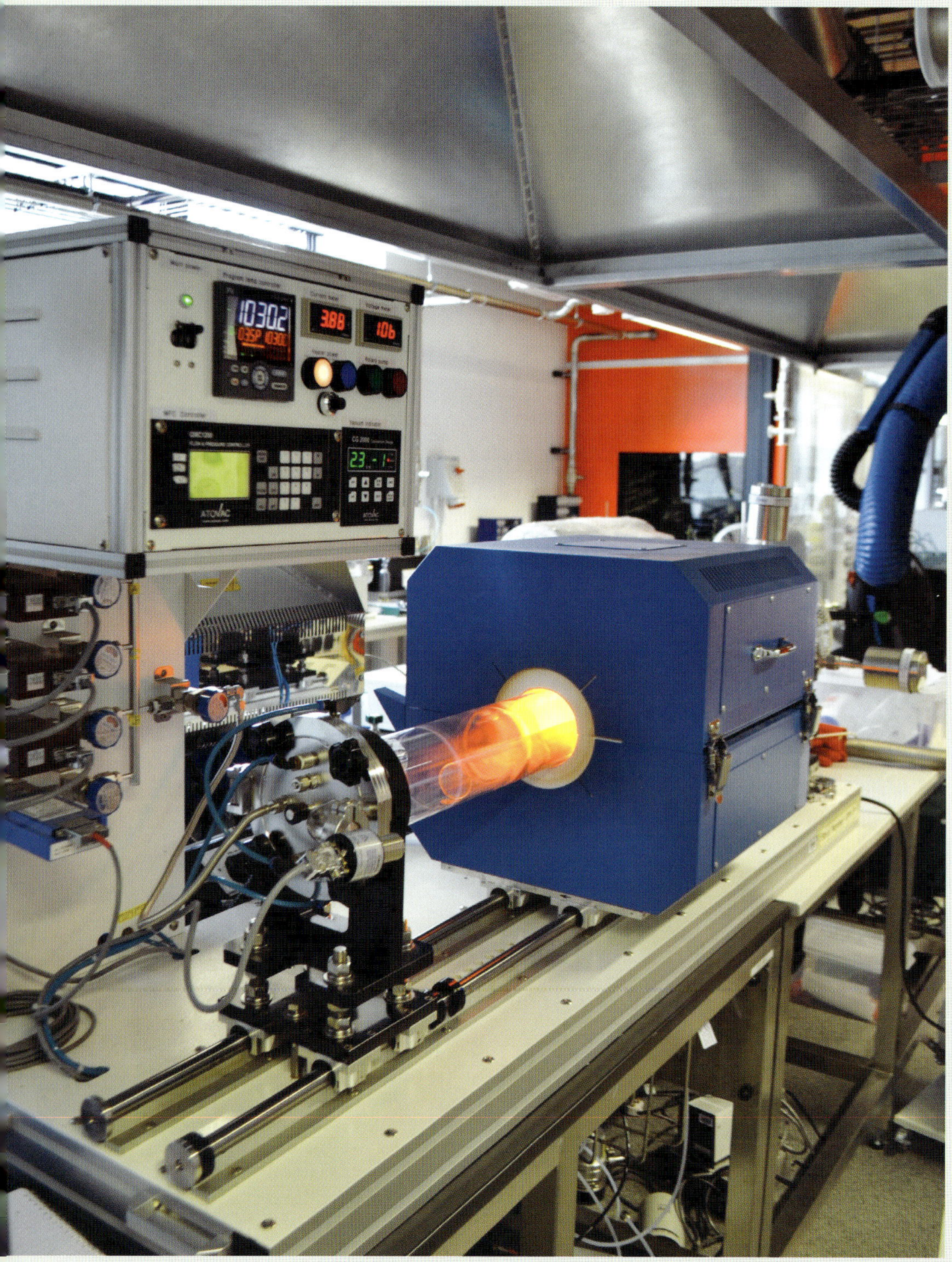

Fig. 47: The furnace lab, photo by Ben Blackwell.

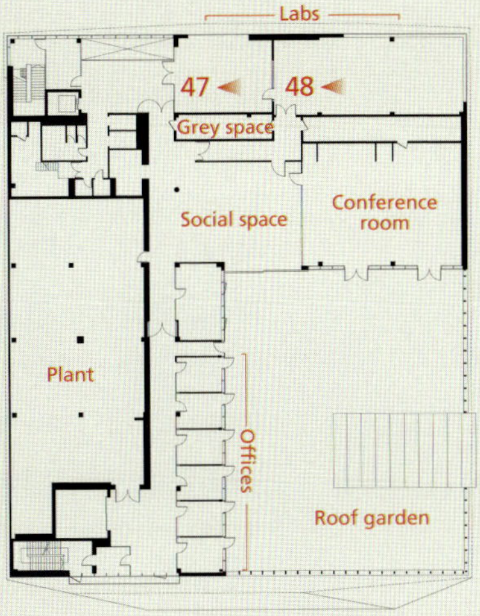

Fig. 48: The chemistry lab, photo by Albena Yaneva.

and seminar space on the 3rd floor, on the other side. In spite of the separations there is still a risk of smells spreading. The chemistry lab also has a negative air pressure which keeps odours inside; the fume hoods in the lab and the extracts constantly take air out. Fresh air is also pushed into the room and all spaces are meticulously air-conditioned. All doors are locked, and so is the corridor leading to the chemistry lab behind the grey space. The access control keeps random visitors away from these spaces. Johns explains that "the services that have to go in come in there through convoluted path; the services — gas, extract, water, etc. — come in down the centre of this corridor and over the chemistry lab, and they do not go over the seminar space."[117] No one enjoying a graphene talk in the conference room or having a chat over a coffee in the social space can suspect the presence of a chemistry world behind these layers of doors, walls and corridors. Nor can they sniff the presence of chemicals betraying the lab's existence. The partitions between chemicals and coffee, between experimental work generating results and discussions around the results is strictly sustained so as to ensure the success of each of these activities.

This separation is important for a working science building. As John clarifies, "it is a research facility with a seminar space; it's not a big seminar space with some research underneath it."[118] Just like no one suspects the existence of a chemistry lab hidden behind doors and corridors, no one is equally aware of the existence of the plant rooms on the same floor (the CUB), just opposite the social space. In fact, one third of each floor is plant space, and two thirds is operational space; and there is a divide between the two types of spaces that acts as a vibration and acoustic buffer (see chapter 4). The sound levels of the plants are below the expected level which is why many visitors passing the plant rooms remain unaware of their existence. One building next to another. One visible, the other one, invisible, secret. Most visitors and researchers can only perceive the visible spaces, as they pass through the operational space of the laboratories without really knowing their impact (detectable only by the smells or the sounds). Once on the 3rd

[117] Interview with John Whittaker, 31.05.2019.

[118] Interview with John Whittaker, 31.05.2019.

floor, they see the roof garden, the social space and the seminar space; they can enjoy a cup of tea while sitting in the social area. Occasionally they see people going out of the chemistry lab, all gowned, wheeling trolleys full of chemicals into the seminar hub, or moving the cryogenic gases and large scales of chemicals around, and they are instantly reminded of the existence of the lab on that floor – reminded also of the nature of the building. However, chemists try to avoid going out of the lab with materials during seminar times and social peak hours. In a way the proximity to social spaces creates more worries for the lab users as it sets constraints for free movement between spaces. Having the lab next to the social spaces and the kitchen makes it difficult for the students: it takes them a while "to learn that they cannot come out of the lab wearing the coats because they are entering a social space; it's just a habit."[119] Now it is a routine that has to be trained into new people to the building. It takes some time to adopt the routine. Thus, while the chemistry world can resurface occasionally and become visible to the social world that unfolds on the 3rd floor, both technicians and building managers ensure that the secret plant building, the CUB we have seen in chapter 4, remains invisible so that its imperceptible, but sophisticated infrastructure of pipes, tanks and cylinders can continue to sustain the existence of the visible NGI.

Just as it is important to maintain the separations between social and lab spaces (full of chemicals, sounds and smells that do not always facilitate social exchange), cleaning the spaces to keep dirt, smell and sounds away is equally important for the image of the labs. The labs are very difficult to clean, and difficult in a different way, depending on the nature of the lab's activities. We have noticed the black spots on the white cupboards and the fume hoods in the energy lab where we met Lewis. The house attendants warn us that "there is graphene floating in the air." There is also a lot of dust coming in the building due to the construction work on campus. While cleaning the labs, Daniela uses a cleaning cloth, yet, the cloth absorbs only a certain amount of the dust. The floors are particularly difficult to clean because the dust settles there, so she uses the scrubbing machine, making sure it is not

[119] Interview with Polly Greensmith, 16.10.2019

too wet; special signs warn the researchers of possible slip hazard. Recently, Daniela had to clean the furnace lab with the help of one of her colleagues and she was struck by how fine graphene is and how deep it gets into surfaces. This lab was not cleaned for a while, and over the time, it got dirtier and dirtier where graphene found its way into the floor itself. To clean it "was just a matter of wetting the floor, mopping it up, getting very, very dirty water out, and cleaning again with clean water. And after a while we got the floor clean, but it did take a long time as graphene was very thick on the floor."[120] They used a special cleaning chemical to polish efficiently. In addition, in the labs there is a lot of equipment lying around and the house attendants are very cautious to dust it. Daniela elaborates "we can't really touch anything. You might see something, it looks like dirt, but it could actually be something to do with experiments. You can wipe around some stuff, but you can't actually touch too much. There are also chemicals, and you don't know how dangerous they are, some of the things can be lethal."[121] Thus, navigating carefully between equipment, samples and the extraction cabinets, Daniela dusts the lab surfaces keeping them clean while remaining vigilant not to interfere in the lab work and interact with harmful chemicals. Cautious not to cause disruptions, always there before the others, always invisible, the house attendants also contribute to the seamless course of graphene work.

All needed for successful graphene work is here: gases and water all supplied 24/7, all in a state of readiness; water constantly pumping all the way around the building; gases in constant circulation, lines that can be purged at any moment. An army of technicians, experimental officers and house attendants are there to sustain this operational pace. An unstoppable rhythm of flows, machines and circuits all around the building support an unstoppable course of research. Built to respond to the competitive pace of graphene work, the standard labs accelerate it even further, allowing easy connections to infrastructure, facilitating a smooth rhythm without disruptions to lab routines. At the same time, they reinforce the specialisation by containing chemicals, hazards and secrecy inside the lab walls. The balance between openness and partitioning in the lab design makes the work tempo even more efficient.

[120] Interview with Daniela Sevelova, 4.12.2019.

[121] Interview with Daniela Sevelova, 4.12.2019.

8b

[M] Open Labs

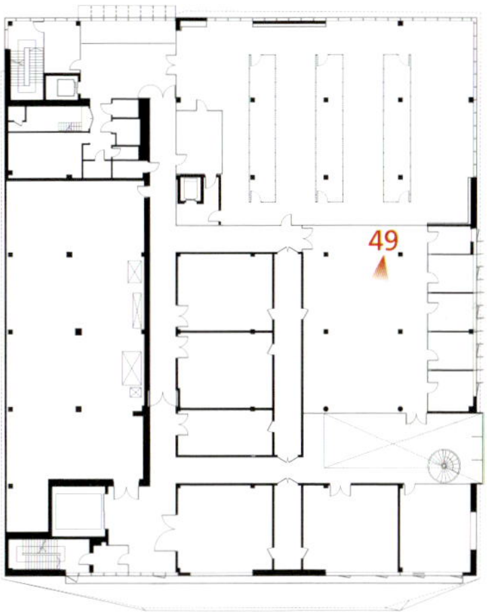

It is important to stress the reasons why we have decided to make some of the laboratories open and did not go for solely enclosed labs. First of all — it is the complete flexibility in using the space. Desks, equipment, proximity between apparatuses — everything can be combined without restrictions. Also, potentially very large equipment could be installed in such laboratories.

Second, access to daylight (already discussed in chapter 2). Third — open space promotes collaboration and encourages more often interaction

Fig. 49: Open lab on the 1st floor, photo by Ben Blackwell.

with colleagues, forces them to get out from offices and walk a step into labs (literally) more frequently.

Fourth, it encourages equipment sharing. Very often equipment purchased by one group would not be utilised 100% of time. This is especially true for characterisation and analytical machines. Sharing such equipment between different groups is a way for more efficient use of resources and promotes trust and collaboration between groups.

Also, importantly, open access laboratories allow for simpler expansion. In the case of the open space labs on the 1st and 2nd floors – one needs only to move the glass walls in order to significantly expand the laboratories (Fig. 49).There are cons as well, though. Obviously, the open space labs do not guarantee privacy, which might be important for commercial projects. Absence of the walls means that the services have to be distributed through the ceiling. There might be crosstalk between equipment, especially acoustic. Access to equipment, which in closed labs can be controlled through the lab access, has to be managed by some other means.

Proximity between labs and offices

The arrangement of offices and labs (with offices situated along the perimeter and the labs inside) immediately solves another issue of proximity between experimental and the writing-up space. Close proximity between the two dramatically improves the efficiency of work: one can set up an experiment, say for half-an-hour, then work away to the desk to do some work on the computer and come back to check the results and to set up a new experiment. This would be impossible if the distance between the two type of spaces is too large.

The same is true for the supervisor-student relations. A door of the supervisor which opens directly to the lab encourages students to walk in and start asking questions. The same is true for the opposite traffic: a professor seeing his/hers student doing experiments right now just outside his/hers office is much more likely to get out and discuss the results in the real time. The proximity between offices and labs also facilitates the exchange of ideas between disciplines. The fact that many offices look like continuation of labs make them much more accessible for students who need to discuss their ideas with colleagues from other groups as well (same students or professors). The students from different groups also share communal offices and exchange information.

Finally, it is also a safety feature. Accidents do happen and with labs being effectively continuously monitored from the offices, it is much more likely that a mistake will be spotted before a disaster has happened, or help (in the form of advice or actual physical help) will arrive in time.

Similar arrangements are implemented in the prototyping room, with one exception that now the actual machine workshop is situated towards the perimeter of the building and the office with glass walls is located more in the interior, towards the entrance to the workshop. The machine floor is full of heavy, high risk equipment (we have 5-axies CNC mill, CNC lathe, manual mill and lathe, drills, etc.), and the particular disposition of the office is implemented in order to avoid traffic of students across the machine floor when they need to come and talk to the technicians in their office. Note, that in the prototyping room the compartments (there are two, apart of the main floor: one for 3D printing and one for braising) are separated from the main machine floor by transparent partitions. The functions for such separations are slightly different in the two cases, though. For the braising room the partition is there to prevent the fumes from entering the main workshop area (they are extracted by powerful extraction system). In the case of the 3D printing lab the partition protects the delicate printers from contamination coming from the outside.

8b

[E] Experiencing Transparency

While most of the standard labs are isolated and enclosed with their own heavy doors, the open labs are connected to offices, corridors and atria in a dynamic, airy and flexible way. There are two big open plan labs at the NGI. The connection between them and the outside world is facilitated by the extensive use of glass (Fig. 49). Here is an open lab with shared equipment that sits on a square plot in the middle of the building surrounded by light coming through the offices. This is one possible way to maximise the space and increase the efficiency of the lab. Ernie recalls that the scientists liked the concept of open plan labs from the start, but they were against open plan offices. They "didn't mind sharing offices, that's not a problem. But having big, open plan office appeared problematic."[122] Talking to scientists at Southampton University (one of the first science buildings designed by Jestico+Whiles architects) during a visit, the NGI team listened to their concerns; most of the researchers found the open plan office environment very distracting, even hard to work in. This lesson was implemented then at the stage of planning the new graphene facility in Manchester. Now, only the PhD students have open plan offices (Fig. 50).

The offices of the senior scientists are immediately adjacent to the open labs, connected by transparent walls that allow some light to come from outside, pass through the offices and infiltrate the labs. There are several academics who oversee that area where 50–60 students can book equipment. Andrey is one of the academics supervising the process, and that is why you can see him around very often in the open lab on the 1st floor: all his students and postdocs are based here.

Let us follow Andrey for a moment as he begins his working day at the NGI. It is 8.30 am. His day starts by checking all the overnight

[122] Interview with Ernie Hill, 14.06.2019.

Fig. 50: PhD students working in an open plan office space next to the open lab on the 2nd floor, photo by Ben Blackwell.

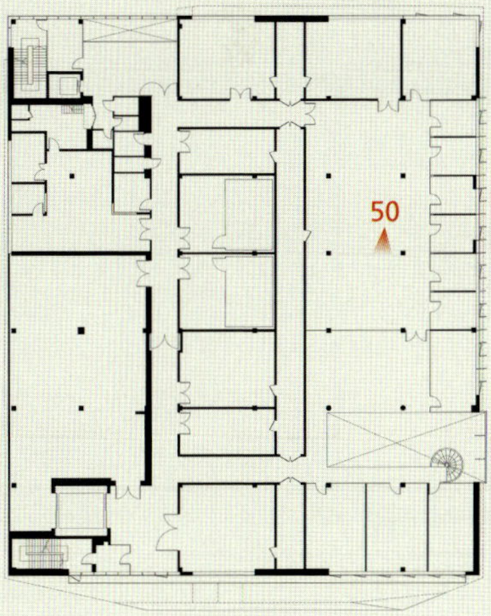

experiments: if the system is working and the equipment is running. He has programmed these measurements in the evening using computer-controlled equipment and has left them running. As Andrey notes, "even when you're not here, the building works. It never sleeps. Definitely in Physics, some of our experiment measurements will take days, that's why you need to make sure that you're continuously running the equipment, and some of the equipment never stops, it runs for weeks, months."[123] That is why Andrey's day begins by checking the pulse of graphene research, testing parameters, making sure that everything is all right. Here he is coming back in the morning, stopping

[123] Interview with Andrey Kretinin, 29.06.2017.

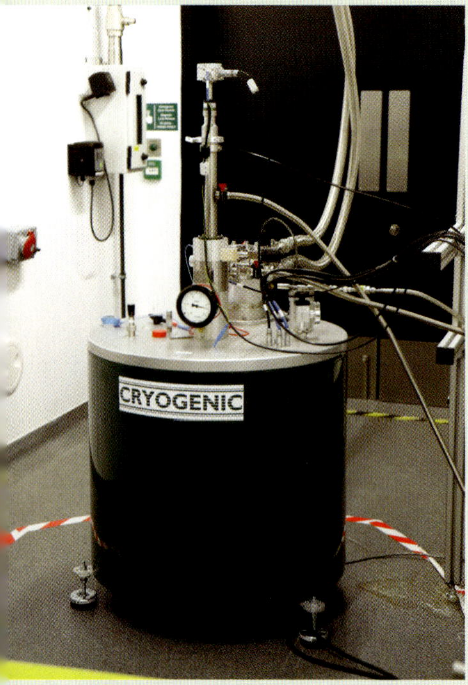

Fig. 51: The superconducting magnet, photo by Simon Mitchell.

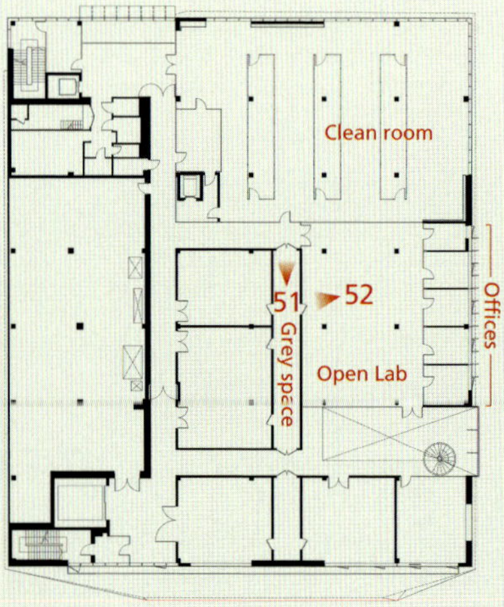

by the superconducting magnet that they bought in 2016 (Fig. 51). He explains,

> "It's the same idea like the magnets in the hospitals for MRI, but it's a smaller size and it gives you much higher magnetic field. We needed for our research to push the extreme boundaries of environment conditions, to see how materials behave; and this set-up requires for example, running water to cool down the compressor, and normally, it's actually inconvenient to have such a device in the Physics building. So, you have to find the cooling water, you'll have to pay a lot for that, but here [at the NGI] the design is such that there's already a special line with cooling water designed specifically for this type of equipment, which makes life much easier. We have all the gases around, like nitrogen or helium or compressed air and we don't need to handle cylinders, because most of the gases which we need are ready; plugged into the wall, which we need to connect."[124]

Here again, like in the standard labs, the infrastructure is in-built, available, in the state of readiness. The magnet is located in the grey corridor, which separates the open lab from the set of individual labs. Andrey is working in that space, around the superconductive magnet, and a distinctive sound comes from inside the magnet. Yet, the system can be entirely controlled from outside, from the open lab (Fig. 52). As the magnet is connected with the computer, some parameters

[124] Interview with Andrey Kretinin, 29.06.2017.

Fig. 52: The scientist Andrey Kretinin working on the computer connected to the superconducting magnet, photo by Simon Mitchell.

appear on the screen. Andrey goes straight to the computer and reads the parameters. He explains, "the sample is measured with this computer and the power supply [controlled by computer] so we're actually detecting the signal coming from the sample and the magnet, the software with the data from the power supply helps the identification of the sample."[125] Everyone can see Andrey reading these results, then going to his office, next to the open lab to check emails.

About half an hour later, his students come in and they start discussing the plans for the day. He elaborates: "because we're all together in one building it's easier to speak to the students immediately when you see them, to check what they're doing, to discuss things."[126] In the open lab, scientists from Andrey's team do electrical and thermal measurements. The characterisation continues: electrical characterisation in Andrey's case means measuring very low currents and very high resistances; thermal characterisation is done by measuring with the laser flash to determine the thermal conductivity

[125] Interview with Andrey Kretinin, 16.10.2019.

[126] Interview with Andrey Kretinin, 29.06.2017.

of materials (how efficiently they conduct heat) and other heat-related characteristics. Here is Abhishek again using the optical microscopes in the same space. We also see the Ultra-High Vacuum (UHV) systems where the flakes are being transferred and assembled in van der Waals heterostructures in high vacuum. This is "a sophisticated piece of kit to stop implantation or reaction to the air and minimize contamination."[127] Andrey sums up: "here we combine equipment to experiment which is not hazardous; that is probably more than half of what we do here."[128] That is why it is an open and porous environment that does not require containment like the chemistry or the furnace labs. The scientists can enter directly from the offices to the open lab, then to the upper clean room to fabricate a sample. The glass wall connecting the clean room and open lab, allows contemplating huge pieces of equipment and gowned scientists busy with sample preparations. While sitting in the office or working in the open lab, Andrey and his students can see other peers being active in the clean room. Glass allows the sound separation of working zones and the visual connection between different working dynamics. On the other end, the open lab has also a glass connection to the atrium where the social spaces are located. And it is all on one floor: the large lab opens to the rest of the spaces: offices, upper clean room, corridors and social spaces, and it is just a few seconds walk. This easy visual connection facilitates the flow of people and things. As Stuart says, "it's a transient space; people walk through it all the time."[129] This can be witnessed especially on a Friday afternoon; after the seminar, quite a few researchers wander by the door. The contrast between an enclosed specialised lab with heavy doors swiftly closing to make sure the chemicals remain inside (and are properly extracted), and the porous membrane-like open lab is striking.

In addition to facilitating transition, the glass connection is also important for accelerating communication. Andrey shares his experience of this: "through the glass walls of my office I can actually see what my students are doing in the lab and I feel being involved

[127] Interview with John Whittaker, 16.10.2019.

[128] Interview with Andrey Kretinin, 29.06.2017.

[129] Interview with Stuart Lockwood, 3.06.2019.

in the everyday life of my students."[130] Glass prompts interaction and "speeds up the creativity process." It allows senior scientists to monitor their students and provide help in case it is needed, to take part in running experiments and sharing ideas. At the same time, even with closed doors, they remain visually connected through the glass walls, and they feel part of the lab, rather than being "locked" into their office, working behind massive doors. Visibility is also important for health and safety reasons. Transparency enhances knowledge of how to use equipment and dedicated spaces, and how to cope with the technical aspect of the building environment. The glass connection makes it easier for scientists to assist each other in adjusting equipment and solving technical problems. Thus, the porous infrastructure of open labs and offices affords "instant communication" and the exchange of both scientific insights and technical tips, contributing to an even more accelerated pace of research. This exposure increases "social" pressure, but overall it optimizes performance. It also makes the working conditions more informal; it is easier to ask for help and engage in discussion. No need to knock on a door. Expanding the overall "dwelling space" of scientists in the continuum of an open lab-office (branching to corridors, clean room and social spaces) creates a healthier, safer and more spontaneous working environment in a compact building where all facilities are brought together.

Open labs also help to encourage the mixture of people. Rahul's office is next to the open lab on the 2nd floor. The open labs and the glass used, according to him, creates a positive impact on the results, "the end of year results so to speak." He expounds, "If there was a way to measure it, I'm sure if you had the same people in a building like this and the same people in a building which is more enclosed, maybe, the opposite of what we have here, I'm convinced that you would be able to, scientifically almost, prove that you get better results in a building like this."[131] The building acts as an experimental machine, breeding collaborations and productivity.

[130] Interview with Andrey Kretinin, 29.06.2017.

[131] Interview with Rahul Raveendran Nair, 04.07.2017.

Both the large open plan labs and the offices are meant to be adaptable and moveable. The offices are designed in a way "that there is the same level of floor-to-floor height even in the office wings, so that change could happen."[132] They are all provisioned with services. Along the corridors and the service walls, a number of blank spigots hide, and they can connect additional equipment if needed. "It is all about that future adaptability, flexibility."[133] Thus all of the office spaces could be converted into labs in a few years' time, if needed; and one type of lab could be retrofitted into another.

The scientists' offices on the 1st and the 2nd floor have two walls of windows, one overlooking the outside, and one overlooking the open lab. Light travels from the outside, through the outer windows, passing through the offices, and the large glass interior windows, it glides into the open labs, and also reaches the clean room on the 1st floor. Other large windows can bring light from the atria around the open labs. Just like the gases and the water that circulate through the entire building, running hurriedly in the pipes, light is another major force circulating through the building. While the office spaces of scientists are part of a spatial engine that facilitates research communication, an engine fuelled by light and sight, the administrators' offices on the 3rd floor benefit from a different spatial disposition: on the outside, they connect to the roof garden (Fig. 15), while the inside windows are linked to the corridor, often crowded due to the proximity of the conference room and the busiest social space on the top floor. They have a glass back door that opens onto the garden, and as Beverley says, "the weather does not have to be nice, because up here we get the sun and it is quite warm and nice."[134] In addition, these offices are all naturally ventilated with window openings controlled by the occupants. As Tony says, "this gives them a kind of environment they can enjoy, but also an environment they can control themselves."[135] The small top windows in Olga's office are designed so well, that, as she puts it, "if it rains it [the rain] does

[132] Interview with Tony Ling, 23.06.2017.

[133] Interview with Stuart Lockwood, 3.06.2019.

[134] Interview with Beverley Brown, 11.10.2019.

[135] Interview with Tony Ling, 23.06.2017.

not come into the room"[136] and this allows her to let the fresh air in her office and hear the rain. The lit, nice and airy environment of the offices is energizing, especially in the winter when it is dark. The glass porosity establishes the constant dialogue with weather, sun and rain, darkness and brightness, thus reconnecting natural ecologies with the social ecology within the building.

However, porosity can also have a disadvantage: the glass windows and doors allow researchers and NGI admin staff to be seen at all time while working in their offices. Sarah explains that "it's hard to tell people 'I need some space. Don't come in!' when they can see that you're in there."[137] For many academics if you're in the NGI, you are considered "accessible." Glass cannot be modified. It is always see-through. It means availability. Behind the glass you are visible, you can be seen constantly, exposed. Transparency thus dictates the social conventions of accessibility and communication. The different pulses of graphene work can be witnessed at all times.

Summing up his experience, Rahul says that "in this building, I just work, and I don't worry about anything."[138] The compact space where "everything is sometimes on the same floor" with easy transitions everywhere and in close vicinity, reduces the stress. Andrey adds that "sometimes, we are under enormous stress from teaching or research, and we spend a lot of time here, and you don't want your environment to make your stress worse."[139] Thus the spatial arrangements of the open labs, the proximity and the visual connections facilitate easy access and speed up the process of work, while at the same time, reducing the pressure and contributing to a balanced and comfortable working environment.

---

[136] Interview with Olga Falko, 31.05.2019.

[137] Interview with Sarah Haigh, 10.07. 2017.

[138] Interview with Rahul Raveendran Nair, 04.07.2017.

[139] Interview with Andrey Kretinin, 29.06.2017.

8c

[M] Grey Space

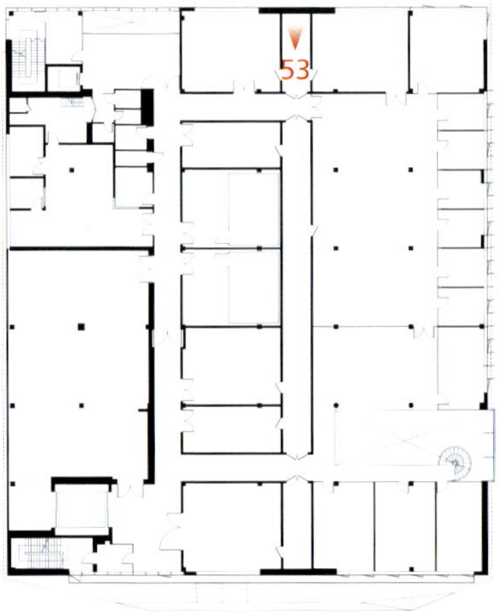

Modern scientific equipment rapidly increases in complexity, vibration and noise requirements. It simultaneously increases the required footprint of the equipment, eating away the valuable space in the labs. One solution to more efficient use of space is the separation of the equipment that requires constant access from the one that can run autonomously. The latter includes pumps, compressors, filters, etc. Such equipment can be placed in spaces with low requirements to

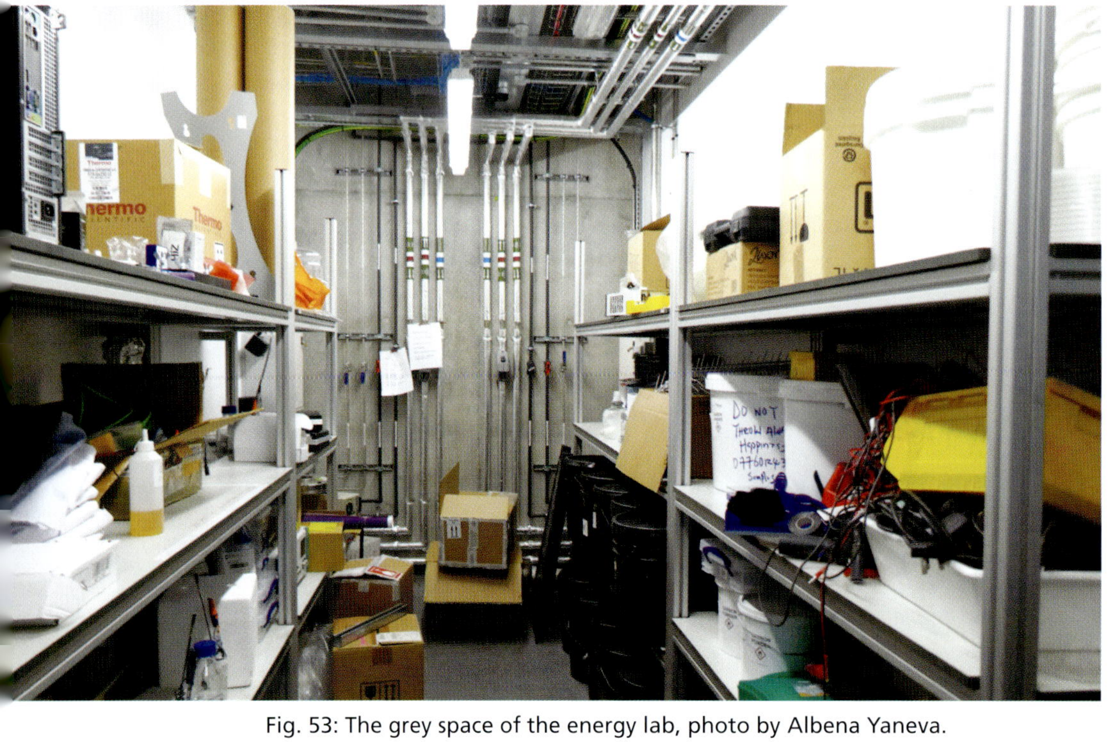

Fig. 53: The grey space of the energy lab, photo by Albena Yaneva.

lighting, air-conditioning, vibrations, etc., saving dramatically on the overall cost of the building. Furthermore, spatial separation of such equipment (which is often a source of vibrations and noise by itself) from the experimental rigs ensures low noise and low vibrations conditions in the research labs.

To this end the NGI has acquired so called **grey spaces**, adjacent to each of the research labs where the auxiliary equipment is placed (Figs. 51, 53). Often the grey spaces are shared between two labs. The concept proved itself extremely viable, with most of the auxiliary pumps, compressors, sonicators, centrifuges and other equipment being situated there, saving space in the main labs and protecting those from noise and vibrations.

Simultaneously the grey spaces serve as distribution corridors for services. Extracts, gases, process cooling water, electric power and other services are terminated in the grey spaces. From here it is easy to supply them to the labs when necessary — again providing dramatic financial saving and flexibility. Also, running services in the grey spaces means that we don't lose the height in the labs.

8c

[E] Experiencing Storage Provisions

The flexible lab rhythm requires more and more auxiliary equipment installed. To respond to this need expressed by scientists in the design process, special grey spaces were created. They are two-metre-wide corridors, which are adjacent to most of the labs, or placed behind them. Within these spaces, we can find all of the air supply, electrical conduits, gas pipes, chilled water, and the isolators. Through the grey spaces the connection to gas lines and the power work is swiftly done. If scientists need to change the nature of their lab or add apparatuses, it is very easy to connect them to these grey spaces. The physical proximity allows installation work to be done quickly.

The idea of having grey spaces between the labs is something that a lot of scientists have not experienced before. Mark finds it really useful. The comparison with the old science buildings imposes itself again. If in the Physics or Chemistry buildings on campus, a research team needs a hydrogen/argon mixture, a cylinder with such a mixture is provided and gets installed in their lab to supply the needed infrastructure. Yet, as soon as a cylinder is introduced in the lab, "it does become quite messy quite quickly, wires everywhere, etc.,"[140] describes the setting Christopher. At the NGI, in contrast, the cylinders almost disappear from the lab landscape thanks to the grey spaces. Instead of messy cylinders in the labs, neat and well-organised terminals for the main house gases (nitrogen, hydrogen, argon) are available, all ready to go and "feed" the labs. If we look at any lab, it has ports coming out of the wall, no local exhaust reach cylinders.

In addition to the fact that they allow quick and flexible retrofitting of the lab, the grey spaces are important in terms of safety. As Mark explains, "we can store chemicals and gases in a space which is not

[140] Interview with Christopher Hyde, 15.12.2017.

occupied by people."[141] Separating substances from people is important for health and safety reasons as researchers in the lab do not have to share the same room as gas canisters and storage cabinets. This allows them also to "keep all the noisy, dirty equipment away from the lab itself" explains Stuart, and "thus, compressors, vacuum pumps, etc., they are kept outside. They can poke them into the labs when needed."[142] Storing chemicals and noisy equipment out of the lab, but in close proximity, helps preserve the lab as a clean, neat and pleasant working environment. Scientists find this as an ideal solution to be able "to keep all the dirty and back of house type of stuff away from the labs." The grey room is also "a space for storing something which you don't use regularly, and you don't need to access every day."[143] For instance in the grey room of the chemistry lab, we find a piece of equipment that can be used in a fume cupboard. It is used once a month for two days. Instead of leaving it in a fume cupboard, the scientists put it in here, and the fume cupboard is available for the current work undergoing in the lab. As the grey spaces are fully locked, they can be also used to store large samples. Thus, separating the equipment and the chemicals in use from those that are not required at the moment and have to be safely stored is another functional separation that works in favour of the neat lab.

The separations are important also for the technicians. James explains that they try to place all of the service equipment in the grey rooms because "if we leave sometimes a chiller out with them [the scientists], and it has a controller, the manufacturer might not want us to adjust that. But that chiller, if it's left out in the lab, some of the researchers may feel like they have the authority to adjust that, whereas it's safer for us to leave it out of their sight, and then it doesn't get adjusted."[144] The grey space, as we see it here, performs another important function in regulating the relationships between the manufacturer of lab equipment, technicians, scientists and the

[141] Interview with Mark Bissett, 30.06.2017.
[142] Interview with Stuart Lockwood, 3.06.2019.
[143] Interview with Rahul Raveendran Nair, 04.07.2017.
[144] Interview with James Fitzsimons, 28.11.2017.

equipment itself; it distributes the control over the manipulation of lab apparatuses differently. In the lab, scientists feel in their territory, entitled to control the equipment; in the grey room, the power of control shifts to the technicians (and the manufacturers' instructions that they comply with). The two spaces, although adjacent, connected, and interdependent, reshuffle the responsibilities of technical and scientific staff. The grey space, thus, has this double function. On the one hand, it keeps the noise, the dirt, the messiness and the chemicals far from the lab, to be able to protect the scientists and their experiments. On the other hand, it keeps the scientists away from special equipment so as to preserve the technology (and the integrity of technicians and manufacturers).

Yet, the grey rooms are "a blessing and a curse as people see them as places to keep stuff."[145] Polly complains that the grey spaces are full of cardboard boxes and that the scientists think, "Oh, I may have to send this piece of equipment back, and they keep the box." Yet, keeping all the boxes, not only eats up space, but creates a fire hazard. We visit the grey room shared by the furnace lab and the chemistry lab on the top floor and we see all these boxes. In the grey room of the energy lab on the 2nd floor, we see another pile of boxes (Fig. 53). It is clear why Polly is concerned. Although the grey space is really useful, it does encourage scientists to hold onto things. They like to keep things: "they will fill all available space, and whatever the space."[146] Resisting change, they are used to their ways of doing things, their routines.

Let us visit the grey space of the energy lab with Lewis, who we met above. Lewis does not use the grey space often but a colleague of his, Richard, uses it on a regular basis as he is in charge of managing the lab, organizing the purchase of equipment and the storage of samples. This grey space is shared with the lab next door. "This is our side and that's their side" explains Lewis, "we mainly use it for storage of equipment that we don't use anymore, whereas the other group, they use it for storage of samples because they are more of a chemistry lab doing research on the chemical modification of 2D materials and

[145] Interview with Polly Greensmith, 16.10.2019.

[146] Interview with Polly Greensmith, 16.10.2019.

their applications in energy storage. They make lots of samples, which they store in and measure."[147] Occasionally Richard can put some samples in there as well, but the energy lab team never makes nearly as many as the neighbouring chemistry lab. Sharing the grey space, although used differently, makes scientists curious about the on-going work of the next-door lab, and can result in collaborations. Watch Lewis: he makes his sample, he prepares the foil, he coats the sample and dries it, he assembles, and he tests. It is like a circle. The other researchers' samples are waiting to be coated; yet, they rarely leave the samples and usually use them within two days. "Things are never left aside for weeks," clarifies Lewis, because of the way their experiments are run. If a sample is made and left for two weeks, it would not be good anymore. That is why everything is done quickly. If they start an experiment on Monday, they have the final device by Wednesday or Thursday and then they test it on Friday or over the weekend. This explains why the energy team usually does not store samples in the grey room. Yet, allowing samples from one lab to co-exist with equipment from another, the grey space can incubate further disciplines' fusions between chemistry and energy.

Fig. 54: The grey space of the furnace lab, photo by Simon Mitchell.

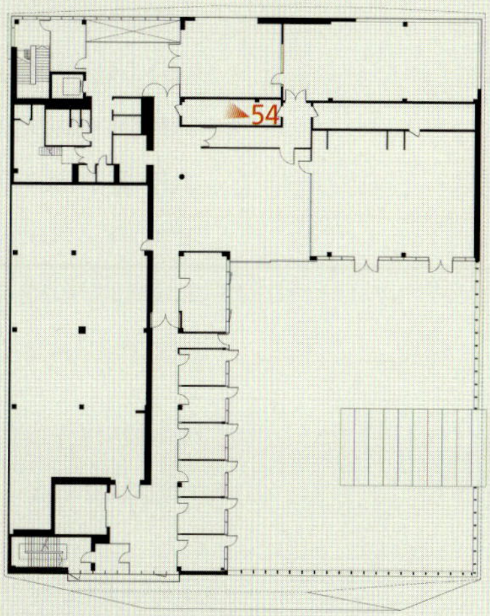

If Lewis rarely uses the grey room, the technician Christopher is often there to provide for his lab. Christopher deals with everything that happens in the labs (as we have seen moments ago), but also with the grey spaces.

[147] Interview with Lewis Le Fevre, 14.12.2017.

He helps to ensure that all of the gases, the air, water, and electrical supplies needed can be "injected" straight into the labs (Fig. 54). Christopher keeps some cylinders connected in the grey space, fitted into a cabinet and securely locked. If scientists ask for some specialized gases to be supplied for a special equipment, Christopher goes and connects the cylinders in the grey rooms through 200 mm ports at the bottom of the walls; through these ports (openings for the passage of communication) he can feed the pipe work. To avoid drilling through the walls, he tries to work out the routes through such ports coming from the grey spaces to the labs, and then connects them. Whenever a new piece of equipment needs to be installed, it takes two to four hours of Christopher's time to take the gas, water or electricity connections needed from the terminals through the wall.

If scientists want to modify one of the fume hoods, Christopher goes into the grey space and he isolates their valves. His work on the fume hood is to ensure that "they [the scientists] are going to be safe because they [the valves] have been isolated."[148] Yet, this only affects that particular hood without disturbing any other piece of equipment in the building and researchers all along the NGI can still carry on with their work. Christopher explains,

> "On the back of the fume hoods you've got eight to ten gases into each one coming down. Halfway down there's a white valve to turn that supply off. And that will only turn off into that fume hood. So, I know that I've turned them off. I put a cap on to lock them off. I have the key to that so no one else can come in and turn them back on. And I know that that gas line is safe secure. I can cut that pipe and I'm not going to get any gas coming out so I'm safe. Because when you're talking about using gases like oxygen, hydrogen, you don't want them mixing in an atmosphere, you'll just explode."[149]

It is important for Christopher to ensure he is safe and that the scientists in the next door lab who want to use the gases are safe using

---

[148] Interview with Christopher Hyde, 15.12.2017.

[149] Interview with Christopher Hyde, 15.12.2017.

them, and their work does not get affected. Here again the separation between people and gases, equipment and the modalities of its control, risk and the techniques for its mitigation, is the key for the smooth functioning of the lab work. The isolation valves ensure that the installation can be continued without impacting the research, and the same goes for the water, the vacuum, and other supplies. While doing the work Christopher isolates every floor and treats every lab independently without disturbing the others, keeping minimal downtime. In this way the lab can be serviced quickly without the technician having to go in there; working remotely from the grey room where the supplies and the valves are, Christopher is able to make significant changes in the lab. "The labs are really quite contained," confirms Stuart, "in the sense that you don't have to have maintenance going in there and switching this and doing that. A lot of it can be done from the grey space without actually disturbing anybody working in there."[150] Thus, by hosting all technical work of maintenance and supply, the grey spaces contribute to minimize interruptions in the hectic pace of graphene research.

The novel design aspect of grey rooms, especially developed for the NGI, is something that Tony and his architectural team took to other scientific buildings. For instance, it has been used in the design of the Cavendish Laboratory at the University of Cambridge (expected to be completed in 2022), one of the world's foremost Physics labs. Commenting on this transfer of design innovations, Tony says, "we've learned a lot from graphene in terms of the flexibility, how to create this, and it's the same requirement that the Cavendish has."[151] This and other inventions are also transferred to other scientific buildings on the campus of Manchester University, like the GEIC and the Royce buildings, where similar grey spaces have been developed.

[150] Interview with Stuart Lockwood, 3.06.2019.

[151] Interview with Tony Ling, 23.06.2017.

Linde
L 12
To Hire Me
Call 0845 609 3333

9

[M] Transportation Routes

The nature of the scientific work prohibits one to predict the experiments one would be doing in a year's time. Instead, a prediction could be made that very likely new experiments will be conducted in the research institute on a regular basis. This creates a necessity of equipment rotation — old one moved out and the new one moved in. Also, quite often equipment vendors and manufacturers are willing to lend their equipment to the Institute for a period from a few weeks to a couple of years, with a view of attracting the large community of researchers in the new capabilities. This creates additional traffic. Easy access to the loading bay and then to the spacious **goods lift** ensures easy access to the building. This should be matched by the equally easy transportations routes through the building itself.

The idea of easy transportation routes is in conflict with the extensive network of services across the building, which eat up width and height from the **corridors** and labs. To this end, both the transportations routes and the services need to be designed synergistically.

In the NGI we naturally chose the starting point of the transportation routes from the goods lift, and the starting distribution point of the service routes to be the opposite — the north part of the CUB. The services cross the corridor between the CUB and the main building in the northern side of the building, and then distributed through the grey space between the dark labs and the open space laboratory. This way the services do not eat up the height of the corridor, meaning that any equipment which fits into the goods lift can then be transported along the corridor. Also, the labs immediately opposite the goods lifts have been designed with doors of extra height and width to accept particularly bulky equipment, which can be wheeled in directly from the goods lift. Continuous motion of goods and equipment means that walls are subjected to extra damage, wear, scratching. To this end rubber stripes are incorporated at the low level of the wall to act as dampers. Also, the walls are made of relatively cheap plastic ("White Rock") which can be easily replaced if scratched or damaged. The plastic can be also written upon by "liquid chalk."

9 [E] Experiencing Circulation

The equipment required for graphene research is usually very bulky and yet must be incredibly stable. Ernie explains that "when you're doing work down to scale, you want things to be incredibly stable; you don't want any vibrating and moving about."[152] However, large and heavy equipment has consequences for the building. Drawing on experience in the other science buildings on campus, which have rooms with small doors and small lifts that make it impossible to move large equipment through, it was established that the NGI building needed more spacious hallways, wider doors and lifts in order to move the large apparatuses around. Thus, fairly early in the design process, it was decided that the corridors should be big enough to be able to relocate the equipment, and that the lift should be large enough to allow for quick transportation.

As the architect explains, the corridors are extra wide "because of the necessity of moving equipment and tools around."[153] Meant to house the large apparatuses and allow a certain number of palette tracks to fit inside, the wide corridors act as thoroughfares for the equipment to be wheeled straight into the labs or to be moved quickly to another lab (Fig. 55). But, a lot of the heavy equipment must also be able to be moved to the basement (to the clean room or for storage). The electron beam machine used for lithography, for instance. The sizeable goods lift is used for that (Fig. 56). However, the large, expensive, and fragile equipment cannot travel without support. It is often placed into other containers for safe travel, which, inevitably, increase the size and the weight. Thus, the electron beam machine, when it is outside the clean room, is placed into an outer container that can be removed, and an inner container, that is clean, and can only be removed inside of the clean

[152] Interview with Ernie Hill, 14.06.2019.

[153] Interview with Tony Ling, 23.06.2017.

Fig. 55: A large corridor, photo by Albena Yaneva.

room — again to avoid disrupting its cleanliness. The corridors need to allow enough space for this entire structure of a "box within a box" to travel throughout the building, both through the corridors and up and down. Stuart sums up the ambition as the need to have space so that "we [they] can wheel equipment in and wheel equipment out."[154] Ernie, in 2015, had the challenging task of getting all the equipment in place and working for the opening of the building. Equipping the building without the huge lift and the wide corridors, he reiterates, would have been a much more difficult task.

Fig. 56: The large goods lift, photo by Ben Blackwell.

Quick circulation also facilitates scientific activities. Tony explains that "you don't want dead-end corridors to be voided; you want people to be in the mix."[155] Thus: how do you get people "in the mix"? You keep the corridors wide to speed up traffic, to keep things moving. They allow researchers to move freely in the spaces. Tools and samples move much more freely and less tentatively without the constant hazard of collision. Stuart recalls the numerous studies conducted on the width of the corridors to make sure that even the largest piece of kit could get around corners. To ensure that the corridor's width would not be too prohibitive for people to manoeuvre their kit around, the NGI design team carefully mapped the traffic of the internal spaces, looking into the issue with finer details, wondering whether certain walls could be removable, putting the door frames and then the doors on, designing the fire doors in certain parts of the corridors as recessed into the walls to make more space. It is important to allow for the

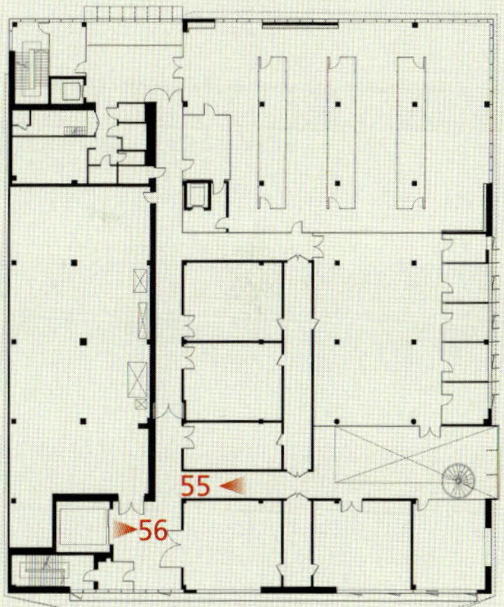

[154] Interview with Stuart Lockwood, 3.06.2019.

[155] Interview with Tony Ling, 23.06.2017.

swift circulation of equipment, samples and people. No one needs to fight for space or squeeze in close with colleagues or apparatuses (as they did in the old clean rooms or as they still do in the Physics and the Material Sciences buildings on campus).

The size of the goods lift is so distinctive that some researchers, affectionately, call it the "world's biggest lift." It is, indeed, the largest lift at the University of Manchester. In dimensions, it is 3 to 3.5 metres, or 10.5 m^2 and can accommodate 55 people with 4000 kg capacity. They like to show off this during VIP events and to transport groups during tours of the building. When the Chinese president came to visit the NGI, the goods lift was carpeted especially for the occasion. As Stuart notes, "the other lifts are quite slim; you can only get three or four people in. But this one you can get quite a big group of people in. So, we had to move them very quickly through the building, in and out. But it wasn't fit for purposes like this, in the sense of moving dignitaries around."[156] In fact, the NGI people liked the carpet so much that they decided to keep it; they can now enjoy a daily "dignitary" experience when taking the goods lift. The other lift in the building at the front entrance, is standard, slim, allowing two or three people only to take it. During conferences and other events, the goods lift can take an entire group of researchers from one floor to another, facilitating the movements from one seminar room to another. While seated with Chris on the ground floor, we watch visitors coming from the lift to the back entrance where we met him. He explains that "these are usually people who have been on a tour of the building with John, Andre, Kostya or Vladimir, and depending on the size of the crowd they will use the large lift."[157] To go down, they descend with the goods lift straight down to the ground level, and the crowd dissipates near the back entrance. Everyone's routines here, in one way or another, involve this lift.

The lift is designed with the foresight that heavy and bulky equipment will need to be moved from the storage space to the labs to be installed. Discussing the lift, Chris excitedly remarks, "you've seen the size of the lift? It can fit a car! That gives you a general idea of the

[156] Interview with Stuart Lockwood, 3.06.2019.

[157] Interview with Chris Livingston, 16.10.2019.

kind of stuff that we can get into the lift."[158] According to Mark, "the goods lift in the back is absolutely enormous" and enthusiastically, he continues, "it was done because in the future there would be lots of heavy equipment that might need to be moved from labs or installed. That kind of forethought is quite important; we don't know how over time the needs of labs are going to change, and putting that infrastructure from the start really helps because some of the equipment we have can weigh tens of tons and can be the size of a car."[159] When a piece of equipment is not needed anymore, due to the quick pace of research, it needs to be relocated, as Mark elaborates, "if I need to move it [the equipment], I can just wheel it out or wheel it into another lab."[160] Thus, the building design enables the car-size equipment to be relocated with ease, responding promptly to the pace of research and technology developments, while being flexible enough for the future of graphene research.

The width of the lift matches the width of the corridors and the width of the doors in at least some of the labs; it is like a continuous large tunnel through which equipment moves from the "stores" downstairs, and up to the different floors, and between each of the labs on the different floors. That is another distinctive feature of the NGI. More traditional buildings on campus do not allow much of the equipment to go through the small doors, lifts, or corridors; as a result, the equipment must be disassembled, transported, and reassembled. Or even, in some cases, walls must be torn down to fit equipment into a lab. All this slows down the work process. In contrast, at the NGI, a huge piece of heavy equipment can travel easily through doors and along corridors, and can be literally wheeled straight into the lab, plugged in and used straight away.

Yet, people and things travel at different speeds in the circulation spaces. When the scientists require a specialised gas, which is not supplied from the gas storage room, or liquid nitrogen, as we have seen earlier, Chris fills the tanks, prepares the cylinders and is in charge of

[158] Interview with Chris Livingston, 01.12.2017.

[159] Interview with Mark Bissett, 30.06.2017.

[160] Interview with Mark Bissett, 30.06.2017.

transporting the cylinders to the labs. But Chris cannot accompany them in the lifts; the gases travel on their own there as they can be harmful, especially when transported within the goods lift. If liquid nitrogen, for instance, leaks, it could suffocate the people traveling with it as it can cause asphyxiation in a tight environment. "If you get trapped in the confined space, it [the gas] can kill you or can suck the oxygen out. It's pretty dangerous," explains Chris, "it is a general rule in the University – you cannot travel with the cylinders, especially if they are full."[161] That is the reason why gases and liquids travel up and down on their own.

Watch Chris for a moment: he uses the lift every day to go up to the kitchen and the toilets upstairs. However, when he transports the gas cylinders, as he cannot go in the lift with them, he takes the stairs. It is tricky to send the cylinders on their solo journey though. Before he can use the stairs, he sets up the lift. A safe key helps him control the lift so no one can get into it while the cylinders are traveling up and down. Watch Chris for another moment: he puts the cylinders on a trolley in the loading bay, connected to the massive lift, and then he loads the cylinders into the lift. Once the cylinders are in the goods lift, he presses the button and programs the lift with the safe key. The cylinders' journey begins. While Chris rushes up the stairs to meet and welcome the cylinders on either the 2nd or 3rd floor, other people may arrive in the lobby near the back entrance and try to use the goods lift. But there is a sign there to indicate that the lift is not available presently; flashing, it signals to them that the lift is being used to transport gas cylinders and liquids. It indicates that a number of nonhumans — gases, liquids, trolleys and a lift — tour the building on their own. Waiting for the flashing signals to stop, the crowd on the ground floor can hear the steps of Chris running up the stairs; in the event that he needs to reach the 3rd floor, they hear him springing up to get to that floor on time to be able to inspect the cylinders. Provided everything is in order, Chris takes the cylinders out of the lift and places them into their respective labs. Then, he can use the lift again to go downstairs, and when the signal changes, other people can use it too.

[161] Interview with Chris Livingston, 16.10.2019.

Human users will crowd into the goods lift too. While they cannot share the lift with gas cylinders, they can share it with bulky equipment. The technician Christopher values the possibility to travel with equipment and the way the building design facilitates the "flow of things." The lift in the Material Sciences building, for instance, allows only seven or eight people to fit into the goods lift, and does not leave sufficient room to transport equipment through the floors. In the NGI, in contrast, the lift size allows large equipment plus anyone who needs to travel with it to share the space, and to be transported swiftly from floor to floor. Polly uses the goods lift on a daily basis to "take equipment up and down from stores," and as she explains, "it's a way of getting to level –2, the big storage room. We put a lot of our crates down there in storage if we're having a piece of kit installed."[162] When scientists need to transport chemicals, they always use the goods lift. Coming out of the chemistry lab, for instance, they need to be very cautious when moving any chemicals in between floors and labs, even buildings; they use a trolley or a box to hold the chemicals. Without taking these precautions, they risk dropping the chemicals or bumping into someone. Dropping the chemicals, especially in the social space, could be extremely hazardous. On other occasions, the lift is used to transport bulky objects to the top floor. Olga recalls that the graphene car (a car from a local manufacturer BAC Mono, which uses graphene parts) was transported by the large lift from the loading bay downstairs, right up to the 3rd floor and then pushed through the corridors so it can reach the large exhibition space on the top floor (Fig. 57). The spacious corridors and goods lift reinforce the notion of speed: the speed of the movements of people and equipment, the speed of research, the speed of maintenance, the speed of experiments, the speed of funding, investment, and interest. The scientists' logic is grounded in this notion of speed. A graphene research project could last months, or may be a couple of years, but never decades. At the edge of innovation, everything speeds up. Therefore, the building must follow along. If the researcher's logic prioritises quick research, "the building has to be dynamic and agile enough to keep up to that

[162] Interview with Polly Greensmith, 16.10.2019.

Fig. 57: HRH Prince William "trying out" the graphene car at the industrial fair, photo by the University of Manchester.

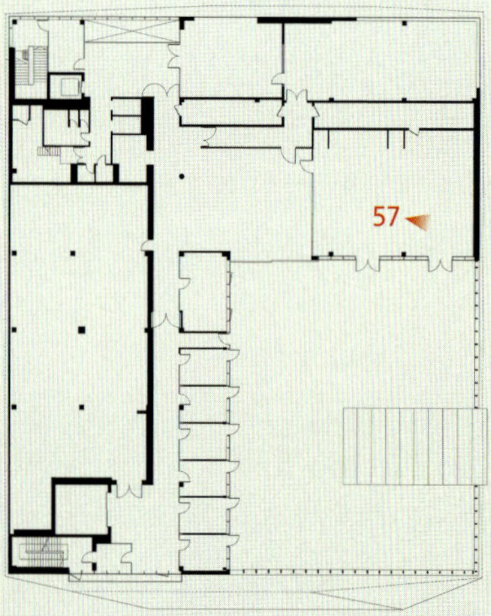

changing research over a period of time."[163] The speed of research, moreover, echoes the speed of engaging with external partners: "the industry doesn't want to wait 15 years, the industry wants to come in and do something very quickly."[164] This requires a very rapid process and a suitable design that facilitates that speed.

[163] Interview with Stuart Lockwood, 3.06.2019.

[164] Interview with Stuart Lockwood, 3.06.2019.

10

[M] Other Functions: Meetings, Conferences, Events

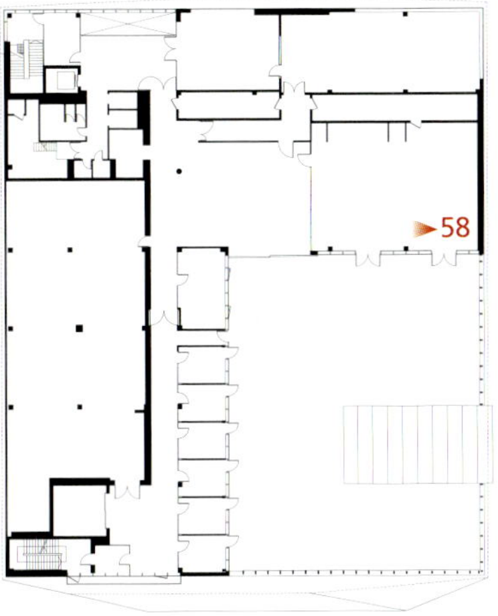

Generally, robust architecture of most buildings sets the functions very rigidly. Instead, the architectural style of the NGI was set to be dynamic, supporting future changes. Similarly, flexibility dominates the current layout of the building — most spaces are designed to be multifunctional and easily convertible to fulfil additional tasks. For instance, the open space lab (discussed in chapter 8b) can be easily configured to accept equipment of any geometry, and proximity to the grey space allows easy access to services distributed from there.

Another good example of flexible, multitasking space is the conference room on the top floor

Fig. 58: The conference room on the 3rd floor, photo by Albena Yaneva.

(Fig. 58). By design, there are a number of meeting spaces in the building: there is one conference room on the 3rd floor, one board room on the 2nd floor and a number of sitting areas across the building. However, with a large number of different research groups in the NGI, with strong presence of industry and intensive commercialisation activity the demand for meeting rooms is even bigger. To this end the main conference room has a transformative design, which can be switched between: (i) two meeting rooms; (ii) one seminar room or (iii) completely open space, which includes the coffee area, and can host around 160 people. All these configurations are easily transferrable from one to another and the staff in the NGI is trained to change between the standard layouts within minutes. The audio/video system, which includes three projectors, follows the room layout, so two parallel meetings can be run easily in this space. There are special spaces along the walls where the unused furniture can be hidden. In case of a particularly large conference being held in the space, the lift lobby is converted into a reception area, making the conference site even more flexible. The atrium area on the 1st and the 2nd floors in the south part of the building can be used as poster areas, for stand-up dining, or even for breakout sessions, as some of them are equipped with large screens.

Another unexpected use of the NGI is as an exhibition space. The ground floor of the building is occupied by the services for the clean room. It is mainly ducting for air supply, extract and circulation. Basically, nothing to see. So, the walls of the ground floor are turned into an exhibition space, thanks to large windows which provide the view to the action-full basement level. Professional painting hanging system is preinstalled (designed by the Whitworth art gallery) and the walls are equipped with the power and internet sockets, in case video screens need to be installed. The location is ideal as the NGI is situated just opposite the Aquatic Centre car park — the arrival point for most people visiting the University, the Aquatic centre and generally the south part of Manchester city centre.

10

[E] Experiencing Communication

The social area on the 3rd floor is experienced as a very adaptable space (Fig. 59). Movable walls are used to close off the room for a conference, or split it up into small seminar areas, or small meeting areas. It can be opened up for a big exhibition, or even a ballroom. All these different arrangements condition different uses of that space and make possible various activities and events.[165] Pointing to the floor, which appears to be made from wood, Stuart reminds us that this is the softest area in the building. He explains that "everything else is really quite hard, in terms of the black plastic walls and the resin floors, and then you go to this wooden bit, and it's actually slightly softer; it's a different colour palette. I think people like that and enjoy being here."[166] This soft space welcomes users. Like the clean room, it is a different "heart" of the building, its social heart.

Let us first turn to the conference configuration. Olga is one of the two administrators working at the NGI. Among the many duties she has (important tasks including supporting research grants management), she oversees the events and the conference room bookings. The configuration of the conference and meeting room is a delicate and intricate affair. The conference room can accommodate 160 people at maximum capacity, but it can also be divided into other configurations with smaller rooms through moveable walls. Olga explains with incredible detail that "if you use the A and B rooms together, it's for 100 people to sit there comfortably, but 135 will fit in

[165] Anyone who works in the NGI building can request that space provided it is available, and it is approved by the head of operations or the director of the NGI. Occasionally, the space is also booked by "external" people.

[166] Interview with Stuart Lockwood, 3.06.2019.

Fig. 59: Foreground: the social space in front of the conference room on the 3rd floor; background: connection to the conference room with a simple door and to the terrace with a glass door, photo by Ben Blackwell

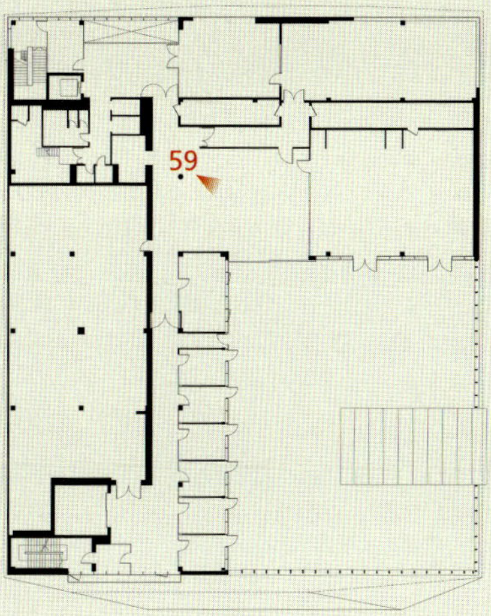

as well. And we have 135 chairs, but when we have bigger conferences what we do is to remove all the walls and bring in chairs from the social area, which will allow us to sit up to 160 people."[167] Usually during the week the room is kept as two meeting rooms. And, on Thursdays, it is set-up as a single space for the big Friday seminar, and the walls get installed again (for the two-room configuration) on Monday.

Planning the room configuration can cause issues. If the room is booked for a small group meeting but immediately following a bigger event, the Friday seminar for instance, the group just uses the larger room. This is to reduce the work for the house services; the standard room layout is kept unless otherwise requested. The house attendant Daniela knows she is needed on the 3rd floor and quickly. She explains that "they tell me, 'please, we need two rooms or one room [...], come and do it,' and I have to do it. I need to do it fast and that is why I need to be available on the 3rd floor all the time. Sometimes they get an email one hour before and the room has to be ready for an important meeting. Now I can do it fast, and when we need to accommodate 100 people my boss brings someone from the other buildings to help me."[168] The walls and partitions can be changed quickly, usually in 15 to 20 minutes. Yet, Olga explains, "it takes time to bring tables and chairs and put them into the room in the order requested."[169] In addition to the standard layout — what they call "the seminar space" — a lecture theatre layout is also possible;

[167] Interview with Olga Falko, 31.05.2019.

[168] Interview with Daniela Sevelova, 4.12.2019.

[169] Interview with Olga Falko, 31.05.2019.

it is usually used for big conferences. The configuration is not just about walls though: the lights are grouped and regrouped according to sections; there are also different modulations of the lamp settings (dim at the front, bright at the back, etc.). Thus, both the moveable walls and the modulated lights create different environments for small and big scale research events.

The researchers find the seminar system run by the NGI a good opportunity to gather once a week to talk about different topics. The graphene seminar is also attended by the technical staff who contributes to some of the papers and helps resolve ongoing issues. Visiting academics and people from the GEIC attend as well. The graphene seminar always runs on Friday, beginning at 2pm and lasts, typically, between 50 minutes and an hour. Usually, one of the postdoctoral researchers takes a turn in organising it and has the responsibility of setting up a programme. Two speakers will then provide short updates of their ongoing work. Occasionally, there are also external lecturers that are invited to give a talk on a particular subject. There are both UK and international speakers vising the NGI for the famous Friday graphene seminars.

While there is no strict seating plan, or formal rules, there are different coloured chairs that orchestrate, and perhaps, provide an indication of some informal social expectations during these seminars. There are red and grey chairs. The red chairs are arranged close to the front table, and it is where the senior academic and administration staff usually tends to sit. The grey chairs are arranged behind them on the rows and they tend to be occupied by students, postdocs and junior scholars (Fig. 58). However, there is no strict order — the seating plan is completely free and ad hoc. There are always a few extra chairs around the walls. Olga explains that "people come with their bags, their coats, and also we have a coat stand outside. Sometimes guests don't feel comfortable leaving their stuff, so they prefer putting their stuff on the chairs."[170] Just like the colour coding of the bay areas in the clean room that prevents cross contamination and the gown colour coding that designates different roles in the lab activities, the colour coded sitting

[170] Interview with Olga Falko, 31.05.2019.

arrangement suggests a differentiated participation in the discussions of the graphene community. Those who pick red chairs in close proximity to the presenter, immediately place themselves in a central position; being closer to the heart of discussions prompts more participation.

It is 31 May 2019. Today, a keynote speaker from Hong Kong is presenting at the graphene seminar. There are around 70–80 people in the room. As guest speakers can come from all over the world no one is surprised with the announcement of today's lecture: a theoretical physicist presents, followed by a couple of questions, one by Mark, and one by Andre Geim, lead scientist at the NGI, who together with Kostya Novoselov was awarded the Nobel Prize for the isolation of graphene in 2010. The speaker comes from a well-known theory group; the collaboration with the Hong Kong research group might be useful for the NGI projects. The theme revolves around the moiré patterns, which is equally of interest to the NGI theoretical physics group; walking around the building, traces of discussions on this topic remain visible on the writable walls. Commenting on the seminar John explains that "five years ago, the discussions were predominantly around 2D materials or graphene, now most of the discussions and seminar focus on the application scale: where it is being used and the interaction of those materials: composites, PV panels, the effect on energy, and how it is being used in various applications outside condensed matter."[171] Occasionally theory talks, like today's, also happen. Commonly the discussions revolve around new materials: how graphene is combined with the other 2D materials in the van der Waals heterostructures that may not have been trialled. There is a good mix of applications or theoretical aspects, and novel ideas discussed.

Sometimes, the conference room is used in an unconventional way, like for business days. Commenting on this use of the room, Olga points out that "we had companies who brought their graphene products, and this place was used as an exhibition hall. We removed all furniture we had, left only a couple of presentation tables, and people had their product displayed on stands."[172] This was the first

[171] Interview with John Whittaker, 31.05.2019.

[172] Interview with Olga Falko, 31.05.2019.

industrial fair with graphene products, and it took place in June 2016. In this setting, the conference room became a flexible space for the presentation of business ideas, and of prototypes. A lot of interesting "graphene related" products were displayed. There was a car (Fig. 57), the bonnet of which is "made by graphene-enhanced materials, so when it smashes, the bonnet doesn't crack."[173] Other graphene products include the graphene guitar. There was also a bike with a graphene-enhanced frame, which, as a result, is much lighter (under 6.5 kg) while remaining as strong as normal bikes. Or, there was a graphene heater, or graphene-enhanced tires for cars, bikes and motorcycles. "My next-door neighbour," Olga proudly declares, "bought graphene tires for his bike, and he says he could ride over the nails or pieces of glass and they don't break. And they're only something like a pound more expensive than the regular ones."[174] Some of the products exhibited at the fair are already on the market. On the occasion of this industrial exhibit, the top floor of the NGI was turned into a display area and all scientists were invited to come out from their labs. The room that witnessed so many discussions around the applications of graphene, also accommodated the first graphene products.

In addition to being used for large scale science and industry events, the conference room is also occasionally arranged for VIP events. As the NGI is a high security building and access to the building can be controlled, very often the university international office and president's office use the building to host such events and there are numerous gatherings every year. For each of these uses the conference room can take the shape that will better suit their format; architecture follows the form of the gatherings.

---

[173] Interview with Olga Falko, 31.05.2019.

[174] Interview with Olga Falko, 31.05.2019.

11

[M] How We Ended Up with the Roof Garden

The roof garden was a bit of a fluke; however, now it plays a significant role in the operation of the building (Fig. 60). During the design stage the main building and the CUB were developed in parallel, and their relative footprint was held in such a way that both buildings would occupy the same number of floors. The optimum was four floors in the CUB. Financially, however, it wasn't possible to complete the whole 3rd floor of the main building, so we ended up with the half-floor being built up and half floor being just an empty roof. The idea came to design a roof garden, which would also help to earn the valuable BREEAM points, which are absolutely vital to secure the funding from European Regional Development Fund. Gaining ecologically-friendly status was crucially important.

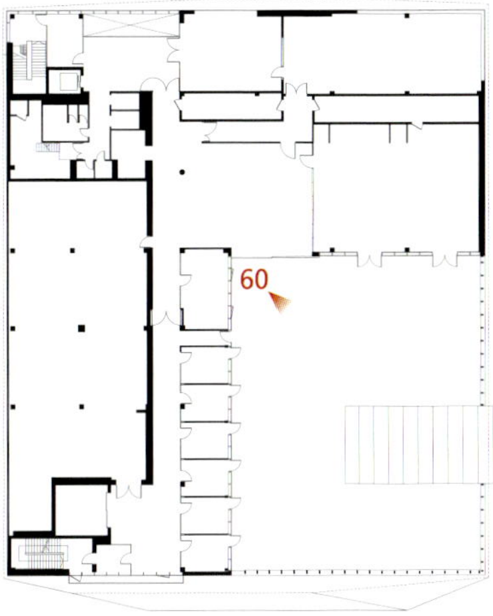

Fig. 60: The terrace and the roof garden on the 3rd floor, photo by the University of Manchester.

11 [E] Experiencing Breakout

While there is no downtime for the accelerated speed of graphene research and while the building never sleeps (and some equipment and the gases provision are never interrupted), scientists who work on graphene do need to slow down. As John jokes, the NGI is not "a complete slaughterhouse for research."[175] He elaborates that "people might just want to have a talk with their friends, not talk about work, uhm, within reason, you know. We allow them to bring visitors into the building, academic visitors; some members bring their families in just to show them the areas where they work. Researchers do need that downtime, that quality time."[176] A number of spaces allow scientists to slow down, to detach themselves from the hectic rhythm of research and experimentation: the top roof terrace and atrium areas. The social spaces provide a welcoming and inclusive environment. "In this building," Rahul says, "the social area is maybe more distinctive compared to the old buildings,"[177] and the attractive social aspects of the NGI makes him spend a lot of time talking to colleagues. Even Sarah, who is often critical in her judgement, thinks that "the building functions really well" and she appreciates the NGI building for the "spaces where you could go and be quiet and relax." She loves spending time here: "sometimes in the evenings I go to the NGI because it's quieter; on the way back from the Material Science building I also walk past the NGI to go home, so I stop and do a couple of hours just to be in there." [178] The attachment that scientists have developed to the building is undeniable. Let us witness them now in the process of experiencing these spaces.

[175] Interview with John Whittaker, 22.06.2017.

[176] Interview with John Whittaker, 22.06.2017.

[177] Interview with Rahul Raveendran Nair, 04.07.2017.

[178] Interview with Sarah Haigh, 10.07.2017.

Roof garden

The most distinctive and generous social space is on the top floor: a large area that opens to the roof garden with the help of a huge moveable glass door (Fig. 59). The top terrace and the garden were designed as a result of the BREEAM rating (there are also solar panels on the roof) and the need to build in an environmentally friendly way. There are 37 different species in the garden (Fig. 61). "The first year it wasn't that colourful," some of the scientists remember, but now it is beautiful, blossoming. Rather than a neat and ordered garden, it was designed to be a wild garden, but "not," they also joke, "because we are not trimming it." This garden also provides connections to other buildings that were not foreseeable: bees travel from the adjacent St. Peter's building, where, on the roof, they have beehives. The green spaces on the roof reinforce the green credentials of the building and allow people who like that type of environment to enjoy the sunshine and the fresh air in their breaks. This is one possible way to open the building to nature.

The garden is probably the most quiet and tranquil space at the NGI, although each space is busy in its own way. The visual connection between the garden and the social coffee space on the 3rd floor is maintained by the glass door. The generous use of glass opens up the social space and brings abundant light and the colours from the garden in. The door is a bit delicate and must be used with caution; a written sign on the door warns us of its delicacy. Everybody, including senior scientists, postdocs and PhD students find the terrace a nice space to relax and socialize. Mark really likes the big garden area. To relax, he and his colleague Rahul, often go upstairs to the roof terrace to sit down for a coffee, and to talk to people. He jokes that "occasionally when there is good weather in Manchester [laughs] we are able to sit outside and have meetings, or when we have visitors, it's really nice out there."[179] Sarah also finds this space wonderful on a sunny day; she likes "to go and hide on the roof terrace and work."[180] Often, you can find her reading some printed work on the terrace. Likewise, Olga, if she has a five minute break, prefers to take it on the terrace, where

[179] Interview with Mark Bissett, 30.06.2017.

[180] Interview with Sarah Haigh, 10.07.2017.

Fig. 61: Scientists having lunch in the roof garden on the terrace, photo by Simon Mitchell.

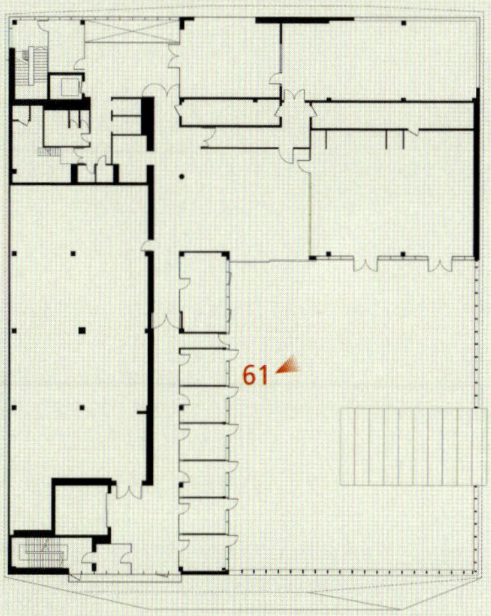

she can relax, drink coffee, and make personal calls that will not disturb her colleague that she shares an office with. The offices on the 3rd floor have doors to the garden as well (as seen in chapter 8b) which allow the administration staff to walk outside straight from their offices and get fresh air. That is why it is so easy for Olga to get out. She says, "If I stay in my office, I would be in front of my computer working. If I really need a small break, I need to go out of the office."[181] To do this, she just opens the office door and she is out, far from the flow of emails, and surrounded by wild plants

[181] Interview with Olga Falko, 31.05.2019.

and bees. On a sunny day, there is a joyful crowd of young researchers (PhD students and postdocs) enjoying themselves, chatting, discussing their experiments. In the summer and the spring, the roof garden looks fantastic, flowers all in bloom.

Social space

The large social space on the top floor that opens up to the garden is the main social area both because of the proximity to the terrace, but also to the conference room (Fig. 59). Every Friday these spaces accommodate a colourful crowd of graphene researchers from all disciplines and at all levels, from postdocs and PhDs to senior graphene scholars and some people from industry; they gather for the seminars (as seen in chapter 10 [E]) and then spread out over the social space and the garden for small talks, meetings and coffee.

On a weekday, however, it is quieter — only occasional small scale administrative or scientific meetings are held in the conference room split into two seminar rooms. But this is only until lunch when it fills up with life again. Lewis, the postdoc we met in the energy lab, likes to spend more time here in the coffee area "because this is much nicer." Most days you can see him having lunch with the people from his lab. But he also comes up here in the morning, after he has set an experiment running, to have a coffee and a chat before the experiment is finished. He spends about 20 minutes finishing his coffee and then goes back to the lab. Commenting on his coffee breaks, Lewis expands, "Yeah, we'll just chat about politics and so on, meaning of life, and all this."[182] We have already seen him spending most of his time in the lab, sometimes eight hours. Yet, during the day he spends at least an hour here for lunch and coffee breaks. It is equally important for him. Everyone who started their PhD at the same time as Lewis are members of a big WhatsApp group, which originally included just the people in Lewis's year (about 17), and then, as more students and postdocs subsequently joined the NGI, they have been added to the group (there are about 40 people now). Sitting in different labs at the different parts of the NGI,

[182] Interview with Lewis Le Fevre, 14.12.2017.

running different experiments, blue gowned or not, they message each other, and they arrange to meet for lunch upstairs. A quickly typed message "I'm going for lunch now, is anyone free?" travels swiftly to all the labs, pings simultaneously in distant corners of the building, on desks and benches, abruptly interrupting the smooth silence of the experiments and the gentle chatter of gases and microscopes. In a few moments, Lewis is up on the top floor, and other colleagues join him. Not all of the 40 can join, but we can usually see between three and 20 people gathering for lunch. Sometimes there are so many people that they cannot find enough chairs to sit together. To have lunch on the terrace is a student and postdoc-led ritual; there is no set time, no established schedule, but rather a spontaneous gathering that forms, as swarms of young researchers from all parts of the building, hungry from the sometimes tedious experimental work, leave their labs, flakes, and experiments to congregate here. The time of the gathering varies depending on how busy they are, on the scheduled meetings in the morning, or on the nature of experiments they are running that day. As the WhatsApp group include many different researchers that Lewis knows, it is always a random selection that is free to join him. Here he is in the space. At the start only two other researchers join him, and as the clock hand approaches one o'clock, more young researchers eventually join to share jokes around a crowded table while finishing their lunch. They pull the tables together, remind themselves that the house attendants want them separated again once they leave. There is always a hodgepodge here though: the space becomes crowded, people eat standing up, chairs are swapped, tables move around, join and come apart.

These lunch and coffee breaks mean a lot to Lewis: "I'd say just having somewhere to sit is enough. Most of the people we have lunch with are all interested in various things."[183] He recently found a lot about politics of Catalonia as they have a few Spanish colleagues from Barcelona and other places, and they have spent a lot of lunch breaks quizzing them on political matters. These discussions and the people involved, help researchers switch off. He says that "As long as you can

[183] Interview with Lewis Le Fevre, 14.12.2017.

talk to someone about something that's not work, it is relaxing."[184] Happy that he can engage in different discussions, Lewis finds it refreshing to have spaces where they can spend time chatting about other things and learning from the cultural exchange with others. "Talking about something else" greatly contributes to the quality of the downtime. This dedicated space helps researchers have a proper detachment, while still remaining in the enclosed working environment of the building. There is a striking comparison to be drawn with the traditional buildings on campus. In the Chemistry building, there is a common room, but "it is dark, and it smells funny," complains Lewis, "and it is busy, and cramped. It is also not big enough for the building."[185] When he works there, he ends up having his lunch at his desk in his office, staring at a computer screen, eating a sandwich, unable to talk to other people. In this setting, it is hard to detach oneself from the work environment.

The large social space on the 3rd floor also has a kitchenette and a coffee machine. Daniela is in charge of the coffee machines on the 3rd and the 2nd floor. They have "lots of coffee addicts here at the NGI," she jokes. She restocks the machine with water, milk, and coffee beans. The 3rd floor machine consumes one large pack of coffee beans on a daily basis. She cleans it, provides cups and keeps everything in order so that all the "coffee addicts" can get their coffee on time. It is such a daily routine for her that, as she says, "I can do it with closed eyes. Every day, 3rd floor, clean the pipes, clean the brewing side and fill it up with coffee beans, and milk and chocolate."[186] It is important to do it regularly because if she cannot clean it one day, due to other more urgent tasks, the next day the coffee machine breaks down as the pipes get clogged — no smell of coffee on the 3rd floor for a day. Just as important, she also maintains the social areas around the coffee machines. There is no microwave in the kitchen. They want to avoid having smell of food coming out of the kitchen and spreading through the offices and the social area on the 3rd floor, especially on the days of

[184] Interview with Lewis Le Fevre, 14.12.2017.

[185] Interview with Lewis Le Fevre, 14.12.2017.

[186] Interview with Daniela Sevelova, 4.12.2019.

the seminars or official visits and events. If researchers bring in their own food to be heated, they are required to visit the closest building (the IT building with the old clean rooms) to heat their food up. It takes time, and if they do not have access to the building, they also need to sign in, go through the ritual — it is a long process. In other words, they will have to make a big detour before joining the others for lunch.

During the lunch break, there is also Abhishek, whom we have met in the Raman lab and in the clean room. He likes relaxing for a while on the big couch on the 3rd floor. He contemplates "the nice view outside." He says: "It all helps me to mentally relax, free and recharge."[187] Then he sits with his colleagues to eat his lunch. He stops by twice a day and stays in the sitting areas for half an hour or more, depending, as he says, "on how interestingly we are talking with my colleagues."[188] He often feels very exhausted after working in the clean room; this can be physically tiresome, as we have seen, because one has to spend hours covered from head to toe in gowns, gloves and facemasks that restrict bodily movements and impede breathing. So, after spending two or three hours in the clean room environment, Abhishek explains, due to the physicality of it, it is important that "we breathe more, drink fresh water. This is required while working in the clean room."[189] The researchers working downstairs next to him in blue gown anonymity will join him subsequently, dressed in their own clothes, moving and breathing freely. Sitting next to Abhishek, they chat and relax, drink water from the dispensers, and go outside onto the terrace to breathe garden-fresh air. Recharged, after an hour, they are ready to go back and embrace the constraints of the clean room environment again.

Abhishek's breaks are often dictated by the nature of the lab work. For example, if a break fills in the waiting time for an experiment or waiting for processes in the clean room to be completed, rather than interrupting the course of work, it can speed up the process as a whole. Sometimes, they are just tired, and they can stop the process and go out. "We can have that interruption or that break any time during

[187] Interview with Abhishek Mishra, 21.11.2017.

[188] Interview with Abhishek Mishra, 21.11.2017.

[189] Interview with Abhishek Mishra, 21.11.2017.

the process, so there is no strict rule,"[190] affirms Abhishek. However, he has to make sure that he does not leave his things unattended in the clean room; he cleans up his working space before he leaves. Any researcher entering the clean room after he has left for his break can occupy the cleaned working space. After resting on the terrace or in the sitting area inside, refreshed and relaxed, Abhishek goes back to the clean room and re-enters. If he has started some critical process, his break is limited by the waiting time, for example it could be 30 minutes. He cannot be late — or, he would worry: "what will happen to the sample after the completion of the process?" Leaving the sample there might be critical as it can degrade. Thus, no matter how interesting the chat with colleagues on the terrace is, no matter how fresh the Manchester outdoor air is, no matter how many joyful colleagues the WhatsApp message has gathered for lunch, Abhishek rushes to the clean room, allowing enough time to put his gown and mask, to collect his sample. Being in the same building, having everyone grouped together in the same place, all working on graphene, encourages a lot more communication between the different researchers both in their labs and in the social spaces.

[190] Interview with Abhishek Mishra, 21.11.2017.

12

[M] Atria, Coffee and Writable Walls

Another way to make people talk and engage in multidisciplinary research is through the design of the atria and the open spaces.

Scientists are encouraged to participate spontaneously in discussions and improvised meetings. Many walls in the labs and corridors are made from a special plastic ("White Rock") and are writable (with liquid chalk). This is supposed to promote spontaneous discussions and offers a possibility to arrange mini seminars in the sitting areas. Apart of the main conference room on the top floor and the board room on the 2nd floor, there are several sitting areas, two of which have access to the writable walls.

At the same time, there are only two coffee machines in the whole building, which is meant to increase the traffic of people in the building (always good to make a couple of minutes break). This promotes the possibility of collisions, making people talk.

12

[E] Experiencing the Social Life of Science

In addition to the terrace and the large social area on the 3rd floor, there are a number of atria and social spaces in the building. Initially the architect wanted a lot of open spaces right up through the building. Ernie remembers: "we did not mind having open spaces for breakout, but not all the way through the building. Why do you need to sit at the bottom and look all the way to the top of the building? Architects always want the natural light coming in from there."[191] After numerous discussions, they decided to only keep this concept in the breakout areas. The glass separations bring in light and the spaces are nice and airy (Fig. 62). This is an aspect of the building appreciated by many researchers. As Andrey points out, "it's very convenient to work here psychologically because you have large open spaces, a lot of light, atriums, and common spaces. It feels much better compared to old buildings from the 1960s, which are basically a combination of shoeboxes. For me, to work here is much more convenient, not only practically, with regard to all necessary infrastructure which we have here for the experiments, but also psychologically."[192] Affording physical and psychological comfort, the NGI building also contributes to reducing the enormous amount of stress from teaching or research. The atria and the social spaces contribute to the comfort with a number of interesting features: openness, comfortable furniture, coffee machines, screens, and writable walls.

Social spaces in the atria

Just as the colleagues of Lewis gather around a device in the lab and

[191] Interview with Ernie Hill, 14.06.2019.

[192] Interview with Andrey Kretinin, 29.06.2017.

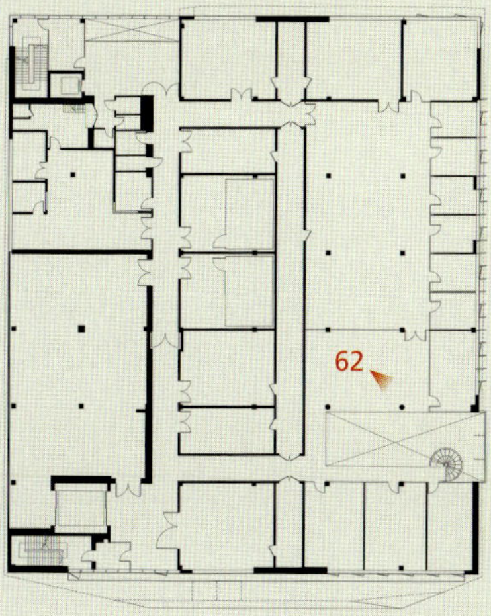

Fig. 62: Atrium, a view to the 1st floor social space and the spiral staircase, photo by Ben Blackwell.

Abhishek's group gather around a sample in the clean room, in their breaks, researchers gather around the coffee machine. There are two coffee machines in the building: one on the 3rd floor in the large space where Lewis and Abhishek were having lunch, and which Daniela is in charge of maintaining, and one on the 2nd floor. The coffee used to be free, but now they need to buy tokens for users in the NGI (those who have their name on the staff list), which cost 50p; this is still cheaper than coffee on campus, which can cost around £2–3 at Starbucks, for instance. One more incentive to keep the scientists inside the NGI longer. Placed in the social spaces, the coffee machines provide a focal point for people to meet, relax, and have a chat. Researchers tend to use the coffee machines and the social spaces close to their labs. Lewis can be seen on the 2nd floor where the energy lab is (and the 3rd floor large space where we saw him moments ago). If the 3rd floor room is occasionally booked for events and cannot be used for lunch meetings, then Lewis and his friends gathered by WhatsApp will move their lunch downstairs. They sit on the couch and chat, drink and relax. Like Lewis, Abhishek can be also spotted using the coffee machine and the sitting area near the Raman lab on the 2nd floor. "There is an advantage," Ernie says, "to get away from the bench or the desk and to get to go into a nice space and relax a bit. That does make things easier as well."[193] The places away from the desk or the lab bench are open sitting areas where discussions between chemists, physicists, material scientists, and biotechnology people can occur at any moment; researchers gather around things: sofas, coffee machines, video walls, writable walls.

Let us have a closer look at these spaces:

In the 1st floor atrium there are some nice spaces with a spiral staircase (Fig. 62), and large windows on the upper level. The 2nd floor just outside the boardroom has another social space with furniture, a writable wall and a coffee machine (Fig. 63). These settings, devices and furniture slow the graphene scholars down, they stop to discuss

[193] Interview with Ernie Hill, 14.06.2019.

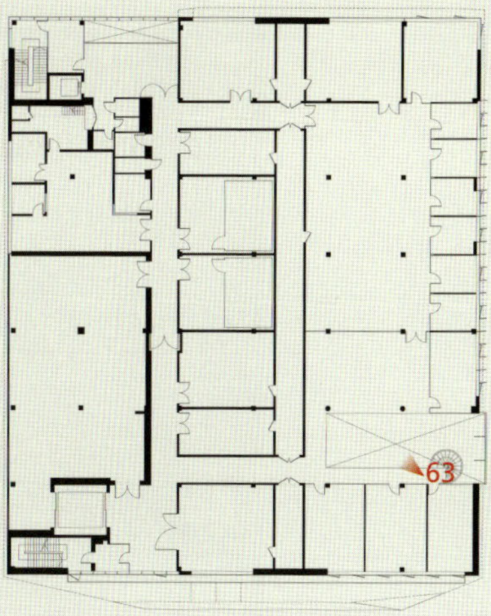

Fig. 63: Atrium, a view to the 2nd floor social space with writeable walls, furniture and coffee machine, photo by Ben Blackwell.

Fig. 64: A closer view to the writeable walls in the social space on the 2nd floor, photo by Simon Mitchell.

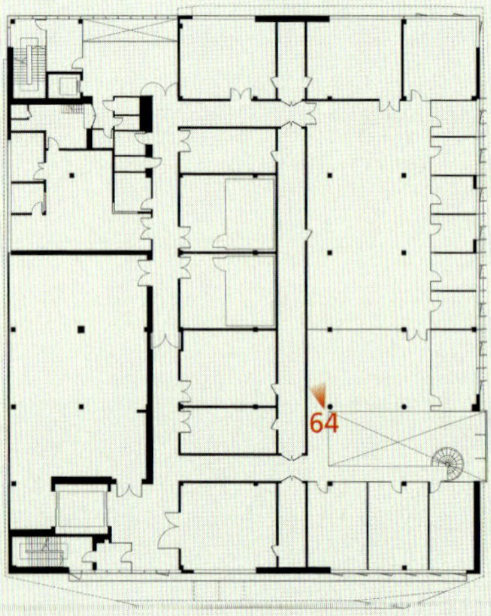

with different groups that do different kinds of research. These are not innocent design features. Instead, they enable thought paths and recipes to mix, groups to mix with other groups. When scientists want to have a group meeting, they do not want to be sat in an office environment, or a lab, or in a formal meeting or seminar environment, they rather prefer a kind of "café" environment. Stuart recalls that in the planning process graphene scientists expressed their wish for a place "where they could relax. Somewhere they could go and have a chill and have those informal discussions."[194] The furniture (comfortable armchairs and designed sofas) contribute to the relaxed atmosphere and maximize the efficiency of the social spaces. Sarah finds the chairs "really cool," and the sofas allow one to have "a bit of a sleep in the middle of the

[194] Interview with Stuart Lockwood, 3.06.2019.

weekend or stretch out." A meeting of the theory graphene group is in progress; their formulae are all over the wall (Fig. 64). Researchers from other areas and other disciplines, experimental scientists, who are less theoretically-inclined, come along with coffees in their hand, sit down and listen. A couple of hours later in the same space, a company holds a presentation, with industrial people working in the NGI; the meeting is open, and other interested people join as well. Then, another group meeting is taking place, which can also mix different subjects together as the groups work simultaneously on different topics — Vladimir's theoretical physics group, for instance, tackles four or five different topics at once. The materials group comes to discuss their tasks on a specific topic. The energy group follows. We can witness in all these situations how the open spaces melt the rigid boundaries, supposedly, erected between theory and practice or science and industry; they facilitate collaborative learning across different levels. Akin to the disciplines that increasingly lack stable boundaries, the social areas also lack fixed walls — except the writable ones. Researchers can eat, read, chat or do talks. In these open presentation areas, no prior booking is needed — there is no rigid registration routine, no dressing up and down into gowns, no rigorous process to pass through — any researcher can just plug in their laptop, use the big screen on the wall, and start small group discussions or use the black writable walls.

In every space the disciplinary boundaries have been removed and new, sometimes unpredictable, fusions become possible. While, for John, this does not "change researchers' personalities," he has "seen it changing the working attitude of different types of physicists, for example. They come in and they are a bit more open to see how a chemist's thought path would work. Because when you get two very different disciplines, it's about trying to get some kind of fusion together."[195] Multidisciplinarity is in action. It is not about the simple exchange of ideas; interaction is not the ultimate goal. Dialogues are not enough. They are just a starting point. Instead, it is about making possible the dissolution of rigid disciplinary preconceptions, the melting of confined professional identities, the amalgamation of research methods, the

[195] Interview with John Whittaker, 22.06.2017.

swapping of techniques and recipes, the exposure to different thought paths, and how all this eventually leads to unpredictable "fusions" emerging through exchange. Ernie affirms this: they all know that the best kind of collaborative work develops from coffee breaks. As he proclaims, "I think Andre and Kostya would agree with that because I seem to remember that it was over coffee that they were talking about the tape peeling technique that they used in surface science that got them to think how this can be used in graphene."[196] Collaborations often spring out of these informal chats. The open nature of the building affords "fusions" to happen "fairly effectively." It is particularly important for research-intensive environments to be conductive to people sharing knowledge. It also helps incoming researchers to get acquainted with the new people more quickly. Multidisciplinarity, in other words, is experienced and enhanced spatially.

The open-plan design contributes to the accessible and open nature of the social spaces. Rahul explains this through the metaphor of transparency: "the transparency afforded by the extensive use of glass forces communication among users and makes it easier to share knowledge."[197] Comparing with the other places where Rahul had worked before, there were not that many social spaces for people to get a coffee and have a chat with colleagues. As currently Rahul shares an office with Mark, he cannot use it for meetings and discussions. Sarah also finds it difficult to hold meetings in the office as she needs a quiet and silent space; she adds that "it doesn't have to be my own, but there has to be an understanding that you cannot talk."[198] Nevertheless, breakout spaces are not quiet. If they need to conduct a formal meeting, they use the boardroom. When Sarah needs to conduct a skype interview, she books the boardroom or the seminar space. Lewis agrees: having a dedicated boardroom for meetings is a great advantage for scientists working here. If Sarah and Rahul cannot use the boardroom, they have to hold their meetings in the social spaces. The boardroom is however different than the open social spaces in the

[196] Interview with Ernie Hill, 14.06.2019.

[197] Interview with Rahul Raveendran Nair, 04.07.2017.

[198] Interview with Sarah Haigh, 10.07.2017.

atria. Rahul finds it difficult to discuss with "the people that report to him" in his office and needs a special arrangement. He is convinced that "there might be aspects of work that are worth discussing while sitting in a sofa, in a more relaxed atmosphere"[199] as it might be helpful in trying to get the message across. Rahul points here to an important nuanced difference between meeting a junior colleague in an office, in the formal setting of a meeting room, or in the relaxed atmosphere of the design-furniture environment of the social space. Open and airy spaces with a comfortable sitting area are predisposed for informal discussions and make it possible to address difficult issues with ease. Thus, we witness that the various material arrangements have a different impact on the type of communication in these spaces.

At the same time the openness of the NGI building and all the social events organised in its premises can be distracting. As Mark puts it: "it has actually had more of an effect than one would expect, especially for 'pure researchers' who are in the lab 24/7 and can be affected by the fact that they are surrounded by social spaces."[200] Commenting on the working schedule, he says: "even when I was here as a pure researcher, sometimes I wished I had somewhere I could go and work by myself."[201] Mark used to work from home "because of the amount of activity in the building sometimes" and the fact that there is "always something exciting happening," some visitors, some interesting seminars going on upstairs or something on in the lab. Overall, it's very easy to "get distracted" by social events in the building because of the many collaborative spaces. With all these activities it was hard for Mark to sit down and write papers. He would have to do his "writing up" from home in the evenings or on the weekends; being in the building, for him, was for practical lab work. Now that his role has changed, and as the head of a group, he participates in the social events as much as he can. Rahul also considers the constant flow of visitors coming every day, and the many meetings taking place in the building as a distraction for his work. The clean room technician Fran also shares

[199] Interview with Rahul Raveendran Nair, 04.07.2017.

[200] Interview with Mark Bissett, 30.06.2017.

[201] Interview with Mark Bissett, 30.06.2017.

that he sometimes misses having a traditional office, where you can concentrate more on your work. Sarah shares an office on the 1st floor with two other academics who use the office as their full-time office space, which makes it very congested. On Friday afternoons, they all gather after the seminars, their students all come into the office to ask questions. "It's noisy," she says, "you can't get any work done, and you just cannot possibly concentrate."[202] Sarah continues: "I have a very good relationship with my office mates, they're great, and good collaborators, but just sharing a space with two academics is not productive. It's not their talking that I mind, it's the fact that we are constantly interacting with students during the day."[203] The busy Fridays look the same for everyone at the NGI: they are hectic, crowded and perhaps, too social.

But the more graphene scholars use these social spaces, the stronger their attachment to the building becomes. It takes time to develop attachments, to "dwell." Sarah and Rahul, now, are in the NGI building so often that they are there even outside of the nine to five office hours. They come to enjoy the quiet and nicely designed atria spaces; here everything is convenient, comfortable, close by and accessible. Sarah likes to use the breakout spaces by the small lifts; like Abhishek, she often sits at the bottom of the spiral staircase. The NGI is home for Sarah now. She shares how important the building has been for her:

> "I have to say that before the NGI was built, I didn't have somewhere to go, to get away from the office, to get away from the Material Sciences building, I mean somewhere to go and to meet people involved in graphene. It was not so easy. I used to go to the Condensed Matter Physics corridor or maybe go for coffee or lunch. If you want to meet somebody from graphene to say 'look, what is this result?', 'it doesn't make sense', I had to go to the corridor in the Condensed Matter Physics in the Schuster Building, wander up and down there until I found someone. Now we go to the graphene seminars.

[202] Interview with Sarah Haigh, 10.07.2017.

[203] Interview with Sarah Haigh, 10.07.2017.

The NGI provides a focal place to go and look for people, and it's more convenient."[204]

When the researchers were located at the Physics building, Sarah used to sit outside on the grass and wait for the right person to come out so she can talk to them. She considered this a better time to catch some colleagues and then walk with them into lunch rather than to disturb them in their offices. When they meet "spontaneously" outside, colleagues are more inclined to talk, walk, get a coffee together, and share insights, rather than being interrupted while they are in the middle of "reviewing their paper" or another important activity. That is why, now, she appreciates the NGI as a place where the gatherings are spontaneous, and the open social spaces facilitate meetings and discussions to occur at any time.

Writeable walls

The entire building is prepared to respond to spontaneous communication. As the corridors are designed to facilitate circulation — there are no dead ends — so that "people can be in the mix" all the time, they also encourage discussions and social interaction. All the walls along the corridors and the social spaces on the 1st and the 2nd floor are writable (Fig. 65). The scientists initially requested that the walls were to be writable to have spaces where they can explore ideas on the spot. The architects proposed a material called "white rock," which is, in fact, a relatively cheap black plastic (the PVC) and Tony found it aesthetically appealing to "have this mysterious black brick inside." Ernie recalls that they had a piece of that black material placed on the walls of the coffee area in the old building, prior to the construction of the NGI. It was there to test it, to make sure it was durable, and that it could be wiped clean without scratching the surface. In the end, they liked it, and they continue to use it in the old clean rooms as well. Then, a decision was taken to use it in the NGI.

[204] Interview with Sarah Haigh, 10.07.2017.

Fig. 65: PhD students using the writeable walls in the corridor for discussions, photo by the University of Manchester.

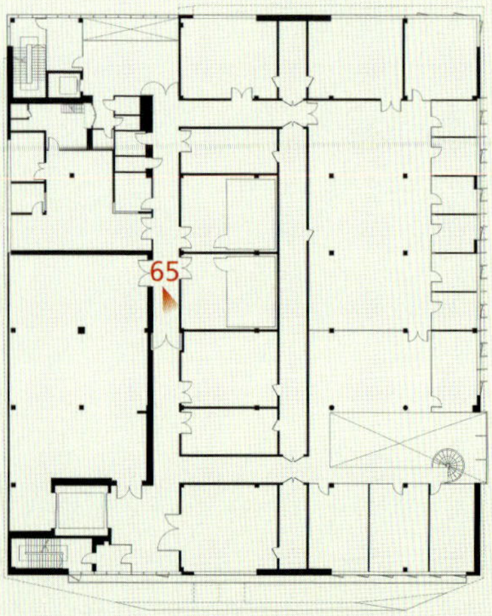

The discussions around the writable walls during the design and planning process were, according to Stuart, "the biggest pain." The "architect was very precious about them." Yet, Stuart, as a representative of Estates on campus, was concerned about the material aspect of the walls. This led to extensive research into the material. It is a soft material, and they worried that if people push up against it, they would leave scars or markings onto it. The anxiety revolved around its maintenance as they wanted the material to maintain its quality, not only until day ten, but up to year ten. In addition, the PVC panels would go right up to the ceiling, but Stuart, at the time, wondered why: "nobody would write on the upper part of the walls, nobody would write on the skirting board. Why are we paying all this money for these spaces to be covered if they will not be used?"[205] After lengthy discussions they suggested cutting the costs. Another cost saving scenario that was put forward was to paint the walls and install blackboards on them. When these different ideas for modifying the black walls were presented to the architect, he was devastated, Stuart recalls. However, after further discussions with the lead scientists, they decided to go ahead with the initial concept of the writable walls (the entire walls are covered by the black PVC panels). Now, the scientists use them extensively. Although the material scratches very easily and it requires careful and adequate maintenance, they "look after it."

The architect's expectation was for the walls to be used to spur ideas. Tony describes it as such: "I am walking down the corridor and I have an idea. I can suddenly write it on the wall. We can have a debate and people can gather and discuss things and we can develop it on the wall."[206] We can see that happening now on a regular basis: scientists and industry people gather around the walls; while they are discussing, they are also writing. Writing is another way, for them, to share insights, but also writing is a means of thinking through the ideas. The walls work well in the corridors around labs and social spaces. This is where most of the new insights emerge but are also scrubbed away on a more regular basis. The writable walls are particularly useful in group meetings. Research gatherings are organised around them (both in the 1st and the 2nd floor social spaces), group meetings are convened around the walls and thoughts get scribbled on their glossy black surfaces. The 2nd floor is the preferred spot of the theoretical physics group, as witnessed above. As we pass by, we can see some writings on the wall, traces left from their meetings (Fig. 64). While it is all written in formulas, it can be translated as: "these are two crystals aligned with each other. And what happens when you rotate them with respect to

[205] Interview with Stuart Lockwood, 3.06.2019.

[206] Interview with Tony Ling, 23.06.2017.

each other?" There is also a structure of a moiré pattern being drafted as well. These walls are very interactive and change content very often: "everyone's thoughts are on the wall, and they get scrubbed off on a monthly basis."[207] They follow the rhythm of discussions and current research topics. James Baker, the current CEO of the GEIC, uses the walls all the time while working in the NGI. In contrast to the writings of the theory group, his writing addresses selling processes to future businesses. James "often stands by the wall and writes on it to show people what graphene is about and what the business, the industry is about."[208] Going around the walls after James has been writing on them, one can "see the technical readiness level graphs that show where everything sits in the life of a product." "You'd see that everywhere, and you'd know James had been there and had been drawing on the wall!"[209] That is a sign that the wall works well, and as scientists repeat on several occasions: "it does something."

Yet, in other places in the building the black walls are used for other purposes. If we inspect the writeable wall in front of the energy lab on the 2nd floor, we find some beautiful colourful diagrams and charts on the wall (Fig. 66). John explains that the energy lab group takes responsibility for this particular wall. They do the cleaning themselves as the house attendants have specific instructions not to touch the walls. The information on the wall provides the means of seeing into the labs nearby, and, these drawings, are not sensitive in terms of intellectual property rights or "innovations" as the work has already been published. The drawings and the diagrams are used as a means of explaining to potential clients and collaborators what the energy group is doing at the moment. It also stops touring groups, or visitors, interested in the laboratory from entering it — everything that they need to know is displayed there on the walls outside of it. In this case, the writings on the wall are "a representation of what is going on in the lab,"[210] of current research and projects, whereas the walls in the

[207] Interview with John Whittaker, 16.10.2019.
[208] Interview with Stuart Lockwood, 3.06.2019.
[209] Interview with Stuart Lockwood, 3.06.2019.
[210] Interview with John Whittaker, 16.10.2019.

Fig. 66: Scientists discussing in the corridor of the energy lab opposite the writeable wall with a presentation of the ongoing research in the lab, photo by Albena Yaneva.

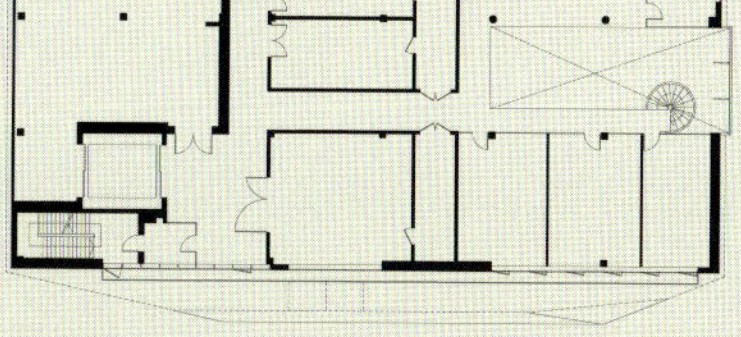

social space used by the theoretical physics group rather serve as a medium for sharing rough thought paths and discussing work in progress. The energy lab "writing is more permanent," John explains.

Yet, sometimes the house attendants are tempted to clean them[211] and scientists from the core graphene team, with frustration, recall this happening when the building first opened doors. Gordon Royle, who worked in Alan Turing building (the Maths building) before working as

[211] There are three of them in the building: Steve working at –1 level, Andy — on the 1st floor, Daniela — on the 2nd and the 3rd floor.

a house attendant at the NGI, compares the mathematicians with graphene scientists, their working habits, their relationship to space, their interactive cultures. "The mathematicians," he points out, "use chalk boards. They write complex equations and stuff like that and they explain things to each other on chalk boards. And our temptation is to clean the chalk boards, but this might be somebody's research!"[212] Daniela also remembers that when she worked in the Shuster Building (the Physics building) eight years ago, she cleaned a board that was not meant to be cleaned: "there was a professor doing his research and all his notes were on the board and he wanted to keep them, look at them and then write again, look at the new notes and then write again, and keep them all. But I deleted them. It was horrible. So, I am scared of boards now… and he was doing research for six months and all his work was on the board and vanished."[213] But, here, all house attendants know they cannot clean any writings around the NGI building. The boards and the writeable walls are not to be touched. This is a standard warning "because if someone has put ten years of research on that wall and you go on and you rub it, he is not going to be happy."[214] If there are boards that should be cleaned, Daniela will be asked explicitly to take the writing down. Yet, every day she looks at the walls, the written chemical formulae and the graphs. These walls also happen to have an impact on those who are not involved in graphene work.

Sometimes, there may be content that is not strictly related to the science happening inside the building. This is what everyone calls "vandalism." That is, any writing that does not include "genuine thought paths," and do not relate to graphene work are considered as "vandalising" the writeable walls as they go against the building program (e.g. jokes, poems, messages, etc.). Everyone remembers the moment when a different type of script, a poem, not a set of formulae, appeared on the wall. It was left by an important Chinese diplomat, a poet-in-residence at the NGI. Yet, it got accidently wiped off. Scientists wondered why it disappeared and assumed it was either a house attendant who must

[212] Interview with Gordon Royle, 13.11.2019.

[213] Interview with Daniela Sevelova, 4.12.2019.

[214] Interview with Daniela Sevelova, 4.12.2019.

Fig. 67: A poem of Lemn Sissay on the writeable wall. *Photo © Jonty Wilde, courtesy Kate Daudy.*

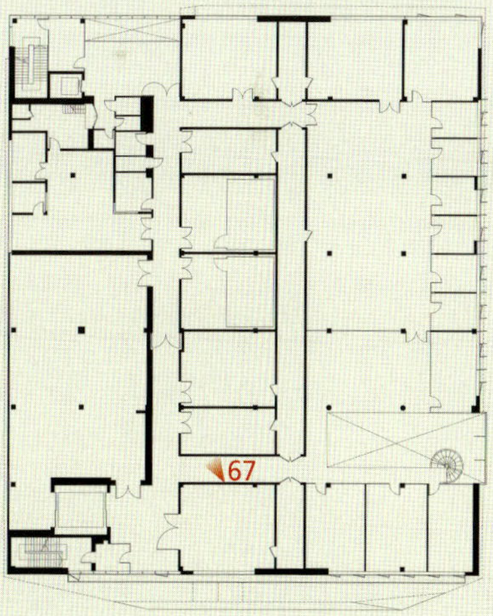

have cleaned it by mistake, or someone walked into it and rubbed off half of it. Lately, another poem has appeared on the walls, written by Lemn Sissay (Fig. 67). The text reads:

“How strong the night lies.
As light aerates the dark.
And atomic dreams multiply.
From a graphene heart.”

Perhaps because it is a poem related to graphene it has remained there longer than some formulae. Far from being an artistic decor of activities, the wall writings actively facilitate both scientific and social interaction among all dwellers in the building. In fact, this is one of the sites where the epistemic and social aspects remain closely entangled.

At the moment when the writable walls were introduced, the habit of discussing something with someone in the corridor and writing on the wall became a routine way of conducting "corridor chats." The only concern they have, Sarah shares, is that "you feel like you have to wash it off afterwards because it's not your space."[215] In the traditional campus buildings, scientists cannot write on the walls in the corridors even if there are dedicated whiteboards, unless the whiteboards are used as notice boards. Used for messages, the whiteboards highlight meetings that are of interest, training opportunities, problems with instruments others might not be aware of. When scientists walk past a board, they can see a message, and they know, "ah, the seminar on Wednesday!", "the registration deadline for that conference is on Friday!" Even though this information is often communicated by email, they tend to forget it, so the board serves as an efficient aid-memoire. The expectation, thus, an inherited habit from other buildings on campus, is that in the shared spaces one can pass messages but can rarely start a scientific discussion. In contrast, at the NGI the corridors host discussions, and the writable walls stimulate group thinking while drafting formulae. Only occasionally do scientists happen to use the writable walls to leave a message, following old habits picked up in other buildings, e.g. "gone to lunch and will be back at half one." However, this is rare. And here, at the NGI, where there is another set of habits, it is experienced as a form of "vandalism": it goes against the new design.

As they appreciated the writeable walls so much, the scientists wanted more of them. They even requested panels on the walls opposite to the glass sliding door leading to the roof terrace, so that they can use the social space on the 3rd floor for working discussions. This was not possible. Yet, similar blackboards or smaller walls were installed in the offices. Sarah and her colleagues use the "funky" blackboard in the office "to explain something to someone." They are better than the students' blackboards where one can write with chalk. These boards last about three days, and as Sarah complains, "you cannot get anything to write properly, and they create dust and it's horrible."[216] Being able to use those

[215] Interview with Sarah Haigh, 10.07.2017.

[216] Interview with Sarah Haigh, 10.07.2017.

funky blackboards without breathing the chalk dust increases the comfort in the shared offices as well as the comfort of sharing knowledge in discussions. To compare with other traditional boards, look at Sarah's whiteboard in her office in the Material Sciences building (Fig. 68). Every couple of weeks she uses the whiteboard with her students, she has "one student who comes in and draws a lot of these things on different occasions." For that particular student, Sarah also draws with pen on paper, takes a photograph of it for her record, and sends the student away with the paper. The whiteboard stays in her office, leaving traces from the most recent discussions with the student, then Sarah writes down the same information, traces from the discussion, in her lab book so she has it as a part of her records. The board is only a temporary support in the process of teaching and thinking together; the inscriptions then travel in different ways, copied on paper, it travels with the student leaving the office of Sarah, and copied once again in the lab book, it travels with Sarah, leaving the small whiteboard in the office. Three versions of the same traces of discussion are spread over the campus. The copies travel to be shared and recorded, to be reused in other reiterations of research in progress, to be developed, to form the basis of protocols for experiments or scientific papers. At the same time, in contrast, at the NGI, the inscriptions stay on the large writable walls and are to be viewed and debated by many. Silence seldom reigns around these walls.

Fig. 68: Scientist Sara Haigh in her office in the Material Sciences building standing in front of a traditional whiteboard, photo by Albena Yaneva.

All of the facilities and their specific design features — from the labs, through to social spaces and writeable walls — facilitate exchange. John sums this up: "we open laboratories, we open writing walls, we open discussion spaces, where anyone working in any discipline can go in and find out what's going on in that particular research group. Even our technical support staff acts as a reference point. Sometimes

'I hear such a colleague is doing this', 'I hear such a colleague's doing that', 'Can you put me in contact with somebody who can help.' If you want to measure that particular photoluminescence spectrum frequency for example, we have this ability."[217] Thus the building promotes, in its workflow, the creation of "a library of information" and "lines of communication." The exchanges that begin in the research labs where ten researchers from typically four or five disciplines work together on a local level, continue and intensify in the meeting rooms and the social spaces. The building efficiently promotes collaborative working and new partnerships.

As the building covers the whole process of scientific work, there is no need to go out; everyone dwells in the enclosed, dense and self-sustained territory of the graphene empire. Working in the building, scientists very often lose track of time. Mark explains that "the temperature control is very nicely done, so it's quite easy for me to spend a lot of time in the building. I forget how long I spend here, sometimes eight to nine working hours, and it never gets uncomfortable."[218] Thus, the pleasing modern aesthetics, the large open air and green space, the abundant light, the atria, the artworks, and the many common breakout spaces make the building a comfortable working environment. There, we can witness an active process of dwelling at two speeds: hectic and competitive, but also, slow and domestic. Both the speedy and the relaxed rhythm encourage interaction, fusions and collaborations. No matter how intense the working pace is, scientists communicate, exchange tips, knowledge, and lab recipes, rub shoulders on the benches and adjust experimental settings together in shared labs or in clean rooms; slowing down, they bump into each other and in this moment of social exchange during breakout time, whether around the coffee machine or the writeable walls, new insights emerge, new research alliances are formed that in return accelerate the rhythm of the graphene machine.

[217] Interview with John Whittaker, 22.06.2017.

[218] Interview with Mark Bissett, 30.06.2017.

13

[M] Veil Design

Scientist approach

The overall motto for the design of the NGI is "flexibility and collaboration." Flexibility is of crucial importance for any research-intensive building (as witnessed in a number of chapters above). It is in the nature of science that it is impossible to predict the future developments. Furthermore — the more unpredictable and volatile your research is — the better. Nobody has got the recipe how to promote the generation of a new idea, but at least the environment should not be prohibitive for such new developments. It is in the nature of scientific research to try novel approaches or even completely new directions every now and then, and the more often we do it (providing there is some scientific rationale behind such trials) — the more chance we have to step into new, unexplored territories. The typical timescale of such trials is months/years.

This is in clear contradiction with the "rigid" structure of traditional science buildings, which are typically built for decades. This mismatch in timescales creates a lot of issues for scientific buildings. Many of them are considered in the other chapters. Here we will concentrate on the functions of the veil for the National Graphene Institute building.

For any building which holds research activity — the external part of the building (walls, perimeter on the ground, roof, underground) is as important as interior, and this is especially true for University buildings. The reason is that modern equipment is often complex, require a lot of services, which are often impossible to predict and account for at the moment of the building being built. Thus, often, when a new process or a new piece of equipment is being introduced into an existing science building a number of questions emerge: Do we have enough space to hold the whole assembly or we need to split the process/equipment between different spaces? How will it interact with the existing processes in terms of noise, electromagnetic fields, light, etc.? Will the current health and safety precautions cover it? Will it even fit through the doors of the building and fit into the lifts? How much does it cost to make all the necessary arrangements to place the new process/equipment inside the building? And we can continue the list.

Thus, often the space outside the building presents a perfect solution to host the new process or equipment or at least parts of them. Such solution would minimise the influence on the other processes in the building, the health and safety restrictions are much more relaxed outside than inside (for instance due to ventilation), there is no problem with access, etc. That's the reason why just after a few years of operation any research-active building looks like a Christmas tree, surrounded by heat exchanges, hanging from every window, gas bottles along the perimeter, ducting and scrubbers on the walls and the roof. And the more active the scientists inside the building, the uglier the building looks from the outside.

The way to overcome this is to provide space outside which can host such auxiliary equipment, but which would look decent even when the space is populated. There are several requirements such space should fulfil: (i) it should provide easy access for the installation and servicing equipment; (ii) provide ventilation for cooling/gas extraction; (iii) provide protection against precipitation, light, wind, etc., if necessary; (iv) provide a barrier for unauthorised access; (v) provide easy access to the interior of the building to feed-in services if necessary, plus more requirements which might be specific in each particular case.

Methodologically it can be done by fitting the outside (walls, perimeter, roof, may be even cellar/ground level) with scaffolding, fitting points, feed-through points, enclosed compartments, service points (power, water, compressed air — whichever necessary) and then covering it with a nice looking membrane/veil. Again, the requirements for such membrane are outlined in the previous paragraph.

This was the solution in the National Graphene Institute. A number of dedicated spaces have been provided outside the building: enclosed storage compartment at the south elevation of the building; enclosed storage for chemical waste; open plinth for liquid nitrogen tanks and filling station; scaffolding to accommodate small equipment along the south elevation of the building. All those spaces (apart of the gas compartment on the roof) were later covered with a veil. The veil is made from perforated (to reduce weight and to allow air access) metal panels, which determine the appearance of the building and provide sufficient protection of the described compartments.

Architect's approach

The overall task for this project was to maximise the functionality of the building, without the compromise on the appearance of the building. Furthermore, the changes to the project have been introduced even during the construction phase. To comply with this agile situation the decision was made to adopt the solution with the external veil, which can be adjusted to any changes in the project with minimum cost. The use of the veil basically decouples the functional properties of the building and its external appearance. Even more importantly, the use of the veil allows fulfilment of the requirement of creation of external storage areas.

The existence of the storage compartments led to the rather complex shape of the external veil. It has been used to our advantage, so even the façade — which do not contain the hidden storage areas — adopted non-planar shape. This gave the building more modern, attractive appearance, underlining the scientific nature of the building by adapting the shape which is reminiscent of the structure of a crystal.

The pattern on the veil is important as well. A decision was made not to create too explicit references to graphene, creating only very subtle allusion to this material. Thus, the perforation, which is required to allow ventilation and to reduce the total weight of the structure, was made of hexagonal holes. Also, the black colour was chosen as a reference to graphite.

13

[E] Experiencing the Building Envelope

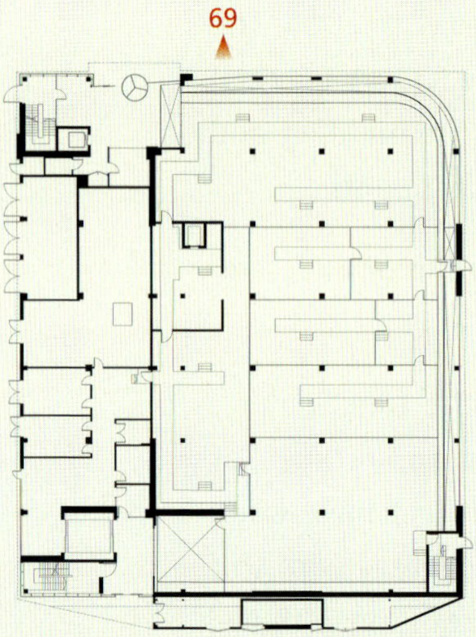

Passing Booth Street West many times, one may notice a large five-storey building taking shape. Cranes and diggers, scaffolding and dust, construction companies and workers with different coloured high-vis vests crowd that part of campus for a while. Slowly, the distinctive blocky silhouette of the building appears and stands out in a dazzling black that breaks the monotonous pattern of red brick buildings on the University of Manchester campus with its unique shape, colour, and sizable volume (Fig. 69).

Fig. 69: The veil, a view from Booth Street, photo by the University of Manchester.

Completed and now full of life, five years after construction, the dust has settled, and the workers have moved onto another site down the road. Neat paths, autumn coloured trees and a giant multi-story parking building have replaced the dirty diggers and massive cranes. Turning around the building, exploring its different facets, it is difficult to locate and grasp its main façade. However, if one moves closer, past the yellow-red autumn trees that block the view, one will find that the structure is covered with a "veil," a fine membrane.

Moving closer and stepping back, zooming in and out, taking various viewpoints, the membrane becomes more and less clear, more and less obscure. A black structure becomes noticeable as one explores the building from a distance, translucent at places, slowly thickening at others. An irregular black veil gently covers a number of joint blocks; in a black jazzy surface geometry, there are glassy and limpid parts that follow solid and opaque parts. Neither obscuring the content behind, nor fully giving away the buzz of "science in action" inside, the veil suggests and finely mediates the delicate relationship between content and cover. Readable at some edges and illegible at others, it discloses the hardly detectable graphene equations inscribed in the perforated hexagonal metal structure, and profiles the scientific lab in a provocative way. Falling discretely and smoothly as a fine veil covering a nucleus of functional units, its irregular angles reveal a shape that is visible behind, yet hardly graspable as a separate volume. Approaching the building, one can begin to distinguish the sign-ingredients of a formula language (E, =, m, v_F^2) and the subtle reference to the hexagonal-lattice of carbon atoms that make up graphene. Running through the veil with different sizes, they join vertically and transversally to make formulae that are only readable by the knowledgeable eye who can notice the "legitimate mathematical jokes" inscribed in them. Mere ornaments to our contemplating eyes, the nanoscientists see graphene in the formulae, so realistic and literal that they can be copied into textbooks; what looks to us like a well-measured and volumetric sequence of darker and lighter black, actually talks about graphene's properties — its electrical resistance, optical transparency, and strength. The dancing variations of equations are marks to read, to make sense of, reminders of what happens behind the veil, and prompts of a significant event that marked the building's beginning: the isolation of graphene.

Far from being decorative elements of the veil, the formulae are legible signs in the building's cladding, the outcome of a compromise between a weighty and opaque black screen concealing the science behind (the typical façade of a traditional campus building) and an explicit bold reference to graphene (i.e. the hexagons). Although the veil is interesting from an aesthetic point of view, everyone who "dwells" inside sees graphene in it. For Ernie, for instance, "the important thing is that it looks like a folded sheet of graphene. It also appears differently in different lights. It's quite subtle."[219] The veil design puts the viewer in the position of a worldly view of science, one that never happens in a "double-click" moment of invention, but like moving closer and farther away, exploring the environs of the building, it is a long and painstaking endeavour, full of numerous reiterations and mistakes in search of the right answer, the right formula — that is, science in the world.

Is the imagery of the veil important for the scientists working in the building? As witnessed earlier, graphene scholars commonly teach and have offices in other buildings on campus, while also working in the premises of the NGI on particular days. They regularly show the graphene building to visitors, and it is often "the wow of others" that makes them appreciate "how pretty the building is." Mark even enjoys sitting in front of the building, contemplating the veil, having a coffee and talking on the phone. For Sarah, the building "looks cool," and the formulae are quite subtle. Walking between two distinct parts of the campus, commuting, as she does, between the red brick tower of the Material Sciences building and the state-of-the art graphene institute, she compares the aesthetics of the NGI with the traditional "dull" campus buildings. Often, when she comes to the institute, she does not notice the NGI façade as "you only notice," she explains, "when you show a visitor and they go 'oh, that's quite cool.'" For her, the fact that it looks pretty "doesn't affect how she works in the building." What is more important, she repeatedly argues, is how the building functions and what it does to her work. The building works in a "cool way" too. Functionality and aesthetic appearance emerge naturally as

[219] Interview with Ernie Hill, 14.06.2019.

two entangled facets of the building. There is an intrinsic functionality in the aesthetic and visual appeal of the veil as it covers and envelops all central and service facilities, equipment and storage on the roof.

However, scientists typically experience the veil and its ornamental formulae effect from the inside, and we witness (ethnographically) how this happens in an experiential way. The expectation is that "we would have this thing that would look like graphene; so, everywhere you look, you find graphene. You cannot get away from it."[220] Mark discusses the enjoyable experience he has in the building with "a lot of really nice views in lots of the places"; for instance, he often goes onto the top roof terrace where the interior part of the veil can be seen (Fig. 70). Here, the formulae are decipherable, tangible, materialised, up-close, at walking distance; they grow, getting closer to the researchers who sit on the terrace, enjoying their lunch. On the terrace, the veil is far from being an obscure silhouette celebrating the graphene breakthrough or an aesthetically pleasing ornamental membrane covering the vibrant scientific life enclosed inside. Instead, out there on the roof, yet still inside the building, close to the wild garden, the flowers and the bees, the perforated texture of the veil and the almost human-sized formulae become an entangled part of the conversations and mundane experiences of graphene researchers. Dynamic and airy, the veil brings the graphene equations closer to the ordinary rhythm of science-making. It speeds up the course of research as a reminder: "everywhere you look, you find graphene."

Thus, neither a solid façade putting a symbolic face over a content box, nor simply an ornamental envelope wrapping up the whole (walls and roof, form and function), the architecture of the veil works as a device that underlines the visible steps in science, the inscriptions, the drafts, the try-outs, the mistakes and re-takes. All this reminds the scientists, industry people, technicians, and visitors that "there is no double-click magic here!" It says: "come and try, make mistakes, start over, and you will be part of it." It is in this continuous dialogue between the formulae hand-written on notebooks and black boards and walls spread throughout the building, and the equations engraved on the

[220] Interview with Stuart Lockwood, 3.06.2019.

Fig. 70: A close up to the veil, a view from the roof garden, photo by Albena Yaneva.

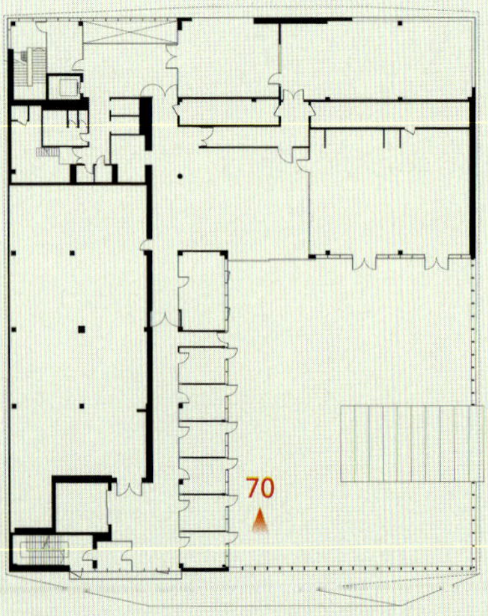

building skin, that we witness how design matters for graphene research, and enacts graphene's future.

Going back in time to recollect the process of making it, the veil was "the worst point of discussions"[221] and negotiations between scientists and architects. It came also very early in the design process. It was "the biggest and longest design decision"[222] that they had to make, recalls Stuart: "we had a variety of different presentations from the architects and none of them really hit the button. We had gone into planning, looked all sorts of aspects of it, different colour arrangements, there were all sorts of different ideas of what it would look like."[223] First, it was decided that the building would be wrapped with a water-proof exterior, an insulated Eurobond panel. From that, there were long and arduous discussions around the colour of

[221] Interview with Stuart Lockwood, 3.06.2019.

[222] Interview with Stuart Lockwood, 3.06.2019.

[223] Interview with Stuart Lockwood, 3.06.2019.

the veil. After looking at a variety of different colours, they eventually settled on black with some reservations: the "downside of it is that it does show dirt."[224] Then, they had "to choose something for the image." This process of negotiation required a lot of experimentation and debate that focussed on what the veil would look like, and what the punctures or apertures within the veil would represent. It took, again, a very long time to get to a decision. Even then various iterations were discussed, more options on its density and options of hexagons piled up. The deliberations were so long that they started causing major concerns about the overall programme of the building. Tony and his team produced and studied hundreds of different options of what the building should represent. This was a moment of intense experimentation, a moment when the visuals proliferated, and hundreds of renderings travelled hectically between London and Manchester.[225] At a certain moment, the scientists remember that the architects came with an image, "like in this movie, The Matrix, where the numbers kind of fall down and then start forming a pattern." [226] This image prompted a suggestion from the scientists: to "put some formulae in"; Kostya had very good hand-written formulae, which they converted and digitised in such a way that they can hardly be recognized as formulae. Both architects and scientists agreed that the formulae should be very subtle. Yet, the University administration requested that the formulae be legible, and the architects and scientists tried several ways — handwritten, typed — then copied all the formulae of graphene there and inserted them into the veil design. At last, after lengthy discussions, the design team abandoned the standard clichéd hexagon. The mysterious undetectable formula pattern won over the explicit little hexagons.

However, the hexagon shape had one advantage: the replacement of the panels would have been simpler. The maintenance of a veil made out of hexagons is relatively effortless as the patterns are straightforward to produce and as they are available "off the shelf." In contrast, the formula panels are bespoke, unique, and have to be

[224] Interview with Stuart Lockwood, 3.06.2019.

[225] David Taylor, *The Right Formula* (Manchester: Manchester University Press, 2016).

[226] Interview with Kostya Novoselov, 12.07.2017.

built and manufactured individually. Moreover, they are oddly angled, moving in different planes. They cannot be fabricated in batches or bought off the shelf, sprayed with paint, and installed. Instead, a special manufacturing process is required for the bespoke veil, which needs to be darkened by a special galvanical process. As a result, maintenance is difficult (as per Stuart's concern) as replacing damaged panels is not easy. To simplify the process or mitigate the difficulty, the drawings are kept for reference, and to identify which panel needs to be replaced they can refer back to the drawings. The imagery of the veil has its "price" — making maintenance more complex.

Ultimately, the veil is the result of a compromise. It emerges somewhere between the initial suggestion from the architects to have an opaque black screen (that would have been too heavy and expensive and similar to the traditional façades on campus) and the explicit reference to graphene and the little hexagons (disliked by most of the scientists but relatively easy to build and maintain). The Matrix-movie moment yielded a very interesting exchange between three different worlds. While, Tony was learning to read and decipher the different formulae of graphene, simultaneously grasping what graphene is and how it is translated into equations, Kostya and his graphene team were learning how to read the different shades of black and grey on the architectural rendering and to imagine the veil on the basis of the visuals produced in the architectural office of Jestico+Whiles in London. Meanwhile, back in Manchester, Stuart, John and others on the facility management team were trying to figure out the technical side, and to anticipate the scope of maintenance work required. In fact, the image of the veil did not emerge in anyone's "mind's eye." Instead, it was the result of extensive exchange between different "labs"—the architects, the scientists, and also the manufacturers and the estate managers. It emerged as the outcome of lengthy material tests and experimentation in which new patterns of collaboration among all these participants involved in design and construction were probed as well. Ultimately, the question shifted away from the symbolic power of the veil: it was not about what it represents, but what it does to scientists and to their daily work on graphene and what it will do in the future to estate managers and builders. Here, graphene pulls everyone into the future in a pragmatic way.

14

[M] Future Services

Apart from the storages and future-proof spaces outside of the building, there are a number of other arrangements which should allow smooth operation of the building for years ahead.

First of all, it is the gas storage compartment on the roof level. Despite the building being equipped with 21 gas lines from day one, it is extremely difficult to predict which chemicals will be required in the future. And if some basic, non-toxic and non-flammable gases could be simply brought into the labs in bottles, the health and safety regulations would require installation of rather complex safety features (extractable cabinets, gas sensors, etc.) when we talk about more dangerous species. To this end an enclosed gas bottle storage has been arranged on the roof level with six gas lines leading directly to the chemistry room. Having the storage outside, in a well-ventilated space means that a large number of gases can be stored there directly, without much modification of the infrastructure. And the preinstalled gas lines will ensure that no expensive and complex modification to the building fabric will need to be done once we need to install a new gas bottle on the roof level.

Starting from the first day of design of the building we knew that there will be a moment in the future when we will run out of the laboratory or office space and will need to expand. There are a number of precautions which will potentially allow to gain space without dramatic changes to the building fabric. First of all, some of the offices (as, for instance, those along the South and the North side of the building) can be immediately converted into labs. Those offices are directly adjacent to the grey space (2nd floor) or to the lab (1st floor) and thus it will be easy to supply those with services. Furthermore, the open space labs on the 1st and 2nd floors can be expanded towards South. In order to do that only the glass walls need to be moved, with electricity supply readily available at the ceiling level.

More radical transformations would include putting floor over the two atriums in the building: one in the North side, right above the main entrance (this space would be suitable for offices); another is just South from the open space laboratories (it would be logical to use the space gained for experimental work). In both cases the provisions for such modifications have been made at the stage of planning and construction (fitting points for beams) — so the modification could be done with minimum disruption.

The roof levels also hold a lot of potential. The load and isolation there are such that it can support light construction — porter cabin or storage. Potentially it can create an interesting, unconventional space if ever required.

Finally, additional precautions have been undertaken if exceptionally tall equipment will have to be installed in the labs in the future. With the ceiling height being 4.2 metres already — the labs are capable to accept pretty much any kind of equipment one can think of. However, the complexity of experiments grows day by day and so is the complexity of the research rigs. To this end several labs on the 1st floor are equipped with 1 metre deep wells (1 × 1 metre in size). While not in use they are coved by metal plates, providing recessed floor. However, in case a particularly tall equipment has to be installed (we had in mind particularly large cryostats) — they can be opened and the equipment placed in the hole. From underneath the wells drop into the plenum area above the main clean room, so they do not interfere with the normal operation.

14

[E] Experiencing Growth

While trying to anticipate the future, graphene scientists and building managers constantly think about and plan how the building will grow, and about the specific opportunities to add, increase, expand, and maximize its efficiency. The NGI building is designed in a way that all the architectural features can be converted at a certain moment into a "useful space." The atria could become labs or offices. The offices can be converted to labs. Even another floor can be added as there are numerous anchor bolts located in the main atria whereupon metal beams could be placed. Anticipating future developments, the NGI remains at odds with the traditional buildings on the campus, not just in terms of aesthetic appearance and structure, but primarily in terms of speed and growth. As John says, in graphene research "we're going on a journey and we don't know where the journey will take us, so from a research point of view that is kind of not mundane, you know, it's kind of exciting, going in this particular direction, but where the ultimate goal is going, we're not sure."[227] The building is a platform for this development, an adaptable platform, an accelerator that opens up the future.

As research buildings change focus inevitably, growth is in the very nature of the scientific building typology. "How can we gain extra space?" "How can we convert one type of space into another?" — these questions are there from the very beginning of the design process. Discussing the flexibility of campus buildings, Richard Cutting, Senior Faculty Project Manager at the Faculty of Science and Engineering, states that the "NGI is an interesting building. It's quite well-designed."[228] It is well-designed for the future. As the lead of the

[227] Interview with John Whittaker, 22.06.2017.

[228] Interview with Richard Cutting, 10.07.2017.

research and technical spaces in the Manchester Engineering Campus Development (MECD) project and the Henry Royce Building, Richard can compare the NGI to other projects on campus. He draws an important distinction between flexible and adaptable spaces. The important element is "getting as much space within the envelope of the building as possible" given the available budget. More lab spaces will be needed; every scientific building will grow at a certain point in time. A five-floor building is bound by the envelope, the roof and the façade — its size is fixed. Adding another floor would be extremely expensive; that is why Richards believes it is important to have vacant space within the existing building, that is, to have a shell that can be filled as the activities inside change and grow. He says that "as long as you've got sufficient capacity in the house gases, in the circuit loads, electrical supplies of the building, if you have that, a small grant of £2,000–£3,000 would be enough to fit out a laboratory."[229] The building is adaptable. This is precisely the difference between flexible and adaptable. The difference is subtle, yet important. For a building to be flexible, it means that anything can be placed anywhere in the building; the "everything everywhere approach," however, can double the cost. "Building adaptable buildings is of greater importance in science."[230] The NGI is distinctive, according to John, because it is "a very flexible facility that is tailored to our needs now, but can also be adapted for future research programmes."[231] They need future proofing of the building. The standard laboratories are adaptable too, and act as a platform where research groups can tailor their labs. In other words, the NGI is both flexible and adaptable; it tries to fit both of these together.

The structural frame provides both the flexibility for service distribution and achieves low vibration performance. "To keep it open and flexible" was an important principle of the overall NGI design, according to Stuart. "They had some dedicated spaces in which they knew what they wanted to do in there. They knew they needed to have a number of valves specifically for certain research streams. But the rest

[229] Interview with Richard Cutting, 10.07.2017.

[230] Interview with Richard Cutting, 10.07.2017.

[231] Interview with John Whittaker, 22.06.2017.

of it was really flexible."[232] The building design matters for the rhythm of work; flexibility in the design leads to flexibility in research. But it is also adaptable: it is extremely easy to change configurations in the building. "Built with future development and expansion in mind," as John reiterates, its very high-spec profile "gives us the ability to run the existing 2D programmes" but also provides "for future development, as graphene and 2D materials research will evolve over the coming decades."[233] Researchers constantly talk about potential, speed, and about the possibility to adapt labs and upscale experiments. They deal with projected changes and think about long-term research developments. Trying to anticipate what future research programmes will bring, what the dwellers in the graphene building witness is an "evolving building" whose plasticity is to be managed while its consistency is maintained. As the technician Christopher explains "you can pop down a floating floor or a ceiling and you've got your isolators or your regulators in there, where we can easily access them to close off lines."[234] Nothing is really fixed in terms of stable architectural features. Flexibility in terms of space and supply of gases and water, is required to allow the research groups to move from a very small benchtop kind of development into a semi-production development. Thus, accommodating different types of research groups in terms of stable atmospheres and environments to give them consistency, the building facilities allow to upscale. This scale-ability is unique.

The building mimics here the unsettled character of graphene research. Investigating the properties of 2D materials and how they interact with each other is often unpredictable, highlighting some of those properties can also produce new research groups who will attempt to harness those properties into the production of a device. Embarking on this journey, the scientists "know that the research they are doing in 2012 is not going to be the research that they're doing in 2015, so our building has to be flexible, adaptable and dynamic enough

[232] Interview with Stuart Lockwood, 3.06.2019.

[233] Interview with John Whittaker, 22.06.2017.

[234] Interview with Christopher Hyde, 15.12.2017.

to be able to look at that, to deal with that and cope with it."[235] As, in graphene research, it is important to engage with external bodies that can invest money and do a bit of research to allow them to be able to move their product forward, the speed of getting to the product stage is equally important. "The research moves very quickly, and there will be people moving in and out of that space, to do that research. But, it's also about moving the products to market as quickly as they can, and that in its own right is dynamic. The GEIC was born out of this." Look at Mark comparing his labs at the NGI with the GEIC one. He explains: "in all of the meetings we've had about the GEIC we would say 'in the NGI it's like this, we want it to be like that,' or 'it's like this and we want it to be different.' This is the point of reference for designing and future-proofing the GEIC."[236] A simple "oh, in the NGI we did it like this, why are you doing it differently now?" or an objection of "one thing we don't like about the NGI is this, can you do it differently?" stirs different designs solutions, connects buildings and labs in the flexible graphene ecology emerging at the campus and city scale, and allows the smooth travel from blue sky science to industry products, back and forth. Supported by a building that runs alongside them, scientists move extremely quickly from the research at the NGI to a unique product, but which could only be done in single batches. To move up onto the next stages, they need the GEIC. The graphene empire expands; it adapts to the urban scale.

[235] Interview with Stuart Lockwood, 3.06.2019.

[236] Interview with Mark Bissett, 30.06.2017.

Conclusion: A New Approach to Science Architecture

> The NGI building is "agile, *it moves*, it does have that dynamic to be able *to move the research*."[237]
>
> "Graphene (and 2D materials) is such a promising field of work, and this definitely has an impact on having a positive mindset to work here; the fact that you know that you're working on something that quite possibly one day might have tremendous applications is inspiring.[238]

Tracing the making of the NGI building and the first years of its existence, this book offered insights into the specificity of this scientific lab and its social life. Drawing on careful analysis of the various facilities at the NGI, as well as the various ways they are experienced, we can witness that as a modern laboratory, the graphene building provides a vital setting for the active shaping of new research habits. It facilitates the development of new partnerships between science, society and industry. Architecture, we demonstrated here, matters for graphene research and helps to accelerate its course.

To conclude, we want to address some questions: What lessons can we learn from the NGI? What are the new challenges for the future architects of science buildings? What is the best method to study the architecture of science? Here are four points that emerge out of our account in response to these questions and form the backbone of a new approach to science architecture.

First, our story captured a number of voices from an array of participants in design and in the use of scientific buildings. In addition to the "usual suspects" that are found in studies of scientific design (the scientists and the architects), we encountered lab technicians, facility

[237] Interview with Stuart Lockwood, 3.06.2019.

[238] Interview with Fransisco Lopez-Royo, 04.07.2017.

managers, gas room and storage room technicians, porters, the admin, experimental officers, house attendants, events managers. Each of them works alongside the scientists to support their research, and assist, in an almost imperceptible way, the maintenance of the NGI's high-spec infrastructure. Drawing on their experiences of the facilities, the book included voices that are rarely encountered in conventional accounts of scientific buildings. These are, as the storeroom technician, Chris, puts it, the "unsung heroes" of lab work. None of the existing studies of lab design have acknowledged them, and yet they are ever-present here. Picturing the world of the graphene building as inhabited by all these actors helps us overcome the perennial cliché of design as a relationship between architects and clients (or scientists) only, or the funders or the politicians that eventually decide on the lab's success.

Second, we witnessed that scientists are a very special type of client, demanding novelty at all levels. The architecture of the NGI has managed to successfully redefine the very meaning of multidisciplinarity.

Mark recalls the excitement of being able to walk through the empty building before it was officially opened, looking at the layout, guessing where the labs would go and trying to imagine all of the spaces. He was "always quite excited about it, about how it was going to function. It was quite nice in terms of researchers working on graphene. It's like a sub-section of a lot of different schools, where there are people from Materials, Physics, Chemistry, Engineering, basically all of the nine Schools across the Faculty (and even other faculties). There are people here who are representatives from all of them, and it's just quite nice in terms of encouraging multidisciplinary collaborations."[239] Now, Mark (as well as the many scientists interviewed and followed ethnographically) even tends to forget that some people come from different schools, or from different disciplines, as they are all working on these similar projects. The Schools and the disciplines no longer matter. This building brings them all together, mixes them up. The excitement of the new lab design merges into an excitement for the existence of a world of science where all disciplinary boundaries are blurred.

[239] Interview with Mark Bissett, 30.06.2017.

Moreover, in devising such a complex building, the NGI overcomes naïve understandings of collaboration as inter-subjective communication. Instead, collaboration is about the exchange of recipes, the friendly trade of tips, the transfer of technologies or the doodling on all surfaces. Far from being a discursive exchange of ideas, multidisciplinarity emerges while sharing spaces and equipment, rubbing shoulders at the lab benches, reading results together or writing on the black walls. In addition to the co-existence of humans, it requires also the co-habitation of diverse lab settings and technologies and their distinct hazards and risk management strategies. Sharing space is also about sharing the fear of explosions that could spread or the hazards of spilling chemicals that are badly transported. It is at the level of these material practices that another type of multidisciplinary exchange transpires. One that allows hypotheses to emerge in the process of sampling or characterization, possible scenarios to be tested, and research leads to be followed. Sharing tools, techniques, protocols, technologies, as well as risks and hazards, implies a type of collaboration that is ontologically different than the exchange of ideas based on results that are commonly communicated in journal articles and discussed in conference rooms, workshops, atria, or other communication spaces. This makes us rethink the role of lab spaces in the new generation of scientific buildings. It is not enough to provide breakout spaces where scientists can meet and exchange ideas. It is, instead, important to entirely rethink the design (and support infrastructure) of the labs as spaces where research problems are shared and eventually, collectively, probed and resolved.

It is in fact quite easy to slip into an analogy: just like in graphene research where the interaction with other 2D materials determines the success of devices (in membranes, in energy, in electronics), the interactive capacity of humans (scientists and industry people) likewise depends on the formation of bonds between different materials. They are all expected to form new bonds, we might say. But the process of formation of human bonds is also carefully mediated by the building architecture. Just as carbon appears in different configurations (graphite or diamond) depending on how the bonds are formed, so are the configurations of humans, and the different fusions of disciplines. And we can continue this symmetric reasoning. The study of the NGI architecture illustrates that scientific design is not simply about connecting, interacting, and bonding human and nonhuman actors. It is rather about actively regulating both the regime of isolation and enclosure for the purposes of non-interference in experiments (as well as for the purposes of secrecy, especially in case of commercially sensitive data) and the regime of communication. These are two key conditions for the success of graphene work. The building design makes possible the co-existence of clean and protected spaces, separated from vibration and electromagnetic interferences and also open and highly interactive spaces for developing new research partnerships. Yet, exchange happens both at the level of the confined spaces (clean rooms, labs and desks) as researchers perform experiments and produce results, and in the open, social spaces (conference rooms and atria) as they share and discuss results. Space matters, on the one hand, as it divides, partitions, isolates, and contains, and on the other hand, as it assembles, reshuffles and brings people and things together, and is being shared. These two modalities have their own merits for scientific production.

Third, architecture matters for graphene research. This does not mean that it can determine the science conducted inside — we are far from the regime of architectural determinism. Nor is architecture irrelevant to the science contained within its walls — we are far from architectural indifference. The design of the NGI mediates the rapid rhythm of graphene research, a hectic tempo of experimentation, and a demanding, highly competitive research culture. Even the spaces that are supposed to provide an "escape" and quality time, the so-called "breakout spaces," happen to be busy spaces of social exchange and continue to accelerate the pace of research. The labs are adapted quickly, the groups are formed and disbanded. The building never sleeps. There are overnight experiments. Busy evenings in the shared labs. Sundays in the clean room. John or Polly spending their holidays monitoring the technical facilities with BMS, and imperative instructions to take time off over Christmas. Indeed, an unstoppable pace of graphene research. The NGI building operates as a machine that intensifies the work on graphene. It is reminiscent to a good scientific experiment,[240] not one which is passive but one that constrains and actively transforms scientific practices. Far from being an invisible decor, its design is experienced as active, influential and transfiguring.

Fourth. This study of the NGI illustrated how hard it is to disentangle technical and aesthetic aspects of the building. All attempts to untangle the technical from the aesthetic features go against the grain of graphene research (e.g. the colour coding system in the clean room, the different aesthetics of the writable walls, the various configurations of the conference rooms, the ample functionality of the mysterious veil). There is invariably an aesthetics in technically good solutions.

Our study showed that architects who think scientists always need open spaces, air and light, establish a generic basis for all scientific activities as fundamentally human. Yet, if designers engage with scientists, to fully understand the nature of their work, like Tony, aesthetics becomes part of functionality, it gains many nuances as it extends and intensifies the functional. Rather than assuming that pure technical rationality comes first, and that aesthetic shape simply follows, as a pretty envelope, we demonstrated that a good science building is one that is simultaneously aesthetic, functional and operational; it is one that symmetrically cares for the human, visual and perceptual qualities, as much as the nonhuman, mechanical and infrastructural performance. Defying the dualism of technology and aesthetics, the NGI successfully illustrates how the new generation of scientific buildings can offer both more efficient and pleasant working environments.

[240] Stengers, I. *The Invention of Modern Science. Minneapolis*: The University of Minnesota Press (2000). Yaneva, A. *Five Ways to Make Architecture Political. An Introduction to the Politics of Design Practice*. Bloomsbury: London (2017).

The design of scientific buildings has been largely explored during the last two decades.[241] The existing research focused either on the technical side of lab design (guidebooks for efficient and sustainable design) or on the human interface (studies of the communication patterns, the informal coffee discussions, the shaping of scientific identities). Both social scientists and architectural scholars with different interests toured the world, to visit, photograph and document these new temples of 21st century science. Yet, they often only scratched the visible surface of scientific design: some of them stayed outside the buildings contemplating their architectural expression and symbolism, others dared to enter and stay for a little while, but only to explore the soft social spaces of scientific communication and the visible architecture (the cafes, the restaurants, the leisure spaces). Yet, to fully understand the new generation of scientific buildings, a more refined gaze at the entire technical and design infrastructure that makes a science lab possible is needed: the gas rooms, the grey spaces, the utilities blocks, the mechanical workshops, and the different ways of servicing them. They all support an uninterrupted course of research.

It is therefore important to devise new types of enquiries that will engage in a longitudinal analysis of the life of a science building by paying equal attention to both the complexity of the design facilities and the variability of human experiences that they enable. All these facets of a scientific building, all unknown, and often invisible routines of science making, contribute to the seamless experimental work, and gradually to scientific discovery. Space matters for science not only because it

[241] Galison, P. and Thompson, E. (eds.), *The Architecture of Science*. Cambridge, Mass.: MIT Press (1999). Livingston, D. *Putting Science in Its Place: Geographies of Scientific Knowledge*. Chicago: Chicago University Press (2003). Gieryn, T. City as Truth-spot: Laboratories and Field-sites in Urban Studies. *Social Studies of Science*, 36, 5–38 (2006). Meusburger, P. The Nexus Between Knowledge and Space. P. Meusburger, M. Welker, & E. Wunder (eds.), *Knowledge and Space: Vol. 1. Clashes of Knowledge: Orthodoxies and Heterodoxies in Science and Religion*, 35–90. Dordrecht, The Netherlands: Springer (2008). Moravanszky A. and Kirchengast, A. (eds.) *Experiments: Architecture Between Science and the Arts*. Berlin: Jovis (2011). Klonk, C. (ed.) *New Laboratories: Historical and Critical Perspectives on Contemporary Developments*. Berlin: De Gruyter (2016). Kaji-O'Grady, S., Hughes, R. & Smith, CL (eds.) *Laboratory LifeStyles: The Construction of Scientific Fictions*. Cambridge Mass.: MIT Press (2018). Kaji-O'Grady, S. and Smith, CL *LabOratory: Speaking of Science and Its Architecture*. Cambridge Mass.: MIT Press (2019).

brings minds together, but because it allows the smooth circulation of flows of gases, water and electricity to run through the veins of a building, thus re-ordering lab equipment, chemicals, instruments and particles, in an active dance, and ultimately changing thought paths.

The current NGI study outlined the importance of scrutinizing the simultaneously unfolding worlds of architectural and scientific ventures. If the perennial question for studies on the architecture of science in the 1990s was to explore the relationship between the building and the shaping of scientific identities,[242] and the identities of the architects who design them, for us the key concern is different. It is important to understand how scientific architecture translates the changing nature of scientific practice today. It reveals the larger challenges and networks of scientific production, the partnerships with industry, the dialogue with the city. Moreover, it is important to unravel how buildings like the NGI "move research," as Stuart likes to say, and accelerate its course. Science, by setting new questions, drives new architectural answers. It leads to new techniques and experimental tactics in the practices of designing architects. These new design solutions, in turn, facilitate new types of scientific endeavours. In other words, it is crutial to explore the shifting practices of scientists and architects as they engage in collaborations and to find new ways to trace their working dynamics.

Graphene is evolving every day. Graphene research is changing lives as we write these lines. Here comes the pressing need for scientific buildings to promptly join the dance of its unstoppable rhythm. One that is expanding. One that is becoming global. One that is speeding up. Architecture provides new choreographies for that dance.

[242] Gieryn, T. Two Faces on Science: Building Identities for Molecular Biology and Biotechnology. P. Galison and E. Thompson (eds.), *The Architecture of Science*, 423–459. Cambridge, Mass: MIT Press (1999).

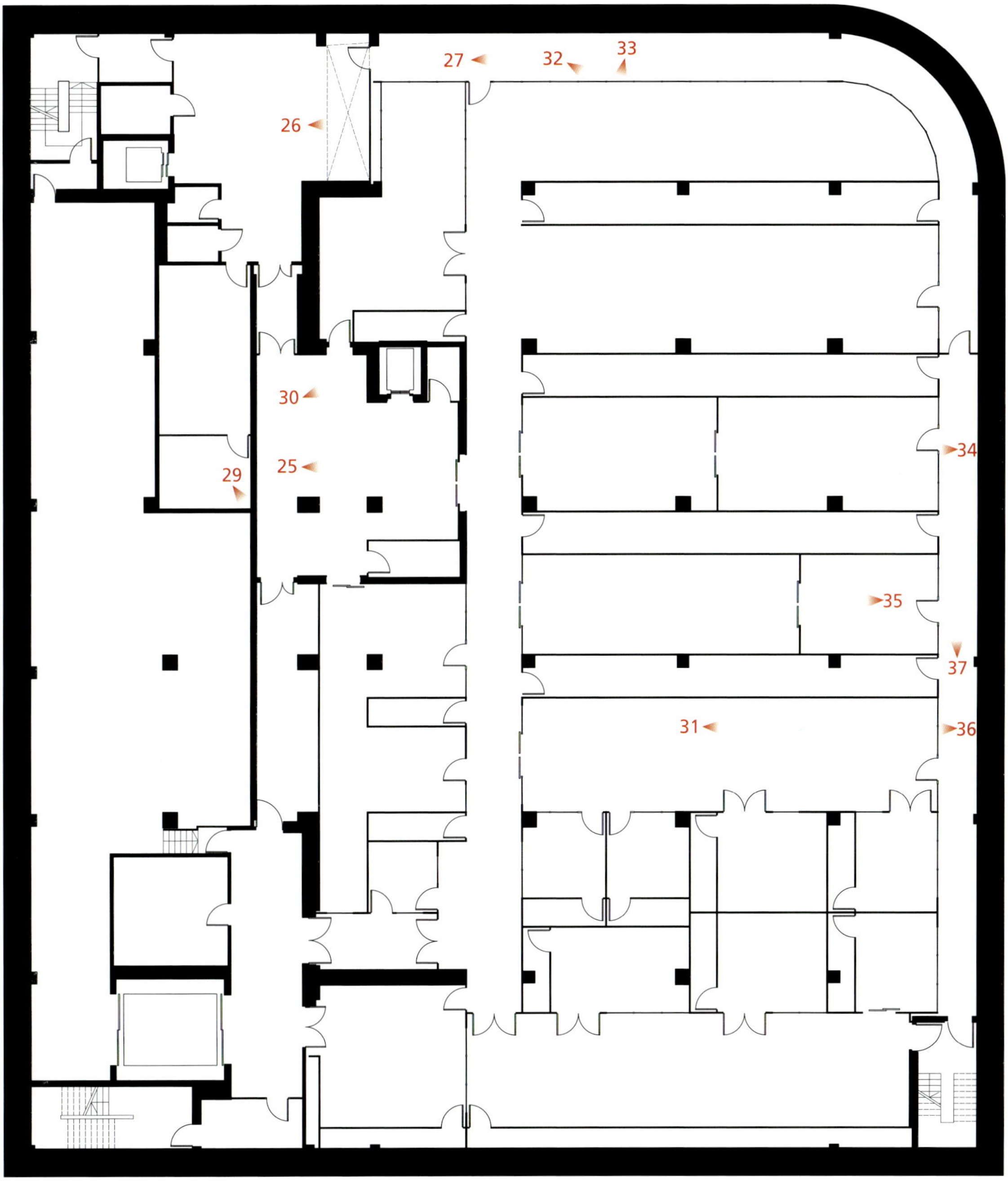

NGI –1 Basement Level

The scale is given by the grid, which is 6600 mm.

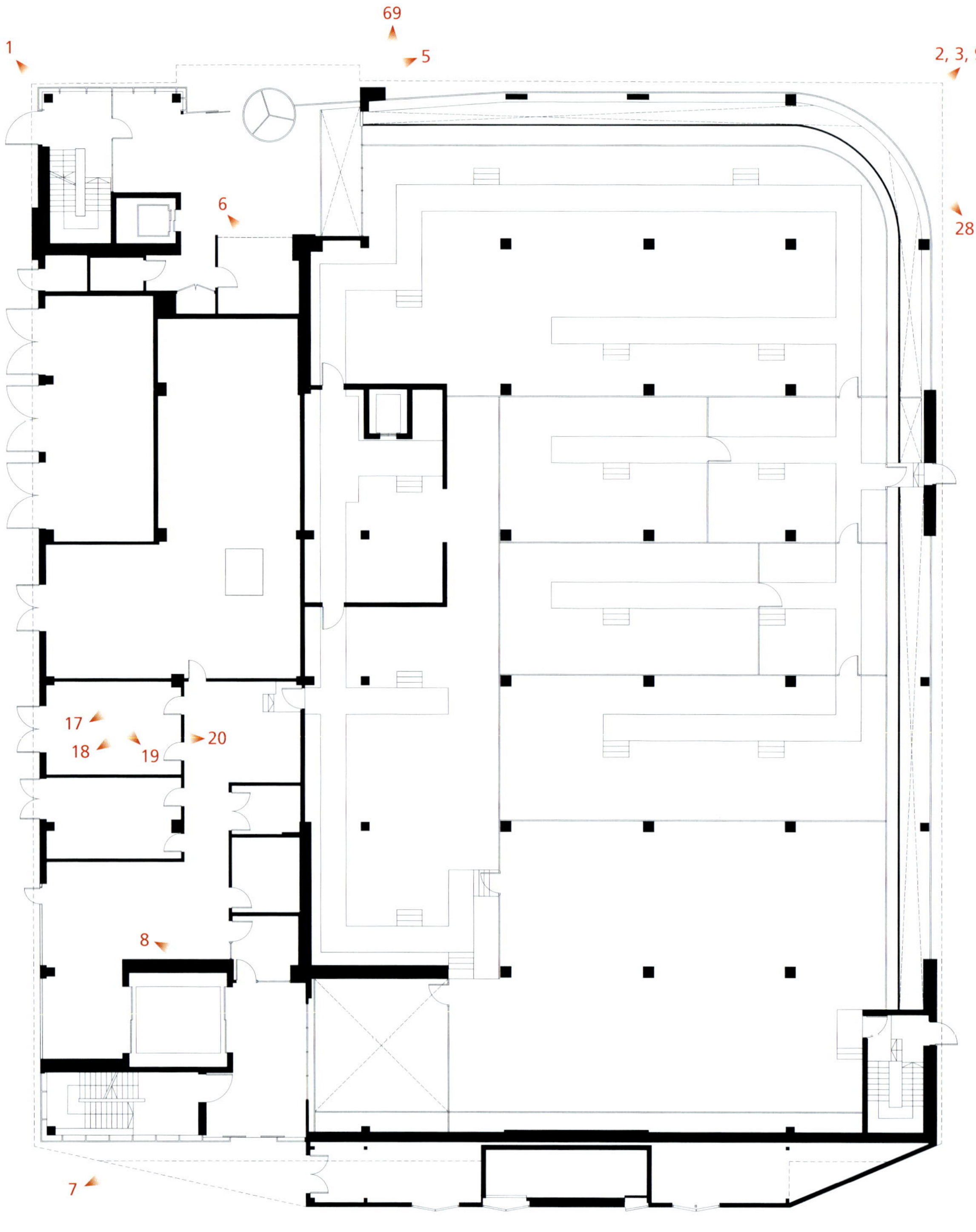

NGI 0 Ground Level

The scale is given by the grid, which is 6600 mm.

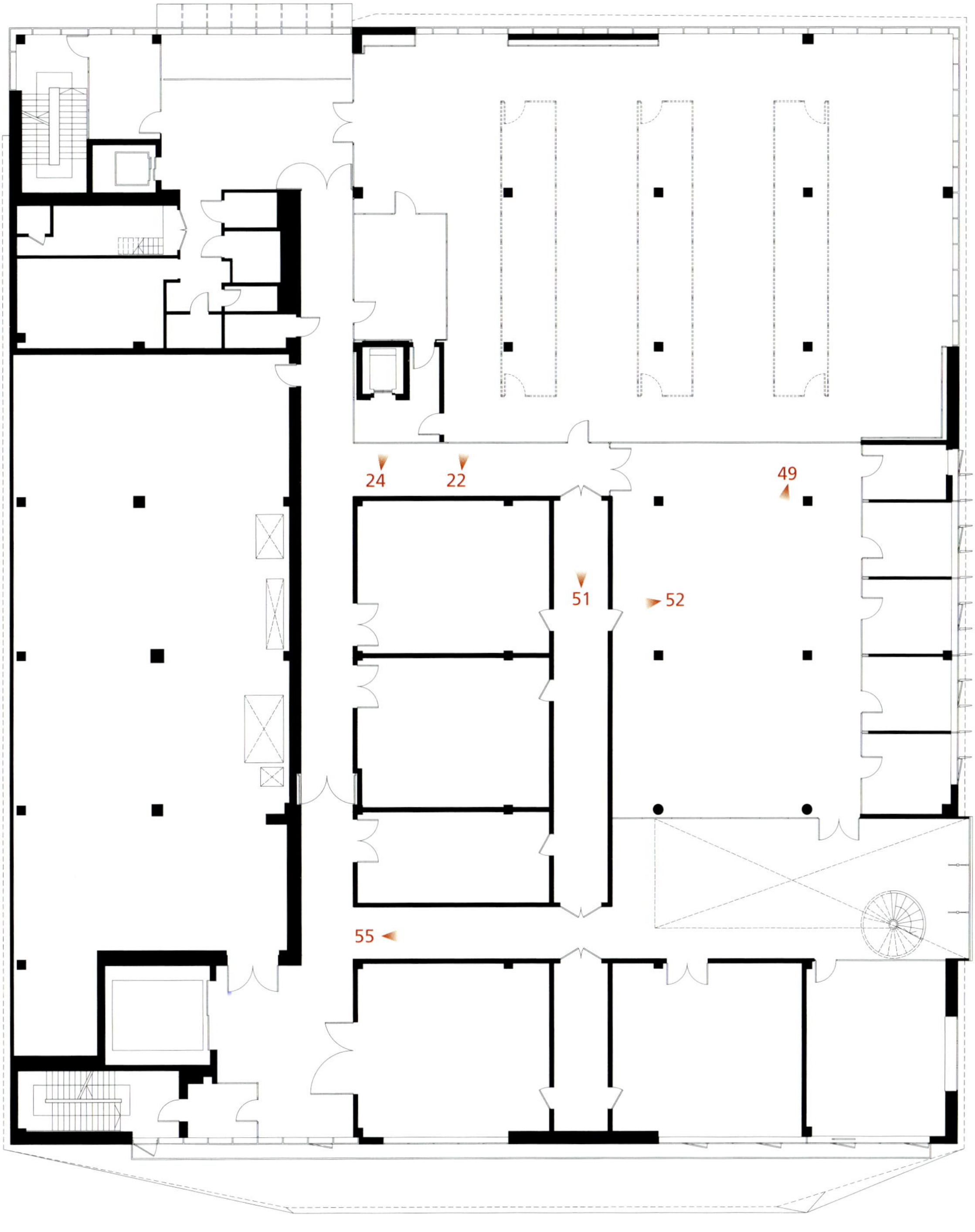

NGI 1st Level

The scale is given by the grid, which is 6600 mm.

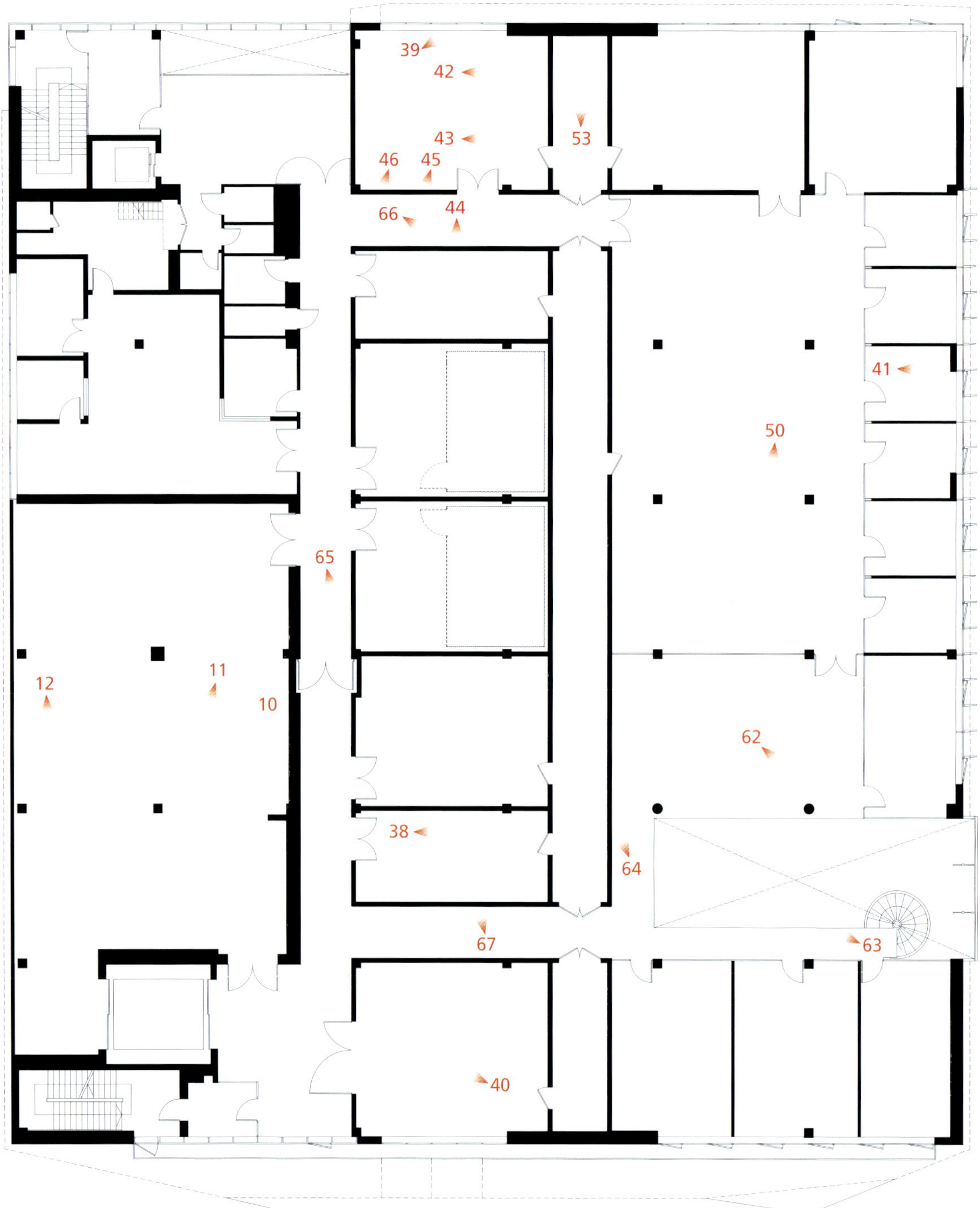

NGI 2nd Level

The scale is given by the grid, which is 6600 mm.

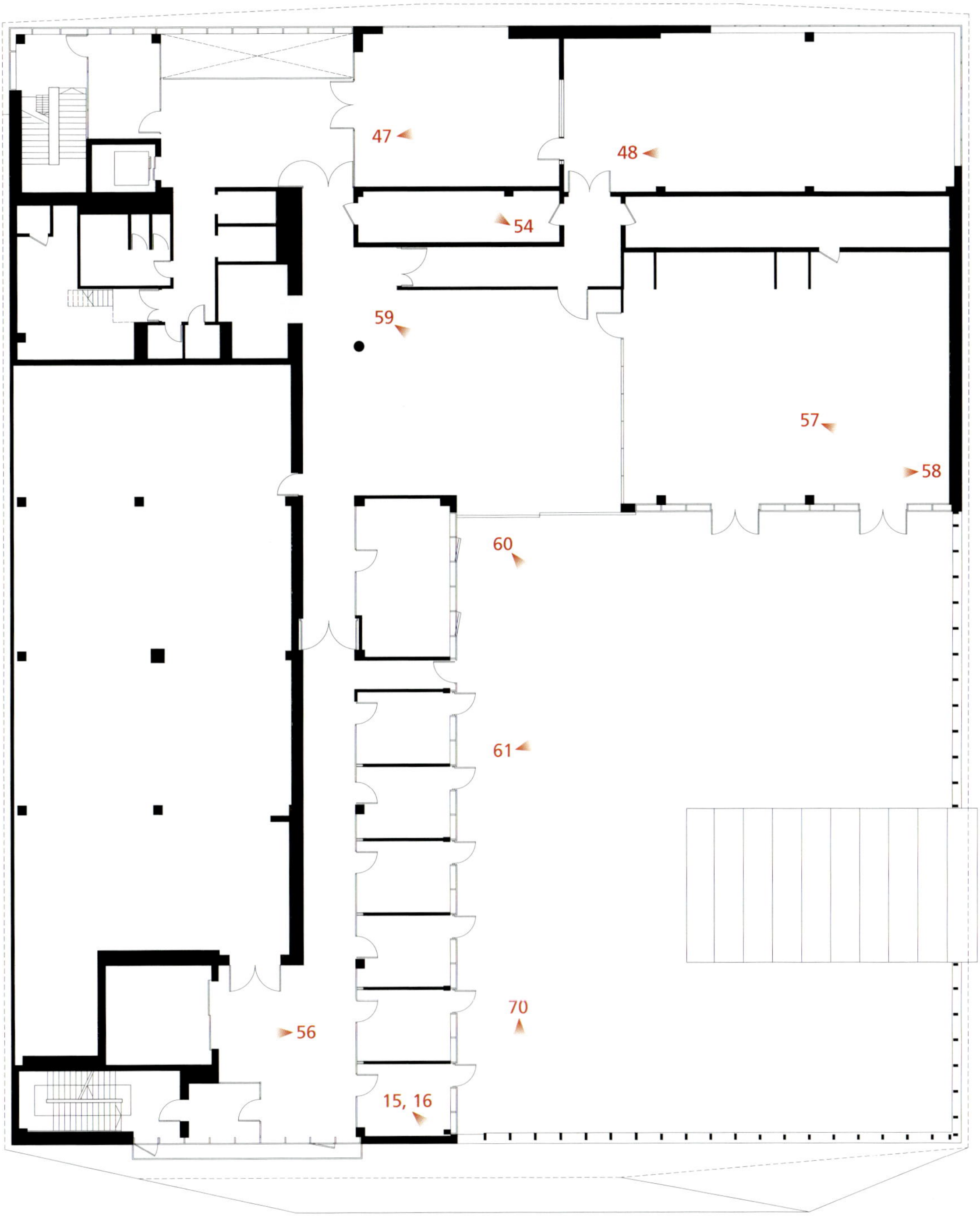

NGI 3rd Level

The scale is given by the grid, which is 6600 mm.

Spiral staircase in the atrium area. The colourful writing is a result of artistic project "Everything is Connected" by Kate Daudy and Kostya Novoselov. *Photo © Jonty Wilde, courtesy Kate Daudy.*

Index

B

C

D

E

M

N

O

P

X